God and Politics

God and Politics

Four Views
on the Reformation of
Civil Government

Theonomy
Principled Pluralism
Christian America
National Confessionalism

Edited by
Gary Scott Smith

Presbyterian and Reformed Publishing Company
Phillipsburg, New Jersey

Chapter 1, "The Theonomic Position" by Greg L. Bahnsen, was previously published in *Transformation* 5 (April-June 1988) and is reprinted by permission.

Chapter 14, "The Theonomic Response to National Confessionalism" by Gary DeMar, is an abridged version of his article "A Response to Dr. William J. Edgar and National Confession," copyright 1987 by American Vision, Atlanta, Georgia 30328, used by permission.

Editing by Edward W. Ojarovsky.
Typesetting by Thoburn Press, Tyler, Texas.
Manufactured in the United States of America.

Library of Congress Cataloging-in-Publication Data

God and politics : four views on the reformation of civil government :
    theonomy, principled pluralism, Christian America, national confessionalism /
    edited by Gary Scott Smith.
        p.   cm.
    Includes indexes.
    ISBN 0-87552-448-6
    1. Christianity and politics—Congresses.   2. Church and state—
Reformed Church—Congresses.   3. Reformed Church—Doctrines—
Congresses.   I. Smith, Gary Scott, 1950-
BR115.P7G56   1989
261.7—dc19   89-3640
                                                                              CIP

95   94   93   92   91   90   89   5   4   3   2   1

To
Patty, Greg, and Joel.

Thank you for
your inspiration, patience,
understanding, and love.

Contents

Foreword

John H. White

In the fall of 1985, the Executive Director of the National Reform Association, Dr. Marion McFarland, and I discussed how the NRA could best challenge the evangelical Christian community, and especially Reformed Christians, to think about what implications Christ's lordship held for civil government. We knew that even Reformed Christians disagreed among themselves on this subject. Our goal was to organize a conference where leading proponents of these divergent Reformed views could interact and discuss their differences.

We realized that such a consultation could succeed only if it were sponsored by a coalition of organizations and planned by representatives of the various Reformed positions. Four organizations agreed to sponsor the conference: The Association for Public Justice, Geneva College, The National Reform Association, and the *Presbyterian Journal* (now *God's World, Inc.*). The planning committee consisted of: Marion McFarland, National Reform Association (co-chairman); John H. White, Geneva College (co-chairman); Will Barker, *Presbyterian Journal*; Carl Bogue, Pastor, Presbyterian Church in America; David Carson, Geneva College; Richard C. Gamble, Westminster Theological Seminary; Tom McWhertor, Association for Public Justice; and Gary Scott Smith, Grove City College. I continued to be amazed at how the Lord enabled this planning committee to work together smoothly and enthusiastically.

We decided to entitle the conference a "Consultation on the Biblical Role of Civil Government" and to hold it at Geneva College, Beaver Falls, Pennsylvania on June 2 and 3, 1987. The purpose of the consultation was to clarify areas of agreement and divergence among Reformed Christians in order to achieve consensus where possible and, where not possible, to promote further discussion of differences. We identified four major positions within the Reformed community with regard to the subject of the conference: theonomy, principled pluralism, Christian America, and national confession. A leading representative of each of these four positions was invited to present a major paper to which proponents of each of the other three positions would respond. The consultation then consisted of four major segments, each of which included one major paper, three responses, and a question and answer period with a major presenter, concluding with his remarks to his respondents. A fifth session was devoted to formulating areas of agreement and disagreement among proponents of these four positions (which appears in this volume as Appendix B). One hundred and ten pastors, professors, journalists, leaders of Christian organizations involved in political issues, and other interested persons attended the consultation, which was by invitation only. The time together was marked by a mutual desire to understand one another and to seek the truth of God's Word. Many participants expressed delight at the openness of the exchange and the respect and love evidenced at the conference.

The following pages are a revised version of the papers presented at the consultation. The authors reworked their manuscripts after the conference to clarify their positions and make their views more understandable to nonspecialists. Their central arguments, however, remain the same.

It is worth noting that in the context of this volume the use of the definite article to introduce the four positions—e.g., "*The* Theonomic Position," "*The* Principled Pluralist Position"—is not meant to imply total agreement among the proponents of any one view. The chapter headings emphasize the four positions set forth at the consultation as they contrast with each other, not the shades of differences within each perspective.

We are grateful to Gary Scott Smith for his diligent and effective work of editing these papers and summarizing the question and answer periods (see Appendix A). We also thank Sharon Myers of Geneva College and Tammy Dibler and Holly Atkinson of Grove City College for their excellent work in typing this manuscript. This volume is offered as a first step in enabling God's people to witness more faithfully and vigorously in the political arena. "Soli Deo Gloria."

Introduction

Gary Scott Smith*

During the nearly two millennia since the birth of Jesus, Christian attitudes and approaches toward the state and political life have been many and varied. In his now classic book, *Christ and Culture* (1951), H. Richard Niebuhr identified and explained five basic historical positions toward culture. A view that Niebuhr labelled "Christ against culture" has been evident since the early church fathers. Tertullian, for example, declared that Jerusalem and Athens (Judeo-Christian teaching and Greek intellect and culture) had nothing in common and that Christians therefore should participate in cultural life as little as possible. Many Anabaptists, from the founding of this movement in the sixteenth century until the present day, have urged Christians to shun cultural and political life because these activities are corrupted by sin. Believers should instead concentrate their efforts on cultivating a deep spiritual life and preparing for heavenly existence.

Throughout the past 450 years many Lutherans have followed Martin Luther's dualistic approach to culture, which Niebuhr called "Christ and culture in paradox." This view stresses that Christians should seek primarily to promote evangelism and discipleship rather than engage in cultural activity. Believing that human selfishness, sin, and ungodliness are pervasive in the world, its advocates maintain that Christians cannot create a righteous society in the world through political action. At best, Christians can retard the spread of evil in their countries.

Most Roman Catholics and many Anglicans historically have embraced an approach to political and cultural life rooted in Thomas

*Gary Scott Smith is Associate Professor of Sociology at Grove City College (PA). He holds the degrees B.A. from Grove City College, M.Div. from Gordon-Conwell Theological Seminary, and Ph.D. from Johns Hopkins University. He is author of *The Seeds of Secularization: Calvinism, Culture and Pluralism in America, 1870-1915* (1985), as well as numerous articles, and has edited (along with W. Andrew Hoffecker) *Building a Christian World View*: Volume 1, *God, Man, and Knowledge* (1986) and Volume 2, *The Universe, Society, and Ethics* (1988).

Aquinas's teachings, which Niebuhr designated "Christ above culture." According to this view, Christians should work to bring all social institutions, including government, under the jurisdiction of the church, an arrangement that characterized much of the Middle Ages. As the "custodian of the divine law," the church should control political life and establish the laws for the state's operation.

Liberal Protestantism, as it developed in nineteenth-century Europe and spread to America, adopted an approach to cultural and political life that Niebuhr termed "Christ of culture." Previously advocated by the Gnostics during the second and third centuries and Peter Abelard in the twelfth century, this position accommodates Christ to culture and sees little tension between the church and the world or between the gospel and the laws of nations. It emphasizes Christ's teachings and actions and those doctrines about Him that seem consistent with the best in civilization.

In contrast to these four views of cultural and political life is the position of Augustine and Calvin, which Niebuhr described as "Christ the transformer of culture." Reformed Christians have traditionally argued that although all people are depraved and sin pervades all human action, God is sovereign over all human cultural activity. God is building a kingdom on earth, and Christians are to respond obediently to God's norms and to serve Him in every area of life, including politics. As Christ's ambassadors in the world, Christians should work to restructure all institutions, heal all broken relationships, and develop cultural life based upon biblical standards.

As this brief discussion indicates, views developed by Christians throughout history have significantly influenced political analysis and activity. The writings of Augustine and Aquinas have been especially important. Augustine's magisterial *City of God*, published in A.D. 410, helped to shape Western civilization's understanding of the role of government and political responsibility for a thousand years. He argued that church and state were "two swords," both under God's authority, both fulfilling God's aims, which should be independent of one another. God ordained the state to restrain human sinfulness, to preserve order, and to promote goodness. Thomas Aquinas, writing in the thirteenth century, agreed with Augustine that the state had a very positive role to play in society. He contended that God had established government to insure peace and stability, defend the community against outside attacks, and promote morality and material well-being among its citizens. In contrast to Augustine, however, he maintained that spiritual authority (the church and its clergy) should supervise and direct civil authority (the state and its rulers). While urging the church and state to work closely together and to respect each other's rights and responsibilities, Aquinas taught that the church should guide the state in its ordering of temporal life. In his hierarchical society the church, because of its higher, spiritual aims, was to dominate all of life: culture, politics, education, family, and religion.

Building on foundations laid by Augustine, John Calvin developed the Reformed theological perspective in the sixteenth century. Calvinism emphasized God's sovereign control over the universe He created, including the process of salvation. First published in 1536, the *Institutes of the Christian Religion*, Calvin's systematic analysis of Christian doctrine, developed the principal features of Reformed theology and significantly shaped its subsequent development. Also expounded by Theodore Beza, Calvin's successor in Geneva, and Heinrich Bullinger of Zurich, Calvinism spread rapidly during the sixteenth and seventeenth centuries on the European mainland among the Swiss, French, Dutch, and Germans. John Knox brought Reformed theology to Scotland in the 1550s, and four decades later Calvinism helped to inspire the rise of Puritanism in England. This latter movement attempted to restore New Testament forms of worship and polity, teach Reformed theological convictions, and promote spirituality among clergy and laity. The Heidelberg Catechism devised in 1563 and the Westminster Standards adopted by the English Puritans in the 1640s strongly influenced subsequent Reformed theological development.

In 1619 the Synod of Dort in response to the challenge of Arminianism delineated five points as essential to Reformed theology: total depravity, unconditional election, limited atonement, irresistible grace, and perseverance of the saints. These five doctrines (commonly known by the acronym TULIP) continue to be a succinct summary and a well-known explication of Calvinism. Total depravity stresses man's innate sinfulness and his inability to earn or even contribute to his own salvation. Because human beings are spiritually "dead," salvation must be God's free gift, not something people can achieve. Since God's choice of some for salvation is not based upon any known factors, Calvinists call it unconditional. The Scriptures, Calvinists argue, teach that the atonement is limited or definite in scope; Christ died only for the elect. God's irresistible grace brings salvation to all those whom He has chosen. People are powerless to resist His grace. Because salvation is a gift of God, not something human beings can earn, it can never be lost. God's grace will sustain the elect to the end of their earthly lives; no one can snatch God's sheep from His fold, nor can they stray away.

Reformed theology was carried to the shores of America by English Puritans in the 1620s. From the founding of Plymouth to the American Revolution, about 80 percent of the colonists were adherents of Reformed theology who belonged to various denominations: Presbyterian, Congregationalist, Baptist, Dutch Reformed, German Reformed, and other smaller Calvinistic communions.

During the seventeenth century the Puritans who settled New England sought to develop a biblical commonwealth that honored God and followed His divinely revealed norms. Believing that they were in the same relationship to God as was Israel in Old Testament times, John Winthrop and his fellow Puritans labored to create a truly Christian society as a model for all the world to emulate. Establishing a covenant with God, the Puritans sought to base their society upon the laws of the Old Testament. As George Marsden has argued, their society acknowledged its dependence upon God, recognized that God ordained government, and affirmed the rule of law. Despite good intentions the Puritan approach was fundamentally flawed. The state was empowered to establish a church, prevent false religion from being taught, require church attendance, banish dissenters, and call church councils. In the Massachusetts Bay Colony only church members were allowed to vote or run for public office. Most grievously, the Puritans' mistaken belief that they were political Israel inspired false pride among them, contributed to their poor treatment of Indians, and thwarted their efforts to develop a more genuinely biblical approach to political life.[1]

Unfortunately, no distinctively Christian political understanding was devised during the colonial period, and the new American nation, as it emerged in the late eighteenth century, was built upon an eclectic foundation. Three major streams converged to give shape to the American political system and to inform its values: the ideas of the radical Whigs or Commonwealth men of early eighteenth-century England (especially the writings of John Locke), the several varieties of the Enlightenment in Europe, and the Judeo-Christian tradition. The views of America's Founding Fathers on natural rights, limited government, and liberty of conscience were strongly influenced by the political writings of Locke and Charles Montesquieu. While the influence of Reformed Protestantism has contributed significantly to American political views, the Ameri-

---

1. George Marsden, "America's 'Christian' Origins: Puritan New England as a Case Study," in Mark A. Noll, Nathan O. Hatch, and George M. Marsden, *The Search for a Christian America* (Westchester, Ill.: Crossway, 1983), pp. 28-47.

can republic rests ultimately upon the broad Western humanist tradition, both Christian and secular.

Although the English law tradition, which helped to contour American society, incorporated many biblical principles and many of the colonists espoused Christian values, our nation has never been thoroughly or consistently Christian. While the ideas and leaders of Reformed Protestantism contributed to the revolt against England, so did Enlightenment reason and radical Whig political ideology. During the Revolutionary era Christians failed to develop a distinctly biblical understanding of political thought that differed sharply with Enlightenment rationalism. Christian and Enlightenment world views, though resting upon very different presuppositions, combined to furnish principles that guided the development of the American political system. Both systems taught that human lust for power must be curbed, that public virtue was necessary to sustain a republic, and that absolute norms should govern political and social life. Based upon these convictions Americans developed a limited government, provided religious liberty, and separated religious and civic institutions. Reformed beliefs about human nature helped to shape important features of the new nation's Constitution such as the separation and balance of powers. In the years following 1789, however, the United States became increasingly pluralistic denominationally and theologically.

American society has continued to blend or amalgamate Judeo-Christian and Enlightenment principles to the present day, and this ideological synthesis still molds our political consciousness and concerns. During the past two hundred years, though, Enlightenment and rationalist views have gained dominance as secularization has advanced in American society, especially after the Civil War. Between 1870 and 1930 naturalistic and humanistic ideas deeply influenced elites in the fields of education, journalism, and the professions. After 1930 these secular ideas began to permeate American public life more broadly, thus reshaping political institutions and traditional views and practices within public schools, and redefining social mores.

Throughout the last two centuries many Christians have actively resisted secularizing and demoralizing trends and have promoted political and social reform. During the Second Great Awakening (1800-1830) Christians created numerous voluntary societies to further temperance, peace, penal reform, and many other worthy causes. Christian convictions underpinned efforts to abolish slavery and attain women's rights during the nineteenth century. From 1870 to 1910 liberal and conservative Christians devised different versions of a "social gospel" that sought to aid the poor, improve working conditions, end corruption in government, and clean up the cities. The Progressive Movement, which achieved many political reforms during the first two decades of the twentieth century, was in large measure inspired by Christian commitments. Many of its leaders—such as Samuel "Golden Rule" Jones, Thomas Johnson, William Jennings Bryan, Jane Addams, and William Allen White—sought to remake America according to biblical principles of righteousness and justice. Between the Civil War and the Great Depression three presidents—Abraham Lincoln, Theodore Roosevelt, and Woodrow Wilson—were especially influenced by biblical ideals as they directed the American nation.

Rejecting or neglecting this rich heritage of political and social involvement, most conservative Christians in the years between 1920 and 1970 retreated from active political involvement and from social reform efforts in what has been termed the "great reversal." While largely ignoring national politics during these years, many conservative congregations developed programs and activities, and evangelicals created numerous parachurch organizations, to assist the poor and underprivileged in their local communities.

Between 1925 and 1945 no major political officials represented evangelical Christians or spoke directly and consistently for their interests and issues.[2] In the late 1920s conservative Protestants campaigned against Catholic presidential candidate Al Smith and fought to prevent the repeal of Prohibition. During the 1930s some fundamentalists—most notably Gerald B. Winrod and Gerald L. K. Smith—gravitated toward fascism. Most fundamentalists, however, concentrated their energies on denouncing the social gospel, communism, and the New Deal. In the 1940s evangelicals gained a new voice in American politics as three of their number—Frank Carlson of Kansas, Dr. Walter H. Judd of Minnesota, and Brook Hays of Arkansas—were elected to (and subsequently served long terms in) Congress. Meanwhile two organizations were created—the National Association of Evangelicals in 1942 and International Christian Leadership in 1943—that helped to reawaken and mobilize evangelical political consciousness and activism. The NAE founded an Office of Public Affairs that from 1943 to the present day has sought to lobby for various issues of concern to evangelicals, especially matters involving

---

2. The material in this section summarizes the argument presented by Richard V. Pierard, "Cacophony on Capitol Hill: Evangelical Voices in Politics," in Stephen D. Johnson and Joseph B. Tamney, *The Political Role of Religion in the United States* (Boulder, Colo.: Westview Press, 1986), pp. 71-96.

missionaries, chaplains, and church-state relations. The ICL sponsored prayer breakfasts in Washington, D.C., and across the nation and worked to help individual politicians develop a biblical perspective on government and politics.

During the 1950s conservative Protestant political activity and interest grew as Presidential Prayer Breakfasts were organized, the words "under God" were added to the Pledge of Allegiance, the phrase "In God We Trust" was adopted as our national motto, and Billy Graham became an informal advisor at the White House. The evangelical political voice increased further in the 1960s as growing numbers of conservative Protestants served both in the House, including James Wright, Jr. (TX), Elford A. Cedarberg (MI), Albert Quie (MN), John Duncan (TN), and John Dellenback (OR), and in the Senate, including John Stennis (MS), John McClellan (AK), Carl T. Curtis (NB), Jennings Randolph (WV), and Harold Hughes (IA). The most significant evangelical spokesmen, however, were John B. Anderson (IL), elected to the House in 1960, and Mark Hatfield (OR), elected to the Senate in 1966.

By the 1970s evangelical Christians were committed to a wide variety of political convictions and political agendas. On one end of the political spectrum, *The Other Side*, founded in 1965, and *Sojourners*, begun as *The Post-American* in 1971, argued for pacifism and economic justice. "Evangelicals for McGovern" supported his 1972 presidential candidacy and his pledge of immediate withdrawal of American troops from Vietnam. More evangelicals, however, voted for Richard Nixon, and many preferred the policies of conservatives Jesse Helms (NC) and John Conlan (AZ). Growing numbers of evangelicals, however, identified with the centralist policies advocated by Anderson, Hatfield, Paul Simon (IL), Governor Ruben Askew (FL) and, most significantly, Jimmy Carter. In 1976 evangelicals divided their votes between Carter and incumbent Gerald Ford, both of whom professed to be born-again Christians.

The election of 1976 gave Democrats control of the Presidency and the Congress and helped to push many evangelicals, especially fundamentalists, into a new coalition with secular conservatives in 1978, labelled the "New Right." In 1979 three organizations were founded to promote a conservative Christian agenda: the Moral Majority, Christian Voice, and the Religious Roundtable. Most controversial and most covered by the new media was the Moral Majority created by Jerry Falwell — pastor of the 18,000-member Thomas Road Baptist Church of Lynchburg, Virginia, President of Liberty College, and preacher on "The Old-Fashioned Gospel Hour." Falwell sought to organize the estimated 50 million born-again

Christians and other Americans holding traditional moral values into a new political force. The Moral Majority has strongly opposed permissiveness, moral relativism, and hedonism, and it has waged war against illegal drug traffic and pornography. Its members have supported a strong national defense, the state of Israel, the strengthening of the family, and the sacredness of human life. The Moral Majority and several other conservative Christian political organizations have conducted voter drives, held strategy sessions, issued ratings of Congressional voting, and published many newsletters. Despite all the attention the secular media have given to the New Christian Right and despite its claim to have determined the outcome of many electoral campaigns, studies reveal that its influence has not been powerful.[3]

Ironically, in the election of 1980, many evangelicals, influenced by the exhortations of the New Right, rejected the two candidates with much more clearly expressed evangelical commitment — Jimmy Carter and John Anderson — and voted for Ronald Reagan. Reagan's opposition to homosexuality, abortion, and the teaching of evolution and his support of prayer in the public schools, tuition tax credits, increased defense spending, a sound dollar, and the dismantling of much of the welfare state made him attractive to many conservative Christians. His approach to politics, however, seemed not to spring from a distinctively biblical perspective.

By the 1980s the number of persons holding public office who identified themselves as Christians was probably greater than at any time since the first decade of the twentieth century. By this time, a wide variety of organizations have been created to instruct Christians about political issues and stimulate their active participation in the political process: the Association for Public Justice, Baptist Joint Committee on Public Affairs, American Studies Program of the Christian College Coalition, Americans United for the Separation of Church and State, Mennonite Central Committee, Peace Section, Christian Life Commission of the Southern Baptist Convention, Friends' Committee on National Legislation, Moral Majority, and many others. Meanwhile Christians sponsor conferences to discuss political matters and publish scores of books about political issues, while the religious press features articles on political topics and the secular media pays considerable attention to the involve-

---

3. See Richard V. Pierard and James L. Wright, "No Hoosier Hospitality for Humanism: The Moral Majority in Indiana," in David G. Bromley and Anson Shupe, *New Christian Politics* (Macon, Ga.: Mercer University Press, 1984), pp. 195-212, and Robert Zwier, "The New Christian Right and the 1980 Elections," ibid., pp. 173-94.

ment of Christians in politics. Peter Benson's and Dorothy Williams's *Religion on Capitol Hill* argues that members of Congress are at least as religious as the general public and that their religious convictions "are strongly connected" to how they vote on specific issues.[4]

Two weaknesses are evident in evangelical involvement in contemporary American politics. First, evangelical public servants represent very different political viewpoints and propose contrasting political programs. On ecopolitical issues, for example, evangelicals "support everything from laissez-faire capitalism to communitarian socialism and much in between."[5] Tragically, these differences prevent Christian legislators from sounding a "clarion call for national righteousness and social justice."[6] These same differences exist among Reformed Christians, and this indictment can be charged against us as well. It is our hope that the dialogue in this book and the thinking it will stimulate can help Christians work toward more understanding and agreement on political matters.

Second, unfortunately many Christian legislators have not developed a consistent biblical world view to guide their analysis of political presuppositions, processes, and programs. Instead, their approach to politics has been determined much more "by personal philosophies and prejudices they bring to the Word of God."[7] Benson and Williams demonstrate that while religious conviction is widespread among members of Congress, much of that conviction is shallow and superficial. They show that Christians in Congress do not operate on the basis of consistent, cogent biblical assumptions but rather on particular types of religious faith: conservatives tend toward "Individualism-Preserving Religion" and liberals toward "Community-Building Religion."[8] Our book seeks to encourage Christians to think seriously about what the Scriptures teach about government and politics and to develop biblically based views to guide their own assessment of these matters.

The political activism of American evangelicals during the past decade has been part of a resurgence of religious involvement in politics around the world. In Iran an Islamic revolution has transformed government and society. In Central and South America liberation theology has inspired political protest and change. Catholicism in Poland has

---

4. Peter L. Benson and Dorothy L. Williams, *Religion on Capitol Hill: Myths and Realities* (New York: Harper and Row, 1982), pp. 82, 143, 156.

5. Robert Booth Fowler, *A New Engagement: Evangelical Political Thought, 1966-1976* (Grand Rapids: Eerdmans, 1983).

6. Pierard, "Cacophony on Capitol Hill," p. 92.

7. Ibid.

8. Benson and Williams, *Religion on Capitol Hill*, pp. 164ff.

helped to stimulate resistance to Soviet policies. Meanwhile in the United States Catholic bishops have continued their longstanding opposition to abortion and have spoken out on nuclear war, Central America, and economic justice.

American Catholics have also joined Protestants in campaigning for voluntary school prayer and in fighting for public funding of Christian schools. Catholics for a Moral America and the Catholic Center for Private Enterprise, Strong Defense and Traditional Values have both taken political positions similar to those of the Moral Majority and the American Coalition for Traditional Values (an umbrella organization for Protestant groups concerned about political and moral issues). As have some conservative Protestant leaders, several archbishops have even endorsed candidates for public office. Many Catholic politicians have moved beyond John F. Kennedy's extreme separation of religion and state to a position, espoused by New York governor Mario Cuomo, which argues that religion can properly help form a consensus concerning public morality. Following traditional Catholic moral theology, Cuomo urges Christians to support legal changes only after a clear public consensus has been formed on particular issues.

Before analyzing the political presuppositions of contemporary Reformed Christians, we will first briefly sketch the development of Reformed Christianity in America since 1800.

During the nineteenth century Methodists and Baptists (most of whom became Arminians) were much more effective than Calvinists in using revivalism and in planting churches on the frontier, and their denominations came to dominate American Christianity numerically. Revolt against Calvinist doctrines was widespread during the years of Jacksonian Democracy (1820-50). Many Americans thought that Reformed convictions of total depravity, unconditional election, limited atonement, irresistible grace, and perseverance of the saints denied human responsibility and free choice and contradicted America's republican principles. While about 80 percent of the colonists were affiliated with Reformed denominations in 1776, by 1850 70 percent of Protestant church members were Baptists or Methodists, most of whom espoused Arminian theology. Some groups of Baptists remained Calvinistic during the second half of the nineteenth century, as did most Presbyterians, Congregationalists, and members of Reformed communions—in all about one-third of American Protestants.

In the first fifty years of the twentieth century Reformed Christianity in America reached a nadir in terms of the number of its proponents, its theological development, and its cultural influence. Since the 1960s, however, a resurgence of commitment to Calvinism is evident in the United States in the growth and vitality of Reformed seminaries and colleges, Reformed presses and publications, and Reformed congregations and parachurch ministries, and in new elaborations of Reformed theology. From the planting of Plymouth Colony to the present day, Calvinism has contributed significantly to the development of American culture, affecting our views of God, humanity, the Bible, and cultural activity, especially vocation.

While considerable diversity of views has existed within the Reformed community in America with regard to political and cultural matters, several major principles have been widely agreed upon. First is the conviction that the Bible is God's authoritative word that addresses all areas of life, including politics and government. Although the Scriptures do not speak exhaustively or even explicitly about all political matters, they provide principles to guide and structure political activity. This means that political life is not autonomous or based upon human predilection and preferences; instead it is subject to transcendent, divinely revealed norms.

Second, Christians have a cultural commission or mandate in the world. The task of God's people is not simply to help individuals commit a dimension of their lives to Christ — the spiritual (as opposed to, say, the physical, aesthetic, and psychological dimensions). Christians are called to subdue the earth in God's name and to have dominion over all aspects of life. God's kingdom is not confined to the institutional church; instead it embraces all areas of life. We are to glorify the Lord not simply through ecclesiastical life (worship, the sacraments, Christian education and nurture, prayer) but by what we do in every sphere of life: marriage, family and home, leisure and recreation, work and economics, art, music, dance and drama, literature and communications, education at all levels, and politics and government. Christ died on the cross, not merely to reconcile individuals to God the Father, but to restore the whole creation to its rightful condition. Redemption therefore involves not only saving the souls of individuals but reconciling the entire world — all its structures, patterns, practices, and relationships — to the Lord.

Through the Holy Spirit God is at work renewing the cosmos and building His kingdom on earth. Christians are God's ambassadors and stewards — the force He uses to renew the world. Through our cultural activities — buying and selling, producing and serving, teaching and learn-

ing, nurturing and homemaking, voting and lobbying—Christians are
to be at work transforming the world from a wilderness to the garden of
God. God is Lord or King of all life. Through these various activities we
can glorify Him, advance His kingdom, and spread *shalom*, justice, and
righteousness throughout the world. God seeks to reconcile individuals
to Himself, thus enabling them to develop a deep spiritual life and build
caring, sharing Christian communities. But He also wants marriages,
family life, education, work, and states to be based upon biblical norms,
to foster healthy relationships, and to serve the human community.

With regard to government, Reformed Christians have agreed on
several basic principles. Because Jesus is Lord of the universe, the
ascended King over all creation, all governments are under His authority. Ultimately, all earthly powers are subject to Him; His authority
transcends that of all earthly rulers. Because this is so, political authority
ultimately stems from God—not from the consent of the governed. Governments must respect, honor, and protect their citizens, not because
they possess certain inalienable natural rights, but because the Creator
of the universe assigns moral worth and value to creatures made in His
image and likeness.

Like modern science, the contemporary state has ignored metaphysical questions and avoided religious commitments. Assuming that there
are no ultimate principles to which law must conform, modern states,
including America, have based their laws upon relativistic foundations.
Repudiating a transcendent source of authority, nations have argued
that they can and should change their laws as social conditions and needs
change. Rarely do states recognize that divine law supersedes human
law or appeal to absolute norms as a basis for particular laws. The abandonment of the traditional Judeo-Christian foundation for government
has produced increasing confusion over the role and tasks of the state.
Consequently, political expediency rather than principles now guide
most political thinking and decision-making in the Western world.

Reformed Christians reject this position, arguing instead that God is
the sovereign governor and judge of both the universe and all nations.
This means that governments are servants, not lords; they exist to
enhance and enrich the lives of their citizens, not to coerce or dominate
them. Governments are not autonomous; they are subject to divine authority and norms. The Bible's teachings are relevant to all areas of life,
including politics. The Scriptures are no more a systematic handbook on
statecraft than they are on science, history, or economics. The basic
principles and specific norms they present, however, should direct how

governments operate, what policies and laws they adopt, and how people participate in the political process.

Specifically, this means that civil officials are God's servants who should rule wisely and justly, look to God's Word for guidance, and respect the dignity of all citizens. God's sovereign reign over the universe also means that governments have only limited authority. Political rulers cannot do anything they wish. God established government to perform important but limited tasks. Whenever a government claims to have unlimited authority or attempts to control all areas of life, it disobeys God and exceeds its mandate.

Reformed Christians agree that the primary task of government is to insure justice among its citizens. Governments accomplish this by establishing and maintaining order, providing for defense and punishment of law-breakers, and making sure that other social institutions—such as marriage, family, schools, work, economics, and media—perform within their divinely assigned spheres. All Christians, not just a select few, have political responsibilities. No one can properly delegate his political duties to others. We all need to assess candidates, analyze issues, vote, and support policies that promote justice and fairness in society. While so doing, we must remember that the state is only one of God's important agents in the world. Christians also serve the Lord and advance His kingdom in the world as we develop strong families, caring congregations, and service organizations.

Politics and morality, Reformed Christians argue, are inseparable. All law rests upon moral conviction, upon beliefs about right and wrong, good and evil, justice and injustice. All law reflects conceptions of the good life, the nature of human community, and of human rights and responsibilities. All politicians, like all persons, function on the basis of ultimate commitments, on underlying convictions, on what they esteem as valuable—in short, on world views.

Recognizing this fact, Christians should seek to challenge other views at the presuppositional level. We should encourage debate and dialogue among Americans about first principles—about the bedrock assumptions that underlie what form of government we espouse, what tasks we would assign to the state, what legislative issues we advance, what parties and politicians we support, and what political decisions we advocate.

The first part of this brief overview has sought to present the various approaches Christians have adopted historically toward culture and politics, to explain the political and ideological foundations of American society, to assess the role Christians have played in shaping American life,

and especially to analyze Christian political response in the twentieth
century. The second section described the development of Reformed
Christianity in America during the last two hundred years and identified
major areas of agreement among Reformed Christians with regard to
cultural and political matters.

We now present four different viewpoints or emphases within today's
American Reformed community that offer distinctive approaches to politics and the state: theonomy, principled pluralism, Christian America,
and national confessionalism.

Part One

Theonomy

From the beginnings of their movement in the early 1960s, "theonomists" (from *theos*, "God," and *nomos*, "law") or "Christian reconstructionists," have called for radical reform of American society and life to bring our nation into conformity with God's laws revealed in the Bible. Led by three major thinkers—philosopher R. J. Rushdoony, economist Gary North, and theologian Greg Bahnsen—theonomists have had a growing influence among American Christians during the past twenty-five years. Rushdoony, who has published more than thirty books primarily on education, law, politics, and cultural analysis, is the head of the Chalcedon Foundation, located in Vallecito, California. North founded the Institute for Christian Economics in Tyler, Texas, and he writes widely on economics, conspiracy theories, computers, and many other issues. Bahnsen's *Theonomy in Christian Ethics* (1977, 1984) is the best one-volume summary of the movement's principles. He is co-pastor of an Orthodox Presbyterian congregation in Orange County, California.

Reconstructionist thought rests primarily on three foundations: presuppositional apologetics, the thorough application of God's law to contemporary society, and postmillennialism. Advanced primarily by the late Cornelius Van Til of Westminster Theological Seminary, the presuppositional approach assumes that God exists, that He has revealed absolute truth in the Bible, and that scriptural teachings should guide behavior in all areas of life. Unlike Christians who use a rationalist apologetic, presuppositionalists make no attempt to prove these axioms by appeals to religiously neutral or independent criteria.

Reconstructionists insist that Old Testament law, moral and civil, except as it is specifically abrogated by New Testament teachings, should be applied exhaustively to present-day nations. All nations, not simply Old Testament Israel, are obligated to live by God's law. While Christ's coming ended the need for the ceremonial laws of the Old Testament, both the moral and civil laws of the Israelite theocracy continue to be

17

binding today. It is these convictions about the applicability of the laws
of the Old Testament that make the theonomic view distinctive from
other Christian approaches to culture.

A person can be a theonomist without accepting the postmillennial
understanding of Christ's Second Coming. Nevertheless, most reconstructionists are postmillennialists; they believe that more and more people will become Christians and that social institutions will progressively
be based upon biblical norms, enabling America to become a theonomic
nation before Christ returns again.

While theonomists disagree considerably over how to apply God's
laws as revealed in Scripture to society, they all wish to create a
theocracy that honors God and obeys His eternal norms. In their recon-
structed society government would be republican and the Bible the basic
constitution. The functions of government would be limited primarily to
providing defense, maintaining order, assuring justice, and punishing
criminals (primarily by capital punishment or restitution). Education
would be a responsibility solely of parents. All taxes upon property
would be eliminated, and churches and other private agencies, not the
government, would provide relief and welfare to the poor.

The reconstructionist movement has had substantial influence among
several groups. Many fundamentalists and evangelical Christians, especially among independent Baptist congregations and within the smaller
Reformed denominations, have embraced theonomy. So have many
charismatic Christians around the world. In addition, home schoolers,
libertarians, and the Religious Right generally have expressed agreement
with and support for at least some aspects of the theonomic program.

Central to Bahnsen's argument in the following chapter is his exposition of Psalm 2, especially verses 11 and 12: "Serve Jehovah with fear . . .
[and] kiss the Son." These words, he contends, are addressed, "not simply to the magistrates of theocratic Israel, but to all kings and judges 'of
the earth'" (p. 30). This passage and other biblical texts command all
political officials to serve the Lord through their administrations. Those
who argue that a nation's government "should not be based upon or
favor any one distinctive religion or philosophy of life (but rather balance the alleged rights of all conflicting viewpoints)" ultimately are disobeying God's commands. By taking this position, pluralists unwittingly
promote "political polytheism"—acknowledging and serving different ultimate authorities (gods) in the area of public policy (p. 30).

The heart of Bahnsen's argument is that "in all of its minute detail
(every jot and tittle) the law of God, down to its least significant provi-

sion, should be reckoned to have an abiding validity—until and unless the Lawgiver reveals otherwise" (pp. 40-41). According to the apostle Paul, the stipulations of God's moral law—whether known through Mosaic (written) ordinances or by general (unwritten) revelation—are universally binding. These laws are valid not only for the Jews of ancient Israel, but for all people at all times. Because Christ completely endorsed the moral validity of Old Testament law, it remains in force unless supervened by later commandments. Christ's rule in the world and the continued applicability of Old Testament laws mean that all civil magistrates today are morally obligated "to be guided and regulated by the law of God" taught throughout the Bible, "*where and when* it speaks to political matters" (p. 42).

1

The Theonomic Position

Greg L. Bahnsen*

Any conception of the role of civil government that claims to be distinctively Christian must be explicitly justified by the teaching of God's revealed Word.[1] Anything else reflects what the unbelieving world in rebellion against God may imagine on its own. If we are to be Christ's disciples, even in the political realm, it is prerequisite that we abide in His liberating Word (John 8:31). In every walk of life a criterion of our love for Christ or lack thereof is whether we keep the Lord's words (John 14:23-24) rather than founding our beliefs upon the ruinous sands of other opinions (Matt. 7:24-27). And as those especially in the Reformed heritage confess, to the extent that our view of civil government (or any matter) does adhere faithfully to Scripture, that view stands above any and all challenges that stem from human wisdom and tradition (Rom. 3:4; 9:20; Col. 2:8).

A Brief Synopsis

Christians who advocate what has come to be called the "theonomic" (or "reconstructionist") viewpoint[2] reject the social forces of *secularism*,

---

*Greg L. Bahnsen received the degrees B.A. from Westmont College, M.Div. and Th.M. from Westminster Theological Seminary, and Ph.D. from the University of Southern California. He is an ordained minister in the Orthodox Presbyterian Church and has taught apologetics and ethics at Reformed Theological Seminary in Jackson, MS. He is author of *Theonomy in Christian Ethics* (1977, 1984), *By This Standard* (1985), and *Homosexuality: A Biblical View* (1978).

1. God's word is, of course, found not only in special revelation (Ps. 19:7-14), but also in natural revelation (vv. 1-6). And to whatever degree unbelievers do civic good, and whenever there has been anything like a reasonably just government in non-Christian lands, it is to be credited to common grace and natural revelation. Scripture is nonetheless our final authority. In a fallen world where natural revelation is suppressed in unrighteousness (Rom. 1:18, 21), special revelation is needed to check, confirm, and correct whatever is *claimed* for the content of natural revelation. Moreover, there are no moral norms given in natural revelation that are missing from special revelation (2 Tim. 3:16-17); indeed, the content and benefit of special revelation exceeds that of natural revelation (cf. Rom. 3:1-2).

2. From the theonomist's standpoint there really is no need for a new or distinctive label, since the position is deemed essentially that of Calvin (cf. his sermons on Deuteronomy), the Reformed Confessions (e.g., the Westminster Confession, chaps. 19, 20, 23,

which too often shape our culture's conception of a good society. The Christian's political standards and agenda are not set by unregenerate pundits who wish to quarantine religious values (and thus the influence of Jesus Christ, speaking in the Scripture) from the decision-making process of public policy. Theonomists equally repudiate the *sacred-secular dichotomy* of life, which is the *effect* of certain extrascriptural, systematic conceptions of biblical authority that have recently infected the Reformed community[3] — conceptions implying that present-day moral standards for our political order are not to be taken from what the written Word of God directly and relevantly says about society and civil government. This theologically unwarranted and socially dangerous stance curtails the scope of the Bible's truth and authority (Ps. 119:160; Isa. 40:8; 45:19; John 17:17; Deut. 4:2; Matt. 5:18-19).

We beseech men not to be conformed to this world, but to be transformed by the renewing and reconciling work of Jesus Christ so as to prove the good, acceptable, and *perfect will* of God in their lives (2 Cor. 5:20-21; Rom. 12:1-2). We call on them to be delivered out of darkness into the kingdom of God's Son, who was raised from the dead in order to have pre-eminence in *all* things (Col. 1:13-18). We must "cast down reasonings and every high thing which is exalted against the knowledge of God, bringing *every* thought into captivity to the obedience of Christ" (2 Cor. 10:5) in whom "*all* the treasures of wisdom and knowledge are deposited" (Col. 2:3).[4] Thus, believers are exhorted to be holy in all manner of living (1 Peter 1:15), and to do whatever they do for the glory

and the Larger Catechism's exposition of the Ten Commandments), and the New England Puritans (cf. the *Journal of Christian Reconstruction* 5, 2 (Winter 1978-79). Even as hostile an opponent as Meredith Kline concedes that the theonomic view was that of the Westminster Confession of Faith (see his review-article in the *Westminster Theological Journal* 41, 1 [Fall 1978]: 173-74).

3. Two pertinent illustrations are found in (1) the Dooyeweerdian scheme of dichotomizing reality into modal spheres having their own peculiar laws and (2) Meredith Kline's idea of dichotomizing the canonical authority of various elements of Scripture, both between and within the two testaments. In the former case, explicit biblical texts pertaining to civil government may not provide a Christian view of the state, for Scripture is said to apply directly only to the modal sphere of "faith" (cf. Bob Goudzwaard, *A Christian Political Option* [Toronto: Wedge, 1972], p. 27). In the latter case, the moral authority of certain elements of Scripture is arbitrarily dismissed on the basis of separating (without conceptual cogency or exegetical justification) faith-norms from life-norms, individual-norms from communal-norms, and "common-grace" principles from "eschatological-intrusion" principles — implying that the most explicit biblical directions about political ethics may not be utilized today (*The Structure of Biblical Authority* [Grand Rapids: Eerdmans, 1972]).

4. Scripture quotations in this chapter are from the American Standard Version, 1901, or from the author's own translation. Italics indicate emphasis added.

of God (1 Cor. 10:31). To do so will require adherence to the written Word of God, since our faith does not stand in the wisdom of men but rather in the work and teaching of God's Holy Spirit (1 Cor. 2:5, 13; cf. 1 Thess. 2:13; Num. 15:39; Jer. 23:16). That teaching, infallibly recorded in "*every* scripture" of the Old and New Testaments, is able to equip us for "*every* good work" (2 Tim. 3:16-17)—even in public, community life.

For these reasons, theonomists are committed to the *transformation* (or reconstruction) of every area of life, *including* the institutions and affairs of the socio-political realm, according to the holy principles of God's revealed Word (thus theonomy). It is toward this end that the human community must strive if it is to enjoy true justice and peace.

Because space will not allow a full elaboration, with extensive qualifications and applications, of the theonomic position in this essay,[5] it may prove helpful to begin with a systematic overview and basic summary of the theonomic conception of the role of civil government in terms of Christ's rule as King and of His inscripturated laws.

1. The Scriptures of the Old and New Testaments are, in part and in whole, a verbal revelation from God through the words of men, being infallibly true regarding all that they teach on any subject.

2. Since the Fall, it has always been unlawful to use the law of God in hopes of establishing one's own personal merit and justification, in contrast or complement to salvation by way of promise and faith; commitment to obedience is but the lifestyle of faith, a token of gratitude for God's redeeming grace.

3. The Word of the Lord is the sole, supreme, and unchallengeable standard for the actions and attitudes of all men in all areas of life; this Word naturally includes God's moral directives (law).

4. Our obligation to keep the law of God cannot be judged by any extrascriptural standard, such as whether its specific requirements (when properly interpreted) are congenial to past traditions or modern feelings and practices.

---

5. A fuller discussion of the fundamental perspective can be found in my two books: *Theonomy in Christian Ethics*, 2d ed. (Phillipsburg, N.J.: Presbyterian and Reformed, 1984) and *By This Standard: The Authority of God's Law Today* (Tyler, Tex.: Institute for Christian Economics, 1985). These texts present the underlying theonomic *orientation* to ethics, in distinction from other theonomic publications (e.g., by R. J. Rushdoony, Gary North, James Jordan) which attempt to interpret and apply the *details* of God's commandments — a necessary task, but one that also leaves much room for controversy and disagreement; at a number of places I myself cannot agree with the exegesis or reasoning attempted in them.

5. We should presume that Old Testament standing laws[6] continue to be morally binding in the New Testament, unless they are rescinded or modified by further revelation.[7]

6. In regard to the Old Testament law, the New Covenant surpasses the Old Covenant in glory, power, and finality (thus reinforcing former duties). The New Covenant also supercedes the Old Covenant shadows, thereby changing the application of sacrificial, purity, and "separation" principles, redefining the people of God, and altering the significance of the promised land.

7. God's revealed standing laws are a reflection of His immutable moral character and, as such, are absolute in the sense of being non-arbitrary, objective, universal, and established in advance of particular circumstances (thus applicable to general types of moral situations).

8. Christian involvement in politics calls for recognition of God's transcendent, absolute, revealed law as a standard by which to judge all social codes.

9. Civil magistrates in all ages and places are obligated to conduct their offices as ministers of God, avenging divine wrath against criminals and giving an account on the Final Day of their service before the King of kings, their Creator and judge.

10. The general continuity that we presume with respect to the moral standards of the Old Testament applies just as legitimately to matters of socio-political ethics as it does to personal, family, or ecclesiastical ethics.

11. The civil precepts of the Old Testament (standing "judicial" laws) are a model of perfect social justice for all cultures, even in the punishment of criminals. Outside of those areas where God's law prescribes their intervention and application of penal redress, civil rulers are not authorized to legislate or use coercion (e.g., the economic marketplace).

12. The morally proper way for Christians to correct social evils that are not under the lawful jurisdiction of the state is by means of voluntary and charitable enterprises or the censures of the home, church, and marketplace — even as the appropriate method for changing the political order

6. "Standing law" is used here for *policy* directives applicable over time to classes of individuals (e.g., do not kill; children, obey your parents; merchants, have equal measures; magistrates, execute rapists), in contrast to particular directions for an individual (e.g., the order for Samuel to anoint David at a particular time and place) or positive commands for distinct incidents (e.g., God's order for Israel to exterminate certain Canaanite tribes at a certain point in history).

7. By contrast, it is characteristic of dispensational theology to hold that Old Covenant commandments should be a priori deemed as abrogated — unless *repeated* in the New Testament (e.g., Charles Ryrie, "The End of the Law," *Bibliotheca Sacra* 124 [1967]: 239-42).

of civil law is not violent revolution, but dependence upon regeneration, re-education, and gradual legal reform.

I shall take the remainder of this essay to develop certain relevant themes within the above framework.

Christ Presently, Supremely Our King

The apostle John opens the Book of Revelation by introducing the resurrected Savior, Jesus Christ, not only as the head of the church with whom He is sovereignly present (Rev. 1:12-20), but also as "the ruler of the kings of the earth" (1:5). One is reminded of the closing of Matthew's Gospel, where, again, not only does Christ promise to be with the church until the end of the age, but also claims for Himself "all authority . . . on earth" (Matt. 28:18-20). These are bold claims. They forcefully counteract the popular tendency to restrict the exalted reign of our Lord to some transcendent spiritual domain or to the confines of the institutional church. Christ is entitled to, and settles for, nothing less than *immanent* authority over all things, including the *political* potentates of this earth, "for he is Lord of lords, and King of kings" (Rev. 17:14).

The above claims are not only bold; they are also somewhat bewildering. At the very time that Christ claimed all authority upon earth, He simultaneously indicated that the nations still needed to be made His disciples. At the very time when John wrote of Christ as the ruler of earthly kings, he was about to launch into a lengthy portrayal of the brutal hostility of those political leaders in his own day to the Savior and His people. How can this paradox be resolved? Is Christ actually the King over present earthly rulers, or do they reign in unbelief and defiance of Him? That both things are true can be readily understood in terms of (1) the broader teaching of Scripture about God's kingdom and (2) the specific teaching of Psalm 2.

1. To avoid befuddling ourselves over the biblical teaching regarding God's "kingdom," we need to recognize three conceptual distinctions regarding it (which many writers today fail to do). First, Scripture leads us to differentiate the *providential* kingdom of God (His sovereign dominion over every historical event, whether good or evil—as in Dan. 4:17) from the *messianic* kingdom of God (the divine rule that secures redemption and breaks the power of evil—as in Dan. 7:13-14). Then, second, the Bible distinguishes three historical phases of the messianic kingdom: the past phase of its Old Testament *anticipation* and foreshadowing (cf. Matt. 21:43), the present phase of its *establishment* at Christ's first coming (e.g., Matt. 12:28), and the future phase of its *consummation* at Christ's second

advent (e.g., Matt. 7:21-23). Finally, as closely allied as the church is with God's kingdom (holding the keys of entrance to its blessing, Matt. 16:18-19), the presently established messianic kingdom of God is still not biblically equated with the *church* (as is linguistically evident from Acts 28:23); the scope of the present messianic kingdom, unlike that of the church, is the entire world, inclusive of the doers of iniquity (Matt. 13:38, 41).

But how can this last point be the case? How can unbelievers who reject the Savior and live wickedly on the earth nevertheless be under the dominion of the Messiah? We can relieve the perplexity of that question by remembering a few relevant points. There is a difference between an objective state of affairs and the subjective recognition of it (e.g., between having tuberculosis and admitting it to yourself). Moreover, there is a difference between reigning *by right* and reigning in *actual fact*, as is evident in any nation at a time of revolution against constituted authority. Accordingly, unbelievers often resist subjectively acknowledging the reign of Jesus Christ over them, but objectively and by right that rule nevertheless belongs to Him—having been appointed to Him by the Father (Luke 22:29; 1 Cor. 15:27-28) and testified to by His resurrection and ascension (Matt. 28:7, 18; Rom. 1:4; Phil. 2:9-11; Acts 17:30-31; Heb. 1:3, 8-9; 2:7-9). Furthermore, like the gospel, which is a savor unto both life and death (2 Cor. 2:14-16), the reign of the Messiah presently breaks the power of sin and rebellion in two different ways: one in *redemptive blessing* (John 3:3, 5; Col. 1:13; Rom. 14:17), but the other in *judgmental curse*—experienced both *now* (Mark 9:1, cf. 13:1-30; Rev. 18; 19:15-16; Acts 12:21-23; Ps. 72:4, 12-14) and *later* in its full fury (Matt. 13:41-42, 49-59; 25:31-34, 41, 46; 2 Thess. 1:4-9). So, then, unbelievers who repudiate the Messiah's dominion are nevertheless under His reign in the form of wrath and curse.

Finally, we should not forget the growth-dimension of the present, unconsummated messianic kingdom. It will gradually become quite large and transform all things (Matt. 13:31-33). That is, the objective reign of the Messiah *by right*, involving judgment upon rebels, will more and more become a recognized reign in *actual fact*, which spreads redemptive blessing. Though in this age the wheat will always live in the presence of tares (Matt. 13:36-43),[8] it will become increasingly evident that this

---

8. The pluralist attempt to find biblical support, however meager, for its unique political tenets looks desperate when it reaches for the parable of the wheat and tares. Surveying the text of this eschatological lesson turns up not the slightest intimation that it pertains to

world is Christ's wheat field (kingdom), not a tare field. Christ is presently reigning, and He must continue to do so until every enemy has been subdued under His feet (1 Cor. 15:25; Heb. 10:12-13), progressively spoiling Satan's house and rescuing the nations from deception (Matt. 12:29; cf. Rev. 20:1-3). In the power of the gospel and the Holy Spirit, "the gates of hell will not prevail" against the onward march of the church of Christ (Matt. 16:18). Many sinners will be saved (Rom. 11:12-15, 25-26), will be nurtured in the commandments of Jesus (Matt. 28:20), and will give Christ pre-eminence in all things (Col. 1:13-20)—including the things pertaining to this present world (cf. 1 Tim. 4:8).[9] The nations will be discipled and will obey the Lord's Word (Matt. 28:18-20). The kingdom of Christ will come to dominate the kingdoms of this world (Rev. 11:15). And as God's kingdom comes, His will shall be more and more done on earth (Matt. 6:10), both ecclesiastically (Mal. 1:11) and politically (Ps. 72). "The government shall be upon his shoulder, and his name shall be called . . . Prince of Peace. Of the increase of his government and of peace there shall be no end, upon the throne of David and upon his kingdom, to establish it, and to uphold it with justice and with righteousness from henceforth even for ever. The zeal of Jehovah of hosts will perform this" (Isa. 9:6-7). The knowledge of the Lord is destined to cover the earth as the waters cover the sea (Isa. 11:9). Concomitantly, the people of God will with Christ exercise the authority of persuasion and of right—rather than military might—over the nations (Eph. 2:5-6; Rev. 2:26-27; 3:21; 5:10; 20:4-6; Luke 22:29-30).

the nature or function of civil government. Nor does it bear upon such issues by logical implication. The type of punishment dealt with in the parable is not temporal at all, but rather the judgment of eternal damnation (the tares are "gathered up" in "bundles to burn," Matt. 13:30). Moreover, the temporal judgments of the civil magistrate have nothing to do with discerning the hearts of men so as to divide the unregenerate ("the sons of the Evil One," v. 38) from the regenerate ("the sons of the kingdom"), but rather with punishing lawbreakers while protecting law-keepers (*regardless* of the wheat/tare distinction). In restraining premature separation of wheat and tares, Jesus was not condemning the moral judgments and divine vengeance expressed through the civil magistrate at all (or else Paul really is to be pitted against Him: cf. Rom. 12:19; 13:4). Surely even pluralists would not protect any and all criminal behavior (e.g., molesting children in professed subservience to "the Evil One") for the sake of "safeguarding the freedom of religion for all citizens"! Accordingly, it is ridiculous for them to suggest that they alone conform to the teaching of this parable, while those who advocate civil enforcement of God's law regarding crime somehow do not.

9. The much-abused statement of Jesus in John 18:36, "My kingdom is not of [*ek*: out from] this world," is a statement about the *source*—not the nature—of His reign, as the epexegetical ending of the verse makes obvious: "my kingdom is not *from here [enteuthen]*." The teaching is not that Christ's kingdom is wholly otherworldly, but rather that it originates with God Himself (not any power or authority found in creation).

28   *Greg L. Bahnsen*

These convictions about the kingdom of Christ will help us understand how it can be that, though many kings of this earth rebel against
the Savior, He is nevertheless their higher authority and ruler (as Rev.
1:5 and Matt. 28:18 teach). Christ is indeed the "King of kings" in a sense
that is both *ethical* (all rulers ought to obey Him and stand under judgment, historical and eternal, for refusing to do so; e.g., 2 Thess.
2:8) and *eschatological* (throughout history that reign which has been proclaimed in principle will see in practice more and more kings submit to
it; e.g., Rev. 21:24).[10]
   2. These general truths about Christ's kingdom receive specific expression in the majestic words of the Second Psalm. David opens with a
scene showing the tumultuous nations united in their agitation against
God (v. 1; cf. Ps. 74:22-23). This is identified specifically as *political*
opposition to Jehovah, stemming from "the kings of the earth . . . and
the rulers" (v. 2). They in particular set themselves contrary to the Most
High, devising evil schemes against Him—specifically "against His
Anointed One," His Christ (cf. the conceiving of a wicked plot against
the everlasting King in Ps. 21:11). Loving to exercise authority over
others (Matt. 20:25), the rulers of this world are hostile to any claim that
God has chosen One to exercise authority over them. This antipathy,
characteristic of all unbelieving kings, was clearly and definitively expressed during the earthly ministry of Jesus Christ and the founding of
His church, as Luke records in Acts 4:23-31. The rebellion against God's
Christ of which David spoke in Psalm 2 is applied to (1) the crucifixion of
the Savior (vv. 27-28) and (2) the persecution of those who proclaim His
sovereignty (vv. 29-30). The civil judges who condemned Christ to die
were united with the covenant people of God who in apostasy called for
the crucifixion of God's Son, saying, "We have no king but Caesar"
(John 19:15). Likewise, when the church of Christ preached that He is
Savior and Lord, the response of the world was (and continues to be)
that this is "contrary to the decrees of Caesar, saying that there is another
King, namely Jesus" (Acts 17:7).

   10. My own eschatological view of Christ's kingdom (notably its growth-dimension) is
historic postmillennial. Premillennial and amillennial brothers in the faith will rather apply
many of the victorious elements of the kingdom mentioned in my discussion to a time *after*
Christ returns. This is not the place to debate such questions. It is crucial to note, though,
that one's *eschatological* (especially millennial) interpretation of the kingdom has no logical
bearing upon the *ethical* aspect of the present, unconsummated kingdom. We should agree
that men, including their political leaders, *ought* to submit obediently to the will of Jesus
Christ, regardless of our differing views about *whether* (or when) many will do so or not.
There are premillennialists and amillennialists who are just as theonomic as some postmillennialists; likewise, there are postmillennialists who are not theonomic.

That against which the rulers of this world rebel is the claim that Christ, God's Anointed, is the supreme King to whom all earthly magistrates must obediently submit. David indicated this in Psalm 2:3, saying that the specific political counsel taken against Jehovah and His Christ had as its purpose to "break their bonds asunder, and cast away their cords from us." Unbelieving rulers despise being ruled by a higher, divine authority; they want to rule according to their own dictates and desires. They wish to be a rule-unto-themselves, autonomous. They choose to "burst the bonds" with God, thus disregarding and transgressing the law of God (cf. Jer. 5:5). God's response to this political impudence is described by David as laughing derision (Ps. 2:4; cf. 37:13; 59:8) and wrathful displeasure (2:5). The Creator laughs at those rulers who vainly attempt to assert their independence of Christ and His rule, and He places them under His dreadful curse. There is no escaping the objective fact that, by divine right, Jesus Christ is God's established King (2:6), figuratively described as enthroned upon Jehovah's holy hill (the temple) in the "city of the great King" (cf. Ps. 48:1-2). God has "anointed [Him] with the oil of gladness above all his fellows" and placed Him upon an everlasting throne, the scepter of whose kingdom is "a scepter of equity" (Ps. 45:6-7) — a clear reference to Christ's ascension (Heb. 1:8-9; esp. v. 3). Likewise, the divine affirmation "Thou art my son, this day have I begotten thee" (Ps. 2:7) — a truth made manifest at Christ's baptism, transfiguration, and resurrection (Mark 1:11; Luke 9:35; Acts 13:30-33) — reaches its culmination at Christ's ascension (Heb. 1:5; 5:5-6).

So, then, the Second Psalm portrays God honoring His Son, the Christ, by enthroning Him as supreme King (which took place especially at the ascension), despite the autonomous rebellion against Him by the kings and rulers of the earth. The divine response to this political opposition is to assert the eschatological (Ps. 2:8-9) and ethical (vv. 10-12) character of Christ's reign, the two aspects of His kingdom we have seen above.

Eschatologically, Jehovah promises His anointed King that the nations unto the uttermost part of the earth will become His ultimate inheritance and possession. Jesus Christ — as exalted King — will have victory over the nations of this world, both by way of a crushing historical judgment against disobedience (v. 9) and by way of giving blessed refuge to the humble (v. 12). Elsewhere in the Psalms David spoke of Jehovah sitting the Lord at His right hand until all His enemies are subdued (110:1), again in the twofold fashion of turning "all the ends of the earth" to Himself in repentance (v. 3; cf. Pss. 22:27; 65:2; 67:7) or "striking through kings in the day of His wrath" (vv. 5-7).

Ethically speaking, the Second Psalm portrays God responding to political opposition against Christ by calling upon "the kings . . . [and] judges of the earth" to become wise and instructed (v. 10). It is utter moral foolishness to disobey the King whom Jehovah has enthroned. It is noteworthy that this verse is addressed, not simply to the magistrates of theocratic Israel, but to all of the kings and judges "of the earth," even (especially) to those who dare to exercise civil rule in defiance of Jesus Christ. We cannot escape the clear biblical truth that each and every earthly ruler stands under the divinely established moral obligation to "serve Jehovah with fear . . . [and] kiss the Son" (vv. 11-12). Serving the Lord with fear unquestionably means obeying His commandments (cf. Josh. 22:5; Ps. 119:124-26; Deut. 10:12-13). Doing homage to "the Son"[11] in the form of a kiss was an ancient ritual by which the authority of a leader was acknowledged (e.g., 1 Sam. 10:1).

We cannot help but see, then, how far the infallible moral instruction of this psalm is removed from the pluralist political theories of our day. By contending that civil policy should not be based upon or favor any one distinctive religion or philosophy of life (but rather balance the alleged rights of all conflicting viewpoints), pluralism ultimately takes its political stand with secularism in refusing to "kiss the Son" and "serve Jehovah with fear." The pluralist approach transgresses the first commandment by countenancing and deferring to different ultimate authorities (gods) in the area of public policy. Instead of exclusively submitting to Jehovah's law with fear and openly following God's enthroned Son, the pluralist attempts the impossible task of honoring more than one master in civil legislation (Matt. 6:24) — a kind of "political polytheism." The Bible warns us how our ascended and supreme King, Jesus Christ, will react to political refusal to do homage to Him and obey His law: He will become "angry [with a wrath readily kindled] and you will perish in the way" (Ps. 2:12). The only safe and obedient political option for the kings of the earth is to "take refuge in Him." Our princes should no more take refuge in themselves, instead of Jehovah, than we should (Pss. 118:9; 146:3).

---

11. The traditional interpretation of the Hebrew is defended in standard commentaries by Hengstenberg, Delitzsch, and Leupold; Kidner prefers to read it "do homage purely (sincerely)" — which will, in light of vv. 6-9, imply submitting to *the Son* anyway.

The Validity and Application of God's Moral Law

If, as we have seen, it is the moral obligation of all present-day civil magistrates to obey the will of Jehovah and serve His Son, they need to know the standard by which their duty before God is determined. Where do civil magistrates find the political dictates of God? Surely not in varying subjective opinions, personal urges, the human wisdom of some elite group, the majority vote, or even a natural revelation that is suppressed and distorted in unrighteousness. It stands to reason that God's objective and unchanging standards for civil government will necessarily be found in the infallible, inscripturated Word of God, where and when it speaks to the subject of political ethics. And only someone ignorant of the literary content of the Scriptures could fail to recognize that the Bible says a *great deal* about the subject of public policy — much of it very direct and detailed (which is precisely its offense to many people today), especially as we see in the law of Moses.

But is it theologically legitimate to make contemporary use of this biblical material on civil law? On the one hand, to deny that these revealed dictates (or at least those in the Old Testament) are unchanging moral absolutes is implicitly to endorse the position of *cultural relativism* in ethics ("They were morally valid for that time and place, but invalid for other people and other times"); this is diametrically contrary to the testimony of Scripture (Mal. 3:6; Pss. 89:34; 111:7; 119:160; Eccles. 12:13; Rom. 2:11). On the other hand, to affirm that the principles for civil government found in the Bible (even the Old Testament) are binding in our day and age might suggest to some people that no differences between Old and New Covenants, or between an ancient agrarian society and the modern computer age, have been recognized. After all, in the Old Testament we read instructions for holy war, for kosher diet, for temple and priesthood, for cities of refuge at particular places in Palestine, for goring oxen and burning grain fields. Obviously, there are *some kinds* of discontinuity between these provisions and our own day. However, the evangelical literature on this subject often teems with hasty generalizations, exegetically unwarranted premises, and fallacious conclusions.

Some of these discontinuities are *redemptive-historical* in character (pertaining to the coming of the New Covenant and the finished work of Christ), while others are *cultural* in character (pertaining to simple changes of time, place, or lifestyle). The latter are unrelated to the former. There are cultural differences, not only between our society and the *Old* Testament, but *also* between modern America and the *New* Testament (e.g., its mention of whited sepulchres, social kisses, and meats offered to idols). Indeed, there are cultural differences even *within* the Old Testament (e.g., life in the wilderness, in the land, in captivity) and *within* the New Testament (e.g., Jewish culture, Gentile culture) themselves. Such cultural differences pose important *hermeneutical* questions — sometimes very vexing ones, since the "culture gap" between biblical times and our own is so wide.[12] However, these differences are *not* especially relevant to the question of *ethical validity*.

It is one thing to realize that we must translate biblical commands about a lost ox (Exod. 23:4) or withholding pay from someone who mows the fields (James 5:4) into terms relevant to our present culture (e.g., about misplaced credit cards or remuneration of factory workers). It is quite another thing altogether to say that such commands carry no ethical authority today! God obviously communicated to His people in terms of their own day and cultural setting, but what He said to them He fully expects us to obey in our own cultural setting, lest the complete authority of His Word be shortchanged in our lives. Moreover, it should be obvious that in teaching us our moral duties, God as a masterful teacher often instructs us, not only in general precepts (e.g., "Do not kill," Exod. 20:13; "Love one another," 1 John 3:11), but also in terms of *specific illustrations* (e.g., rooftop railings, Deut. 22:8; sharing worldly goods with a needy brother, 1 John 3:17) — expecting us to learn the broader, underlying principle from them. Again, those biblical illustrations are taken from the culture of that day. After the New Testament story of the good Samaritan, Jesus said, "Go and do likewise" (Luke 10:37). It does not take a lot of hermeneutical common sense to know that our concrete duty is *not* thereby to go travel the literal Jericho road (rather than an American interstate highway) on a literal donkey (rather than in a Ford) with literal denarii in our pockets (rather than dollars), pouring wine and oil (rather than modern antiseptic salves) on the wounds of those who have been mugged. Indeed, one can be a modern "good Samaritan"

---

12. Is that gap as wide as the Grand Canyon or merely a crack in the sidewalk? (Rodney Clapp suggests that these are the alternatives in "Democracy as Heresy," *Christianity Today* February 20, 1987, 22.) It would be terribly misleading to answer either way. First, the "gap" obviously *varies* from precept to precept in the Bible; some are more distant to our lifestyle than others. The question calls for dangerous oversimplification. Second, the metaphors suggested are obviously *extreme*; between those extremes there surely exist other (more reasonable) answers pointing to mediating degrees of difference. Finally, one would be seriously misled to think that this question of culture gap is any more uncomfortable for (or critical of) theonomists than it is for *any other* school of thought committed to using the ancient literature of the Bible (whether Old or New Testament) in modern society. The alternative — which any believer should find repugnant — is simply to dismiss the Bible as anachronistic.

in a circumstance that has nothing to do with travel and muggers whatsoever. Unfortunately, though, this same hermeneutical common sense is sometimes not applied to the cultural illustrations communicated in Old Testament moral instruction.[13] For instance, the requirement of a rooftop railing (Deut. 22:8), relevant to entertaining on flat roofs in Palestine, teaches the underlying principle of safety precautions (e.g., fences around modern backyard swimming pools), not the obligation of placing a literal battlement upon today's sloped roofs.

There are, then, *cultural* discontinuities between biblical moral instruction and our modern society. This fact does not imply that the ethical teaching of Scripture is invalidated for us; it simply calls for hermeneutical sensitivity. In asking whether it is theologically legitimate to make contemporary use of biblical (especially Old Testament) precepts pertaining to civil law, then, our concern is more properly with *redemptive historical* discontinuities, notably between Old and New Covenants. Clearly, the Scriptures teach us that a new day arrived with the establishment of Christ's kingdom, the New Covenant (Luke 22:20; Jer. 31:31-34; Heb. 8:7-13; 10:14-18), and the age of the Spirit (Acts 2:16-36; Luke 3:16-17)—a day anticipated by all the Old Covenant Scriptures (Luke 24:26-27; Acts 3:24; 1 Pet. 1:10-11). What differences with the Old Covenant era have been introduced? Only the King, the Lord of the covenant, who speaks by means of the Holy Spirit is in a position to answer that question with authority. Thus, we look, not to sinful speculation or cultural tradition, but to the inspired Word of Christ to guide our thoughts regarding it. There we are taught that the New Covenant surpasses the Old Covenant in (1) power, (2) glory, (3) finality, and (4) realization. Such discontinuities must not be overlooked, and yet, in the nature of the case, they presuppose an underlying unity in God's covenantal dealings. The historical changes in outward administration and circumstance grow out of a common and unchanging divine intention.

The Old Covenant law as written on external tablets of stone accused man of sin, but could not grant the internal ability to comply with those demands. By contrast, the New Covenant written by the Holy Spirit on the internal tables of the human heart communicates life and righteousness, giving the *power* to obey God's commandments (Jer. 31:33; Ezek.

13. Just here Christopher J. H. Wright has misconceived and thus badly misrepresented the "theonomic" approach as calling for a "literal imitation of Israel" which simply lifts its ancient laws and transplants them into the vastly changed modern world ("The Use of the Bible in Social Ethics: Paradigms, Types and Eschatology," *Transformation* 1, 1 [January-March 1984]: 17).

11:19-20; 2 Cor. 3:3, 6-9; Rom. 7:12-16; 8:4; Heb. 10:14-18; 13:20-21). Although the Old Covenant had its glory, the sin-laden Jews requested Moses to veil his face when revealing its stipulations, for it was fundamentally a ministration of condemnation. But the New Covenant redemptively brings life and confidence before God (2 Cor. 3:7-4:6; Rom. 8:3; Heb. 4:15-16; 6:18-20; 7:19; 9:8; 10:19-20), thus exceeding in unfading *glory* (2 Cor. 3:9, 18; 4:4-6; Heb. 3:3). Moreover, unlike God's Word to Old Covenant believers, special revelation will not be augmented further for New Covenant Christians; it has reached its *finalized* form until the return of Christ. This New Testament Word brings greater moral clarity (removing Pharisaical distortions of the law [Matt. 5:21-48; 23:3-28] and unmistakably demonstrating the meaning of love [John 13:34-35; 15:12-13]) and greater personal responsibility for obedience (Luke 12:48; Heb. 2:1-4; 12:25).

Finally, the New Covenant surpasses the Old in realization. To understand this, we must take account of the fact that the laws of the Old Covenant served two different purposes. Some laws defined the righteousness of God to be emulated by men (thus being moral in function), while other laws defined the way of salvation for the unrighteous (thus being redemptive in function). To illustrate, the law forbidding us to steal shows what righteousness demands, whereas the law stipulating animal sacrifice shows what must be done by a thief to gain redemption. This distinction between justice-defining and redemption-expounding laws was proverbially expressed by the Jews: "To do righteousness and justice is more acceptable to Jehovah than sacrifice" (Prov. 21:3). It was also evident in the prophetic declaration from God, "I desire goodness, and not sacrifice: and the knowledge of God more than burnt-offerings" (Hos. 6:6; cf. Matt. 9:13; 12:7). Accordingly, the New Testament teaches that there are some portions of the Old Testament law that were "shadows" of the coming Messiah and His redemptive work (Heb. 9:9; 10:1; Col. 2:17). They were deemed weak and beggarly rudiments that served as a tutor unto Christ and taught justification by faith (Gal. 3:23-4:10). Paul called them "the law of commandments contained in ordinances" which imposed a separation of the Jews from the Gentile world (Eph. 2:14-15).

These descriptions do not accurately apply to moral laws of the Old Testament, which for instance, forbid adultery or oppressing the poor. Such laws do not foreshadow the redemptive work of Christ, show us justification by faith, or symbolically set apart the Jews from the Gentiles. Laws pertaining to the priesthood, temple, sacrificial system, and the like do accomplish those ends, however, and are to be considered "put out of gear" by the coming of that reality they foreshadowed. This is the logic pursued by the author of Hebrews, especially in chapters 7 through 10. For instance, the coming of Christ has brought a change of law regarding the priesthood (Heb. 7:12), and the administrative order of the Old Covenant is vanishing away (8:13). By realizing the salvation foreshadowed in the Old Covenant, the New Covenant supercedes the details of the Old Covenant redemptive dispensation. We no longer come to God through animal sacrifices, but now through the shed blood of the Savior—in both cases, type and reality, acknowledging that "apart from the shedding of blood there is no remission" from the guilt of sin (Heb. 9:22).

In connection with the superceding of the Old Covenant shadows, the redemption secured by the New Covenant also *redefines* the people of God. The kingdom that was once focused on the nation of Israel has been taken away from the Jews (Matt. 8:11-12; 21:41-43; 23:37-38) and given to an international body, the church of Jesus Christ. New Testament theology describes the church as the "restoration of Israel" (Acts 15:15-20), "the commonwealth of Israel" (Eph. 2:12), the "seed of Abraham" (Gal. 3:7, 29), and "the Israel of God"; (6:16). What God was doing with the nation of Israel was but a type looking ahead to the international church of Christ. The details of the old order have passed away, giving place to the true kingdom of God established by the Messiah, in which both Jew and Gentile have become "fellow-citizens" on an equal footing (Eph. 2:11-20; 3:3-6). It is important for biblical interpretation to bear this in mind, because certain stipulations of the Old Covenant were enacted for the purpose of distinguishing Israel as the people of God from the pagan Gentile world. Such stipulations were not essentially moral in function (forbidding what was intrinsically contrary to the righteousness of God), but rather symbolic. This accounts for the fact that they allowed Gentiles to do the very thing that was forbidden to the Jews (e.g., Deut. 14:21).

Accordingly, given the redefinition of the people of God in the New Covenant, certain aspects of the Old Covenant order have been altered. (1) The New Covenant does not require political loyalty to Israel (Phil. 3:20) or defending God's kingdom by the sword (John 18:36; 2 Cor. 10:4). (2) The land of Canaan foreshadowed the kingdom of God (Heb. 11:8-10; Eph. 1:14; 1 Pet. 1:4), which is fulfilled in Christ (Gal. 3:16; cf. Gen. 13:15), thus rendering inapplicable Old Covenant provisions tied to the land (such as family divisions, location of cities of refuge, the levirate).[14] (3) The laws that symbolically taught Israel to be separate from the Gentile world, such as the dietary provisions (Lev. 20:22-26), need no longer be observed in their pedagogical form (Acts 10, esp. v. 15; Mark 7:19; Rom. 14:17), even though the Christian does honor their symbolized principle of separation from ungodliness (2 Cor. 6:14-18; Jude 23).

Therefore, the redemptive dispensation and form of the kingdom in the Old Covenant has dramatically changed in the New. The New Covenant surpasses the Old in power, glory, finality, and realization. In short, the New Covenant is a "better covenant enacted upon better promises" (Heb. 8:6). Even those aspects of the Old Covenant *law* which typified the kingdom of God and the way of redemption (e.g., priesthood, sacrifice, temple, Promised Land, symbols of separation and purity) were speaking to the *promises* of God, preparing for and foreshadowing the salvation and kingdom to be brought by the Messiah. Thus the discontinuities between Old and New Covenants that we have been discussing actually point to a more elementary, underlying *continuity* between them. At bottom, the two covenants are one, although they differed in administrative outworking according to their respective places in the history of redemption. All the distinctively Jewish covenants of the Old Testament are "the [plural] covenants of the [singular] promise" (Eph. 2:12). However many were the Old Covenant promises of God, they are all affirmed and confirmed in Jesus Christ (2 Cor. 1:20). Thus it was preposterous, Paul said, to set the Mosaic covenant of law against the Abrahamic covenant of promise (Gal. 3:15-22). So then, we find in the Scripture a substantial covenantal continuity of promise underlying the important administrative or formal discontinuities between Old Covenant anticipation (shadows, prophecies) and New Covenant realization (fulfillment).

Regarding the promises pertaining to redemption, then, we may rightly speak of the "better promises" of the New Covenant. They *differed* from the Old Covenant provision by being the fulfillment of that to which it looked ahead, giving both covenants the *same* intention and objective. The differing covenantal administrations of God's *promise* are

---

14. Ronald J. Sider is thus mistaken in imagining that the validity of the Old Testament law would entail the necessity of a Jubilee restoration of land to original owners today; he forgets the special place and treatment given to the Palestinian Promised Land and the (objective) New Testament rationale for alteration regarding it ("Christian Love and Public Policy: A Response to Herbert Titus," *Transformation* 2, 3 [July-September 1985]: 13). He also, without exegetical justification, treats the sabbatical and Jubilee provisions as though they were a matter for civil coercion, in addition to being enforced by direct imposition of supernatural judgment (p. 14).

due precisely to the historical character of His redemptive plan. However, regarding God's *law*, one nowhere reads in Scripture that God's moral stipulations share the same historical variation or anything like it. The Bible never speaks of the New Covenant instituting "better commandments" than those of the Old Covenant. Far from it. Instead, Paul declared that "the [Old Testament] law is holy, and the commandment is holy, and righteous, and good" (Rom. 7:12). He took the validity of the law's moral demands as a theological truth that should be obvious and presupposed by all, stating without equivocation, "We know that the law is good" (1 Tim. 1:8). That should be axiomatic for Christian ethics, according to the apostle.

Contrary to those today who are prone to criticize the Old Testament moral precepts, there must be no question whatsoever about the moral propriety and validity of what they revealed. It should be our starting point — the standard by which we judge all other opinions — that the law's moral provisions are correct. "I esteem *all* Thy precepts concerning *all things* to be right" (Ps. 119:128). Accordingly, James reminds us that we have no prerogative to become "judges of the law," but are rather called to be doers of the law (4:11). And when Paul posed the hypothetical question of whether the law is sin, his immediate outburst was "May it never be!" (Rom. 7:7). God's holy and good law is never wrong in what it demands. It is "perfect" (Deut. 32:4; Ps. 19:7; James 1:25), just like the Lawgiver Himself (Matt. 5:48). It is a transcript of His moral character.

Thus, the suggestion that theonomists concentrate on "abstract personal laws instead of on knowing the Lawgiver" is not only a cheap shot, it also rests upon a devastating theological error. God's law is not abstract (if it were, fewer people would be offended by it); neither is it impersonal. It so perfectly reflects God's own holiness (Rom. 7:12; 1 Pet. 1:14-16) that the apostle John categorically dismissed anyone as a *liar* who claimed to "know God" and yet did *not* keep His commandments (1 John 2:3-4). God's law is a very personal matter — so much so that Jesus said, "If you *love* Me, you will keep My commandments" (John 14:15, cf. vv. 21, 23; 15:10, 14). It is characteristic of the true believer to have the law written upon his heart and delight inwardly in it (Jer. 31:33; Rom. 7:22; Ps. 1:1-2) just because he so intimately loves God, his Redeemer.

Paul teaches elsewhere that *all men* — even pagans who do not love God and do not have the advantage of the written oracles of God (cf. Rom. 3:1-2) — nevertheless know the just requirements of God's law. They know what God, the Creator, requires of them. They know it from the created order (1:18-21) and from inward conscience, the "work of the law" being written upon their hearts (2:14-15). Paul characterizes them as "knowing the ordinance of God" (1:32) and, thus, being "without excuse" for refusing to live in a God-glorifying fashion (1:20-23). This discussion indicates that the stipulations of God's moral law—whether known through Mosaic (written) ordinances or by general (unwritten) revelation—carry a universal and "natural" obligation, appropriate to the Creator-creature relation apart from any question of redemption. Their validity is not by any means restricted to the Jews in a particular timeperiod. What the law speaks, it speaks "in order that *all the world* may be brought under the judgment of God" (3:19). God is no respecter of persons here. "*All* have sinned" (3:23), which means they have violated that common standard of moral integrity for all men, the law of God (3:20).

A good student of the Old Testament would have known as much. The moral laws of God were never restricted in their validity to the Jewish nation. At the beginning of the Book of Deuteronomy, when Moses exhorted the Israelites to observe God's commandments, he clearly taught that the laws divinely revealed to Israel were meant by the Lawgiver as a *model* to be emulated by all the surrounding Gentile nations:

> Behold I have taught you statutes and ordinances even as Jehovah my God commanded me, that you should do so in the midst of the land whither ye go in to possess it. Keep therefore and do them; for this is your wisdom and your understanding in the sight of the peoples, that shall hear all these statutes and say, Surely this great nation is a wise and understanding people. . . . What great nation is there that hath statutes and ordinances so righteous as all this law which I set before you this day? (Deut. 4:5-8).

All "the peoples," not just the Israelites, should follow the manifestly righteous requirements of God's law. In this respect, the justice of God's law made Israel to be a light to the Gentiles (Isa. 51:4). Unlike many modern Christian writers on ethics, God did not have a double standard of morality—one for Israel and one for the Gentiles (cf. Lev. 24:22). Accordingly, God made it clear that the reason why the Palestinian tribes were ejected from the land was precisely that they had violated the provisions of His holy law (Lev. 18:24-27). This fact presupposes that the Gentiles were antecedently obligated to obey those provisions. Accordingly, the psalmist condemned "all the wicked of the earth" for departing from God's statutes (119:118-119). Accordingly, the Book of Proverbs, intended as international wisdom literature, directs all nations to obey the laws of God: "Righteousness exalts a nation, but sin is a disgrace to any people (14:34). Accordingly, the Old Testament prophets repeatedly excoriated the Gentile nations for their transgressions against God's law (e.g., Amos, Habakkuk, Jonah at Nineveh). Accordingly, Isaiah looked forward to the day when the Gentile nations would stream into Zion, precisely that God's law would go forth from Jerusalem unto all the world (2:2-3).

Two premises about the law of God are thus abundantly clear if we are faithful to the infallible testimony of Scripture: (1) The law of God is *good* in what it demands, being what is natural to the Creator-creature relation. And (2) the demands of God's law are *universal* in their character and application, not confined in validity to Old Testament Israel. Consequently, it would be extremely unreasonable to expect that the coming of the Messiah and the institution of the New Covenant would alter the moral demands of God as revealed in His law. Why, we must ask, would God feel the need to change His perfect, holy requirements for our conduct and attitudes? Christ came, rather, to atone for our transgressions against those moral requirements (Rom. 4:25; 5:8-9; 8:1-3). And the New Covenant was established precisely to confirm our redeemed hearts in obedience to God's law (Rom. 8:4-10; 2 Cor. 3:6-11). Should we sin because we are under the grace of God? Paul declared, "May it never be!" Being made free from sin we must rather now become the "servants of righteousness" (Rom. 6:15-18). The grace of God has appeared and Jesus Christ has given Himself to "redeem us from all lawlessness and purify unto Himself a people . . . zealous of good works" (Titus 2:14; Eph. 2:8-10).

While the New Testament condemns any legalistic (Judaizing) use of God's law to establish one's personal justification or sanctification before God, and while the New Testament rejoices in the fact that the work of Christ has surpassed the legal foreshadows and rituals of the Old Covenant, we never find the New Testament rejecting or criticizing the *moral demands* of the Old Testament law. They are at every point upheld and commended.[15] Thus Paul firmly taught that "every scripture" (of the inspired Old Testament) was "profitable for instruction in righteousness" that we might be equipped for every good work (2 Tim. 3:16-17). James is equally clear that if someone is guilty of breaking even one command-

---

15. The antitheses of Matt. 5:21-48 are not an unfair *ex post facto* condemnation of the Pharisees by a higher standard than that which they already knew. They prove to be a series of contrasts between Jesus' interpretation of the law's full demand and the restrictive, external, distorted interpretations of the law by the Jewish elders (cf. 5:20; 7:28-29; e.g., 5:43, which does not even appear in the Old Testament).

ment of the law, he has broken them all (2:10) — indicating our obligation to every one of them. Jesus rebuked Satan (and many modern ethicists) by declaring that man should live "by every word that proceeds from the mouth of God" (Matt. 4:4). This is the uniform New Testament perspective and presumption regarding the laws of the Old Testament. His Word teaches, however, that we should countenance such change in particular cases *only when* God Himself teaches such. We are not arbitrarily to assume that His commandments have been repealed, but only where, when, and how He says so.

The decisive word on this point is that of our Lord Himself as found in Matthew 5:17-19. Since the moral demands of God's law continue to be deemed good and holy and right in the New Testament, and since those demands were from the beginning obligatory upon Jews and Gentiles alike, it would be senseless to think that Christ came in order to cancel mankind's responsibility to keep them. It is theologically incredible that the mission of Christ was to make it morally acceptable now for men to blaspheme, murder, rape, steal, gossip, or envy! Christ did not come to change our evaluation of God's laws from that of holy to unholy, obligatory to optional, or perfect to flawed. Listen to His own testimony:

> Do not begin to think that I came to abrogate the Law or the Prophets; I came not to abrogate but to fulfill. For truly I say to you, until heaven and earth pass away, until all things have happened, not one jot or tittle shall by any means pass away from the law. Therefore, whoever shall break one of these least commandments and teach men so shall be called least in the kingdom of heaven (Matt. 5:17-19).

Several points about the interpretation of this passage should be rather clear. (1) Christ twice denied that His advent had the purpose of abrogating the Old Testament commandments. (2) Until the expiration of the physical universe, not even a letter or stroke of the law will pass away. And (3) therefore God's disapprobation rests upon anyone who teaches that *even the least* of the Old Testament laws may be broken.[16] In all of its minute detail (every jot and tittle) the law of God, down to its

---

16. Attempts are sometimes made to evade the thrust of this text by editing out its reference to the moral demands of the Old Testament — contrary to what is obvious from its context (5:16, 20, 21-48; 6:1, 10, 33; 7:12, 20-21, 26) and semantics ("the law" in v. 18, "commandment" in v. 19). Other attempts are made to extract an abrogating of the law's moral demands from the word "fulfill" (v. 17) or the phrase "until all things have happened" (v. 18). This, however, renders the verses self-contradictory in what they assert.

least significant provision, should be reckoned to have an abiding valid-ity — until and unless the Lawgiver reveals otherwise.

Of course, nothing that has been said above means that the work of Christian ethics is a pat and easy job. Even though the details of God's law are available to use as moral absolutes, they still need to be properly interpreted and applied to the modern world. It should constantly be borne in mind that no school of thought, least of all the theonomist out-look, has all the answers. Nobody should get the impression that clear, simple, or uncontestable "solutions" to the moral problems of our day can just be lifted from the fact of Scripture's laws. A tremendous amount of homework remains to be done, whether in textual exegesis, cultural analysis, or moral reasoning — with plenty of room for error and correc-tion. None of it is plain and simple. It must not be carried on thought-lessly or without sanctified mental effort. Moreover, in all of it we need each other's best efforts and charitable corrections. Only after our ethical senses have been corporately exercised to discern good and evil by the constant study and use of God's law — only after we have gained con-siderably more experience in the word of righteousness (Heb. 5:13-14) — will we achieve greater clarity, confidence, and a common mind in applying God's law to the ethical difficulties that beset modern men. Nevertheless, even with the mistakes that we may make in using God's law today, I prefer it as the *basis* for ethics to the sinful and foolish specu-lations of men.[17] It would be absurd for a man to resign himself to poison just because medical doctors occasionally make mistakes with prescrip-tion drugs.

The Distinction Between Social and Political Ethics

The preceding discussion has brought us to two conclusions thus far: (1) the presently established messianic kingdom of God requires all civil magistrates to acknowledge the supremacy of Jesus Christ and perform their public tasks in obedience to His will; and (2) even though the promises and changed administrative form of the New Covenant surpass the Old Covenant, the moral law of God found in the Old Covenant

---

17. It can hardly be well-reasoned criticism of theonomic ethics that some "potentially dangerous ideas" could arise from following the holy laws of God in Scripture. We live in a fallen world where adherents of any and *every* political philosophy (including attempted biblical ones) will err in carrying out their ideals. That being the case, it only makes sense to err on the side of the angels, starting with the best (indeed, infallible) ideals available to men. Just imagine what "potentially [nay, actually] dangerous ideas" have stemmed from *not* following God's law, but rather the human speculations found in Rousseau, Marx, Buckley, Galbraith, and many others!

(when properly interpreted in light of its cultural setting) is axiomatically good and universal in character. That law was completely upheld by Christ in its moral validity even in its least command, except where and when God revealed otherwise. These two biblical premises lead us to the conclusion that all civil magistrates today are under moral obligation to be guided and regulated by the law of God (throughout the Bible) *where and when* it speaks to political matters. To be properly understood, this conclusion calls for drawing a distinction between *social ethics* (in general) and *political ethics* (in particular). The failure to observe such a distinction is perhaps the most damaging oversight in contemporary evangelical thinking about the ethics of life-in-community.

It is crucial to distinguish social from political ethics so that we may mark off, within the context of public moral duties and responsibilities, a *delimited* realm where the state has authority to enforce civil sanctions against misbehavior. Not all sins against the law of God are properly to be treated as crimes, and therefore we must (in an objective fashion) circumscribe the authority of the state to inflict punishment upon its citizens. This viewpoint stands diametrically opposed to the axiom of Lenin that "we have no more private law, for with us all has become public law." Were the sphere of sin (even public or interpersonal sin) to be equated with the sphere of the state's legal prerogative to impose punitive sanctions, the state would be placed in the position of God Himself. But the state does not have the right to scrutinize and judge every social misdeed. Nor does it have the responsibility to produce every social virtue. The state is neither competent nor empowered to judge the private lusts of an individual's heart or even his selfish use of money in light of a neighbor's need.

The special characteristic that marks off the state from other institutions within society is its moral authority (not simply raw power) to inflict public penalties for disobeying civil statutes. It is an institution distinguished by coercive authority. Paul accordingly symbolized the distinctive function of the state as that of "bearing the sword" as a "terror" and "avenger of wrath" to evildoers (Rom. 13:4), a prerogative denied to both the family (Deut. 21:18-21) and the church (2 Cor. 10:3-4). Because the state possesses this awesome prerogative to use compulsion in enforcing its dictates (whether by threat of death, monetary fine, or imprisonment), the state must be carefully and ethically limited in its proper jurisdiction. If the state lacks moral warrant for imposing a civil penalty upon someone for violating a public statute, its punitive action reduces to the situation where the will of the stronger overwhelms the desires of the weaker. "Without justice, what are states but great bands of robbers?" asked Augustine. Unless the state has a moral warrant for its use of force in particular cases, the state's use of capital punishment is indistinguishable from murder; imprisonment would be no different from kidnapping, extracting a monetary fine the same as theft. Therefore, lest our states become "lawless" and "beasts" (2 Thess. 2:3; Rev. 13:16-17), there must be objective limits to legal coercion — a law above the civil law to which appeal can be made against injustice and oppression. This objective criterion is the revealed law of God as it prescribes civil penalties for misdeeds. God's law enables us to distinguish consistently and on principle sin from crime, personal morality from civil legality, social from political ethics, where the state may properly legislate from where it must not interfere.[18]

Evangelical ethicists of both politically conservative and politically liberal varieties have transgressed the principle offered above. Those with conservative leanings have tended to promote ethically commendable goals (sobriety regarding alcoholic beverages, restriction of smoking tobacco, intervention to curtail the geopolitical spread of communism) by less than ethical means, calling upon the state to exercise its power of compulsion where no biblical warrant for it can be cogently adduced. Likewise, those with liberal political leanings have tended to promote

---

18. David Basinger faults this criterion (rather superficially) on the ground that sincere Christians disagree in interpreting the Bible as to what are punishable crimes ("Voting One's Christian Conscience," *Christian Scholar's Review* 15, 2 [1986]: 143-44). But given that reasoning, the Bible should *equally* be precluded from being the basis of our theological distinctions, matters of doctrinal truth, or church polity — again, because sincere believers have unresolved disagreements there. Moreover, even Basinger's own suggestion of a political standard (viz., those values which all men, believers *and unbelievers*, propound in common) would fall under his own censure; it is surely not a "common value" among men that political power should be restrained by values that are agreed upon by everyone! Besides, the only truly "common" values (if any) that are explicitly endorsed by absolutely all men are unhelpful verbal abstractions (e.g., "fair play," "justice"), which lack particular applications (the very thing over which men notoriously and sharply disagree). Ronald Sider suggests that the principle to be used for distinguishing between social sins to be dealt with solely by the church and crimes to be punished as well by the state is the libertarian ideal: "persons should be free to harm themselves and consenting associates . . . as long as they do not harm others or infringe on their rights" ("An Evangelical Vision for Public Policy," *Transformation* 2, 3 [July-September 1985]: 6). Such a principle is not only ambiguous, arbitrary, and inconsistently applied (see Greg Bahnsen, *Homosexuality: A Biblical View* [Grand Rapids: Baker, 1978], chap. 6), it is simply not biblically derived. This is a fatal defect for a Christian. Not surprisingly, it leads Sider to a complete *reversal* of the explicit teaching of God's law: applying to the *state* what is appropriate only to the church (penal redress of racial discrimination in a matter of private property), and restricting to the *church* what God's law actually requires of the state (redress of adultery and homosexuality)!

ethically commendable goals (racial integration, food or medical care for the poor, public education) by less than ethical means, calling upon the state to exercise its power of compulsion where no biblical warrant for it can be cogently adduced. No matter how ethically good these various projects may be, attempting to get the *civil* authorities to *enforce* them *without warrant* from God's Word is to capitulate to the unprincipled position of Thrasymachus, who taught that what counts as "justice" is simply whatever happens to be in the interest of the stronger faction in society. Ironically, when the strong arm of the state is courted in the name of "public justice," as defined by some evangelical's personal *opinion* (whether conservative or liberal), it is usually at the cost of *depriving* others of their justice—their *genuine* rights (e.g., to choose for what causes to contribute their lives or earnings), as revealed by the just judge of all the earth (cf. Gen. 18:25; Deut. 2:4).

The state that overextends its authority to promote or enforce whatever aims it wishes, however otherwise commendable (e.g., sexual harmony between husbands and wives, prudent financial savings plans, regular brushing of one's teeth), is a state that has abused its power. That power has, after all, been *delegated* to it from God (Rom. 13:1; John 19:11), and God clearly, explicitly *forbids* kings to swerve to the right or to the left from the well-defined path of His law (Deut. 17:18-20). Indeed, the memorable words of our Lord in Matthew 22:21 inescapably teach that there must be a defining limit upon "the things which belong to Caesar." When Caesar demands of his subjects more than what is his—more than what is "due" to him (Rom. 13:7)—Caesar's government inevitably acts as a "throne of wickedness . . . which frames mischief by a law" (Ps. 94:20).

So, then, the state's "sword" which should not be used "in vain" (Rom. 13:4; cf. "vain thing" in Ps. 1:1), is not under the capricious or autonomous direction of the civil magistrate. He will eventually give an account of his judicial actions to the "King of kings" (1 Tim. 6:15), the "ruler of the kings of the earth" (Rev. 1:5). The fact that the civil magistrate makes something a law does not confer the sanction of God upon it. When the civil magistrate (God's "minister") exceeds the limits of delegated power by enforcing laws not authorized by God, he comes under God's wrath and curse: "Woe to those who enact evil statutes" (Isa. 10:1). The proper domain and divine calling of the state is that of civil justice, protecting its citizens against violence (whether in the form of foreign aggression, criminal assault, or economic fraud). In order that men may live together in tranquility and peace (1 Tim. 2:2), the state has been empowered with "the sword" for the *specific purpose* (note the telic construction and divine commission in 1 Pet. 2:14) of "avenging wrath" against those who do evil (Rom. 13:4). "For this cause," God says, taxes may be legitimately collected (v. 6). Beyond this the magistrate may not go. He is to establish the land by justice which is steadfastly followed in the courts (Prov. 29:4; Amos 5:15). God's Word does not, however, authorize the civil ruler to be an agent of charitable benevolence, financial welfare, education, and mercy.[19] Nor does it grant the state the prerogative of promoting or enforcing the gospel, much less to be a "policeman of the world." States that assume such functions take on a messianic complex, attempting to save men or the world in ways God never intended for them. The state's way of dealing with social evils is limited to those marked out by God's revealed law.

---

19. Specifically at this point we must make principled objection to the civil proposals and oppressive, preferential methods of helping the poor (illegally intruding into matters of private property and the free market) advocated by Ronald Sider in *Rich Christians in an Age of Hunger* (Downers Grove, Ill.: Inter-Varsity Press, 1977), notably chap. 9, "Structural Change." His expressed aim of relieving poverty can hardly be faulted, but his suggested *means* of achieving that aim — enlisting the coercive lordship of the civil state (e.g., foreign aid, guaranteed income, governmentally set prices, international taxation, tariffs [for some, not all!], land redistribution, population control) — must be rejected for its lawlessness. He asserts, "Yahweh wills institutionalized structures (rather than mere charity) which systematically and regularly reduce the gap between the rich and the poor" (p. 209, note the telling expression "mere charity"). The only *morally approved* "institutionalized structure" given by God to accomplish such an end, however, is the free market — the very institution over which Sider's proposals ride roughshod. His methods amount to legalized theft by the state.

The biblical way to deal with the physical needs of the poor in society is by means of voluntary personal charity (love willingly extended from the heart, 1 Cor. 13:3), obedience to relevant laws of God (e.g., about lending, gleaning), and the corporate church's tithe-supported diaconal ministry (e.g., 1 Cor. 16:1-2; Rom. 15:25-27). It is not a biblical approach to use state compulsion through taxes or economic barriers that men are forced to honor upon threat of civil punishment. There is certainly a difference between the social demands of benevolence and the political demands of justice; the former calls for one to act according to grace, the latter to perform an enforceable obligation. No one may justifiably claim gracious treatment as a "right" (which conceptually entails a corresponding duty of someone else). Much less may the state, like a middleman broker of power, enforce a claim to gracious treatment on the behalf of others (welfare recipients). As Carl F. H. Henry recently stated the matter: "The business of government is to provide justice, not charity redefined as wealth redistribution by taxation" ("The Gospel for the Rest of Our Century," *Christianity Today Institute* [January 17, 1986]: 25). God does indeed expect kings to "deliver the poor and needy" (Ps. 72:2-4, 12-14), but this means, according to this text itself, that they are to "break their oppressors" by securing fairness in the courts and protecting them from "fraud and violence" (Lev. 19:15; Exod. 23:3, 6; Ps. 82:1-4; cf. Prov. 22:22-23; 29:14). It suggests nothing of state-enforced welfare programs or state interference in the free market.

The Role of Civil Government Is to Enforce God's Criminal Law
When our Christian reflections upon political theory are guided by all
of Scripture and only Scripture, we are led finally to the conclusion that,
in submission to the presently established messianic kingdom, all political leaders are ethically obligated to enforce those civil provisions in the
moral law of God—and only those provisions—where He has delegated
coercive power of enforcement to rulers. In short, it is the civil magistrate's proper function and duty to obey the Scripture's dictates regarding crime and its punishment. The law of God is not a "textbook" of
statecraft, as though all the statutes any culture would ever need (e.g.,
traffic laws), and precisely in the wording a complex technological society might require to address, (e.g., computerized theft, copyright in-
fringement), could be read verbatim right out of Deuteronomy and into
every country's civil code. As noted previously, much homework remains to be done in interpreting and applying God's laws to our modern
world. However, what modern legislators, magistrates, and judges
should be concerned to apply and enforce in the state are the precepts of
God's law.

Although this idea has long been a virtual staple of the Reformed social outlook, many respond to it today with intellectual shock and ada-
mant personal rejection. A common reason for this is that people adhere
to a particular interpretation of church-state separation that actually
parallels the sacred-secular distinction we previously found biblically unacceptable. There are writers who will concede that God's law is valid in
personal, ecclesiastical, or social ethics, but then they utterly deny its
continuing validity in *political* ethics. Such a distinction hardly arises
from the literature and teaching of the Bible, much less the ancient and
medieval worlds. It is much more in tune with the mentality of modern
Enlightenment-sponsored rationalism, which quarantines politics, along
with other material concerns such as history and natural science, from
religious revelation.

That mentality has been especially fostered by one misguided American
conception of the "separation of church and state." We must realize that
such a slogan is not biblical in wording and is conceptually ambiguous.[20]
It should not be taught that the *institutional* separation of the state from

---

20. Cf. Greg Bahnsen, "Separation of Church and State," taped lecture no. 346 from
Covenant Tape Ministry, P.O. Box 7134, Reno, NV 89510), for an analysis of the different issues commonly grouped together under the rubric of "separation of church and
state." This collection of multiple senses under one expression is easily conducive to logical equivocation.

the church (something both crucial and biblical) has any logical bearing upon the transcendent moral authority of Jesus Christ over each and every sphere of life (whatever their institutional forms). The doctrine of church-state separation does not entail the separation of the state from *ethics*, and it is precisely to such ethical concerns that the law of God speaks. Ironically, as things turn out, it is precisely those who do *not* acknowledge the law of God as their political norm who readily disregard and overturn the proper separation of church and state. They do so by taking ethical norms that are exegetically addressed to and intended appropriately for the church (a redemptive institution characterized by mercy and persuasion) and applying them instead to the state (a natural institution characterized by justice and coercion). Thus the moral obligations addressed to the church in particular (e.g., to care for the poor and practice racial nondiscrimination) are transferred to and laid upon the civil state in general.[21]

The relevant moral question is whether or not the infallible Word of God countenances *an exception* from God's law for modern civil magistrates. Such an alleged exemption must be *read into* the text of Scripture rather than taken from it. It thus reveals not the mind of God but the extraneous presuppositional baggage of the interpreter. The premise that today's political leaders are exempt from obligation to the relevant dictates of God's revealed law falsely assumes that the political validity of God's law applied solely and uniquely to Israel as a nation. Of course, there *were* many *unique* aspects of Israel's national experience; important discontinuities existed between Israel and the pagan nations. Only Israel as a nation stood as such in an elect, redemptive, and covenantal relation with God; only Israel was a type of the coming kingdom of God, having its kingly line specially chosen and revealed, being led by God in holy war, and so on. But the relevant question before us is whether Israel's standards of political ethics were *also* unique. Did they embody a culturally relative kind of justice, valid for only this ethnic group? Happily, not all Christians take that view for granted,[22] but all too many thoughtlessly do.

21. One example is Richard J. Mouw, *Politics and the Biblical Drama* (Grand Rapids: Eerdmans, 1976), chap. 4, where God's will for the *church* is explicitly used as a model for *civil political* theory. This results in Mouw criticizing civil legislation, for instance, against sexual promiscuity (which legislation God prescribes) and commending redistributive economic legislation (which God's law prohibits)!

22. "Though we cannot address secular society in the terms God addressed Israel, nor presuppose [that God has] a covenant relationship [with any modern nation], it is nevertheless valid to argue that what God required of Israel as a fully human society, is consistent with what he requires of all men. It is therefore possible to use Israel as a paradigm for social [and] ethical objectives in our own society" (Christopher J. H. Wright, "The Use of the Bible in Social Ethics III: The Ethical Relevance of Israel as a Society," *Transformation* 1, 4 [October-December 1984]: 19).

The error of that assumption is evident, first, from what the Bible teaches about the civil magistrates in the Gentile nations surrounding Israel. If *they* were expected to uphold and enforce the civil provisions of God's law, the natural inference would be that magistrates outside of Old Testament Israel in the modern world (being in a parallel situation) are likewise charged with obedience to the same provisions. From our previous discussion of Psalm 2, it has already been made clear that Gentile and pagan magistrates were seen as morally obligated to submit to the rule of God, even though they were, in the nature of the case, operating outside of Old Testament Israel. Similarly, referring to the kings outside of Israel, David declared in the longest psalm extolling the law of God (Ps. 119) that he "would speak of [God's] testimonies before kings and not be put to shame" (v. 46). This statement clearly assumes the validity of that law for such nontheocratic kings. We know from David's last words that, based on divine revelation, he was convinced that "he who rules among men must be righteous, ruling in the fear of God" (2 Sam. 23:3, where the categorical thrust of the words "among men" is especially to be noted).

The wisdom literature of the Old Testament, intended for practical guidance on an international scale, reinforced this perspective of David: "It is an abomination for kings to commit wickedness, for a throne is established on righteousness" (Prov. 16:12)—just as the throne in Israel was to be established on righteousness (Ps. 72:1-2) because righteousness is the foundation of God's throne (Ps. 97:2). Thus all rulers were seen as belonging to God (Ps. 47:9): "God is the King of all the earth. . . . God reigns over the nations; God sits upon His holy throne" (vv. 7-8). Indeed, in "all the nations" God Himself stands in the assembly of the "gods" (judges, rulers) and "judges among them" (Ps. 82:1, 6-8). They are expected to "do justice" for those who are afflicted and needy (vv. 3-4). There is no hint here that "justice" means welfare payments and redistribution of wealth; it rather means refusing to show judicial partiality to the wicked and, thereby, "delivering [the needy] out of the hand of the wicked" (vv. 2, 4). This is accomplished by the "gods" handing down judgments based upon the law of "God," the Most High and final judge of all mankind.

In that light, the personified Wisdom of God declared: "By me kings reign and princes decree justice; by me rulers govern, and nobles, *all* the judges *of the earth*" (Prov. 8:15-16). Therefore, God's Word teaches that every political ruler of the earth is subordinate to the moral authority of God and the holiness of His throne. Rulers have been established to deal with the "transgressions of a land" (Prov. 28:2) and are morally required in their sphere of authority to condemn the wicked (Prov. 17:15). As Paul later taught in Romans 13:3, all rulers (Jewish and Gentile alike) are to be a "terror to the workers of iniquity" (cf. Prov. 21:15). For this they must rule according to the just dictates of God's law. Any ruler who departs from this standard and treats the wicked as righteous will be abhorred by "nations" (Prov. 24:22), not simply by Israel.

The law revealed by Moses to Israel was intended to be a model for surrounding cultures. As we saw earlier, Moses declared in Deuteronomy 4:5-8 that *"all* this law which I set before you this day" (v. 8) — not simply the personal, familial, redemptive, or ecclesiastical aspects of it — was meant to be imitated by the Gentiles. Accordingly, the Old Testament prophets applied the very same standards of political ethics to pagan nations (Hab. 2:12) as they did to Israel (Mic. 3:10), and their prophetic condemnations for disobedience to God were applied to pagan cultures as a whole, *including* the sins of Gentile kings and princes (e.g., Isa. 14:4-20; 19:1, 13-14, 22; 30:33). By contrast, Ezra the scribe praised God for inspiring the pagan emperor to establish magistrates beyond Israel who would punish criminals according to the law of God (Ezra 7:25-26).

In light of this cantata of evidence, it is futile to think that Gentile rulers in the Old Testament were exempt from the politically relevant stipulations of the law of God. And if *they* were not so exempt, what biblical rationale might be advanced for exempting *rulers today* who operate outside of the theocratic land of Old Testament Israel? The only conceivable one is the argument that the New Testament introduces a completely new regime of deontological ethics from that of the Old Testament, a hypothesis that has already been refuted exegetically and theologically above. The fact is that the *New Testament itself*, as much as the Old, teaches that civil magistrates (even those outside of the Jewish nation) are morally bound to obey the political requirements of God's law. We can see this in that the most evil political ruler imaginable, "the beast" of Revelation 13, is negatively described as substituting his own law for that of the law of God, figuratively written upon the forehead and hand (vv. 16-17 in contrast to Deut. 6:8). Those who oppose this wicked ruler are, by contradistinction, twice described as believers who "keep the commandments of God" (12:17; 14:12). Paul condemns this wicked ruler precisely as "the man of lawlessness" (2 Thess. 2:3), indicating his guilt for repudiating the law of God in his rule.

The way Paul looked upon the civil magistrate, even the emperor in Rome, was that he should behave as "a minister of God" (Rom. 13:4) who "avenges wrath against evildoers." In this passage the "vengeance" is clearly intended to be God's (cf. 12:19; 1 Pet. 2:14), and accordingly "evil" is defined by the law of God (cf. 13:8-10). Unless civil rulers serve God by enforcing His just laws against criminal behavior, they will indeed "bear the sword in vain" (v. 4). This political use of God's law to punish and restrain crime is precisely the illustration Paul employs for a "lawful use of the law" in 1 Timothy 1:8-10. It cannot, therefore, be deemed out of place in New Testament ethics. Since the civil magistrate has been commissioned to bear a sword for the punishment of evildoers according to the avenging wrath of God, the magistrate will *need* the law of God to inform him as to how and where God's wrath is to be worked out in the state. A magistrate who renounces the penal directives of that law therefore forsakes his commission to be "the minister of God." He retains the form of the civil office without its substance and thereby deifies his own political wisdom or desires.

There are those who, as a starting point in their political theorizing, recoil from the very idea that the penal sanctions of God should be enforced by modern magistrates. For example, Ronald Sider, without presenting any argument or evidence, treats this assumption as a benchmark for testing and rejecting the theonomic view[23] — as though it were somehow a priori obvious that the civil penalties prescribed by the law are morally horrid. Such an approach implicitly ridicules the political wisdom of God Himself. That attitude is sometimes fueled without warrant by our own misinterpretation of what God's civil law actually does and does not require. (For example, Sider indulges in the common error of thinking that the Old Testament prescribed civil punishment for failing to worship God—which would imply positive "enforcement of religious belief" today). But there is no warrant for this preconceived negativity toward God's law beyond cultural tradition or personal disdain; for that reason it comes under Christ's censure in Matthew 5:19. Moreover, there is no better political standard to offer than God's law. Without it we are left with either unredressed criminal anarchy or arbitrary and manipulative penalties determined by sinful overlords.

The attitude we are considering stands squarely against that of the apostle Paul, who insisted, "If I am an evildoer and have committed anything worthy of death, I refuse not to die" (Acts 25:11). In fact, Christ Himself excoriated those who laid aside the penal provisions of the law in order to honor their own human traditions (Matt. 15:3-5). The Bible

23. "Christian Love and Public Policy," p. 13.

stands squarely against the personally chosen starting point of those who recoil from the law's penal sanctions. It insists "we know that the law is good" (1 Tim. 1:8-10). According to its infallible teaching, it is *necessary* to execute civil penalties against criminal behavior (1 Pet. 2:14; Prov. 20:2, 8), and to do so without exception or mercy (Deut. 19:13, 21; 25:12). Moreover, it is prerequisite that those civil penalties be exactly *equitable*, requiring neither more nor less than civil justice dictates (cf. "according to his fault" in Deut. 25:2, "worthy of death" in Deut. 21:22, and "eye for eye," etc. in Exod. 21:23-25). On this issue the teaching of Hebrews 2:2 is especially pertinent. There we find explicit New Testament endorsement of the abiding ("steadfast") justice of the penal sanctions prescribed in the law of Moses. According to God's unerring evaluation, "*every* transgression and offense received a *just recompence* of reward" in the law delivered from Sinai. Therefore, to repudiate those sanctions is to be impaled upon the horns of a painful ethical dilemma: either one gives up all civil sanctions against crime, or one settles for civil sanctions that are not just. Both options are clearly unbiblical and will produce abusive political effects in practice.

We are driven to conclude that there is no biblical justification for teaching that, as a category, the "political" provisions of God's Old Testament law have been abrogated. All the relevant biblical evidence, whether about Old Testament Gentile rulers, New Testament magistrates, or necessary and equitable penal sanctions, moves in entirely the opposite direction. God is never pictured as having a double standard of political ethics, as though it were any less necessary to punish rapists, kidnappers, and murderers with a "just recompence of reward" (cf. Heb. 2:2) in Old Testament Israel than across the geopolitical line into Gentile territory or across the time line into the New Testament era. The justice of God's law, even as it touches political matters like crime and punishment, is not culturally relative. It is not surprising that our most pressing criminal problems today (e.g., disdain for the integrity of life, for proper sexual relations, and for property; criminal incorrigibility) are precisely those matters which are addressed with firmness and clarity in God's law. Its divine direction has been set aside, however, in favor of the "enlightened" speculation and self-destructive fashion of this world instead.

Biblical Christians are not "legal positivists" who deny any conceptual connection between civil law and morality. We realize that all civil law arises from and gives expression to a particular moral point of view (or more widely, a world-and-life view). The question is not, therefore, *whether* the state should enforce some definable and coherent conception of ethics, but rather *which* ethical system it should enforce. It is impossible for the state to avoid constraining the behavior of its subjects according to statutes that reflect some moral philosophy. We have argued above that for the Christian this moral philosophy is taken from the infallible Word of God in the Scripture of the Old and New Testaments. It must not be based upon the autonomous philosophical speculation or the social traditions of men, which are alike afflicted by man's fallen condition and can, therefore, offer no reliable ethical guidance.

The Need for Reform

The fact remains, however, that within society there are plenty of unbelieving people who would readily challenge the veracity and authority of God's Word. The Christian lives in a world that is in rebellion against Jehovah and His Christ—a world where non-Christians often outnumber or carry more influence than believers within a particular society. A plurality of perspectives compete with each other for a following. If the law of God is the moral ideal to be followed politically, and if the practice of one's political order is contrary to it, what measures are believers to take in hope of correcting the situation? This question, as every other ethical question, must be addressed by the law of God itself. That moral code not only sets forth standards to be followed by those in political power, it lays down principles of conduct to be followed by those who wish to *bring about* a more just political order.

Accordingly, let me end this essay by observing that a commitment to the law of God does not encourage, but rather forbids, the use of violence today (2 Cor. 10:4; Matt. 26:52) and the use of revolution (Rom. 13:1-2; Titus 3:1) to institute closer conformity to the will of God. Simply put, the law of God is not to be imposed by force upon an unwilling *society*. Of course, there will always be *individuals* upon whom the laws of society need to be imposed (whether these are precisely the laws of God or not). That is, there will always be a criminal element who will not regulate their actions by the restraints of civil law. Imposing society's civil (not ecclesiastical or personal) standards upon these individuals through application or threat of penal sanction is both right and inevitable (Rom. 13:3; Prov. 20:8, 26). The kind of imposition of which we disapprove, however, is the use of coercion or violence to compel a corporate society to submit to the dictates of God's law. That very law directs God's people to rely upon and utilize, instead, the means of regeneration, re-education, and gradual legal reform to bring about a reformation of their outward political order. Christian political concern will advance very little indeed if it ignores the fundamental spiritual need of men to have their hearts changed from above.

Hence we would make evangelism, prayer, and education critical planks in the Christian's strategy for eventual political change. At the same time as we are offering Christian nurture and re-education to converts (regarding socio-political morality, among other spiritual lessons), we must likewise engage in intellectual persuasion and apologetical appeals to the unconverted, aiming to change and correct their value system and to promote the advantages of the Christian view on political issues. Beyond this, Christians should use the lawful means available in any particular society to work toward reconstruction of the legal, judicial, and political framework of that society. Christian legislators, judges, magistrates, and aides ought to labor for progressive amendment of the statutes and legal proceedings of the state, bringing them more and more into harmony with the principles of God's law for political authorities. Complementary and necessary to such reform is every believer's moral obligation to make use of his political voice and vote to support those candidates and measures which best conform to the rule of God's law. In all of this, it should be manifest that peaceful means[24] of political change are to be utilized by those committed to the law of God and its modern application — not anything like "holy war," revolutionary violence, or "the abolition of democracy."[25]

---

24. This restriction to peaceful means of (positive) political *transformation* or reform does not, as such, address the issue of (negative) *self-defense* against the illegal assaults of state officials (say, in a Christian school) or against a murderous political regime that is beyond judicial correction (say, in Hitler's Germany or Idi Amin's Uganda).

25. The last phrase is misleadingly applied to theonomists by Rodney Clapp in "Democracy as Heresy," p. 17. Surely Clapp is aware that the word *democracy* is susceptible to an incredibly wide range of definitions and connotations (e.g., from an institution of direct rule by every citizen without mediating representatives to a governmental procedure where representatives are voted in and out of office by the people, to the simple concepts of majority vote or social equality, etc.). The definitions of *democracy* are so varied that J. L. Austin once dismissed the word as "notoriously useless." While there are some senses of *democracy* that theonomists (and all Christians, even Clapp) would want to shun, we are certainly not opposed to *democratic procedures* as commonly understood.

2

The Principled Pluralist Response to Theonomy

*Paul G. Schrotenboer**

The Calvinist tradition has stressed that theological and lifestyle issues should be decided on the basis of the teaching of Scriptures and the subordinate church standards. Calvinists have emphasized that the Spirit of God enables Christians to know the will of God. Word and Spirit are inseparable as we seek to discern God's will. As the Westminster Confession of Faith states, "The supreme judge" in all controversies of religion is "the Holy Spirit speaking in the Scripture" (I, 10).

Our effort to apprehend God's will should also be communal. It is "with all the saints" that we must seek to understand the love of God (Eph. 3:18, NIV). Thus we Christians must continue to ask God to guide us as we listen and speak (Ps. 25:4, 5). Our agreement on what the Word and Spirit teach about civil rulers is the measure of our success.

My approach rests upon John Calvin's affirmation that civil rulers have one of the highest callings in the service of God. Christians can best fulfill this calling, I believe, by accepting the model of sphere sovereignty or "differentiated authority." This model teaches that God is the sole sovereign who has delegated authority to people in the various life zones where they carry out their God-given assignments. These life zones are all directly subordinate to God and are mutually coordinate one to the other, each with its own task and authority. In critiquing Greg Bahnsen's theonomic perspective, I will strive to be consonant with this view, and, more importantly, with Holy Scripture.

Theonomy teaches that the Mosaic legislation is normative for statecraft today, except where the New Testament indicates it has been set aside. Thus theonomy is concerned directly with the normativity of God's law for human affairs. That God's law holds for all creatures is not

*Paul G. Schrotenboer received his Th.D. from the Free University of Amsterdam. He currently serves as the General Secretary of the Reformed Ecumenical Council.

in question among Reformed Christians. For we can all identify with the apostle Paul who, even when he said he became as one not having the law to those who did not have the law, added that he was not free from God's law but under the law of Christ (1 Cor. 9:21). Paul's words strongly suggest that while God's law abides forever, now that Christ has come it should be adapted in new ways as we use different approaches with different people in working for the coming of Christ's kingdom.

Reformed Christians also agree that the law of God, as given in the Scriptures, is comprehensive; it is valid not only for our worship and personal relations, but also for societal activities, including statecraft.

The issue on which there is not full agreement among us is the form of the law of God that holds today. That the law has many forms is apparent. Bahnsen argues that "we should presume that Old Testament standing laws continue to be morally binding in the New Testament, unless they are rescinded or modified by further revelation" (p. 24). The question is, Which laws are "standing" and which are not? Those which are permanent are, of course, normative today; but how do we distinguish?

To understand how the law of God holds for us in statecraft today we need to clarify four issues: (1) the place of Israel, particularly under the leadership of Moses, in the all-encompassing plan of human redemption; (2) the role of the multi-faceted law of God in the life of Israel; (3) the meaning of Jesus' fulfillment of the law; and (4) the role of the Holy Spirit in discerning our contemporary civil responsibilities.

The Place of Israel in God's Plan of Redemption

Israel in its entirety — in its civil, ceremonial, and moral aspects — was a preparation for the coming of Christ. As a covenant nation, established by the initiative of God, it foreshadowed the coming Messiah, who would be the Passover lamb, the great high priest, the royal son of King David, and the fulfiller of the law. At the end times the Messiah will also be the great judge.

While the descendants of Jacob lived in Egypt, they were not yet a nation, and their life could not be differentiated in such areas as the ecclesiastical, the civil, and the industrial. At that time all life centered on the family. The apostle Paul refers to the minority (nonadult) status of God's people when he describes them as being under tutors until the age of majority when Christ came in the fullness of time (Gal. 4:1-7).

Israel, an assemblage of twelve tribes, was meant to be a model to the nations. To enable them to do that, God gave these tribes a model set of laws — ready made — which the nations could admire and, hopefully, imitate (Deut. 4:5-8). This was part of their covenantal response to God's grace, to be a blessing to the nations. However, Israel failed miserably. Instead of being a blessing, the Jews were a stumbling block to the nations. As a result they were sent into exile.

For our purpose three things stand out about Israel's place in Moses' day: (1) the nation as a whole was a preparation for the coming Messiah; (2) the state of this tribal people was undifferentiated; and (3) despite their model legislation, Israel failed to obey God's voice.

The Role of the Law in the Life of Israel

The laws God gave to Israel were appropriate for the new nation as God's special people (Exod. 19), as a kingdom of priests and a holy nation. The Pentateuch contains a long list of specific regulations, some of which, as Bahnsen recognizes, are culturally conditioned. Some laws, commonly called ceremonial, relate more directly to the cultic practices. Other laws are civil and social (hygienic, dietary). These regulations were not, however, strictly delineated into civil, moral, and ceremonial laws, as if ancient Israel were a highly developed society. We cannot simply lift the laws meant for Israel out of that differentiated society and try to fit them, with little adaption, into our highly developed society.

The Pentateuch also has summary statements of the law as in the Decalogue (both in the Exod. 20 version and the Deut. 5 update) and in Leviticus 19. Moreover, the Old Testament contains comprehensive commands such as in Leviticus 19:18; Deuteronomy 5:10, 12-13; 6:4-6; and Micah 6:8 ("What does the Lord require of you . . . ?" NIV).

Because the Old Testament records various types of law, we should try to determine which are "standing" and which were transitory. The least likely ones to warrant the "standing" category are the specific laws given to regulate Israel's societal structure, which at that early stage was very primitive. Those which have abiding significance, as Jesus taught, are the comprehensive laws of love (the great commandment) and of justice; these along with mercy and faithfulness, are the weightier matters of the law (Matt. 23:23).

As we seek to discern our civil responsibilities today, we should be guided by the abundant scriptural teaching that for civil government, justice is the name of the game. Bahnsen has given us a list of texts that stress this civil task (for which we should be grateful).

What carries over from the Old Testament civil legislation as permanent (to the extent that it was then embryonically differentiated as civil) is that God wills that justice prevail — and justice in the Old Testament is inseparable from release from oppression. The form in which justice is to be maintained, however, should fit the situation.

Jesus' Fulfillment of the Law (Matt. 5:17-19)

What is the nature of the discontinuity between the "law of Christ" (1 Cor. 9:21) and that of the Old Testament? Jesus clearly did not intend to break completely with the Old Testament or to abolish the law and the prophets. The discontinuity therefore is not complete. Nevertheless, the new and the old are not completely identical either, because Christ fulfilled (*pleerosai*) the law. He is the end (*telos*) of the law to all who believe (Rom. 10:4). Therefore Christ's function was more than simply to confirm the law.[1]

Jesus *came* not to abolish the law and the prophets, but to fulfill them. That is, His life's mission, the work the Father gave Him to do (John 17:4), was to bring to fulfillment all that was yet preparatory and incomplete in the Old Testament and in itself ineffective. It was in order that the Scripture might be fulfilled that events went as they did in Gethsemane and on Calvary (Matt. 26:54). In Him promise became fulfillment, and the new age began.

The Mosaic laws governing Israel's life were part of God's larger redemptive relationship with Israel, and Israel, the seed of Abraham, was His agent to bring blessing to the nations. Similarly, Christ's fulfillment of the law must be seen in the wider context of His redemption of His people and the reconciliation of the world. We misunderstand Jesus' words about His work of fulfillment, as recorded in Matthew 5, if we limit their reference to certain regulations, such as the "redemptive" as distinct from the "moral," or simply say that He confirmed them.

Obviously, advocates of principled pluralism find a different kind of discontinuity than Bahnsen does between the work of God in Israel and His work in Jesus Christ in the days of His flesh.

The discontinuity in one sense is greater, as we see it, because the civil regulations *as such* no longer apply. Strangely, the greater discontinuity is a consequence of the greater scope of the Old Testament prefigurations of Christ's redemption and the greater range of His fulfillment. In this sense the continuity is greater. Because Christ brought together all the lines of redemptive history, there is a sharp discontinuity with the earlier cultural forms, which, as shadows, should fade away when the Light of

---

1. Paul in Rom. 15:8 says that Christ confirmed the promises made to the patriarchs, but there he uses the word *bebaioosai* (confirmed), not *pleerosai* (fulfilled) as in Matt. 5:17.

the World shines in full strength. Nevertheless, a great continuity appears in the onward march of the truth of God.

In a very real sense, Christ brought to fulfillment all of Israel's life. As Hosea taught, Jesus identified Himself with Israel as a nation of God's people, and therefore His return from Egypt as a child fulfilled Hosea's backward look to the Exodus. Matthew could say that Hosea looked forward to Jesus even when the prophet looked backward to the Exodus only because of Jesus' identity with His people.

There is one encompassing Word of God; there is one comprehensive covenant—taking in all people, the entire creation, and all ages. Whatever discontinuity there is, it evolved within the fulfillment (from promise to deliverance) of God's plan of restoring the creation in Jesus Christ.

The distinction Bahnsen makes on page 34 is questionable: "Some laws defined the righteousness of God to be emulated by men (thus being moral in function), while other laws defined the way of salvation for the unrighteous (thus being redemptive in function)." This distinction seems to imply that the laws that define the righteousness of God and that men should emulate are not redemptive. This restricts redemption to those injunctions which relate directly to the removal of sin and guilt, the ceremonial laws. Salvation, seen in biblical light, is far broader than that. Salvation is as wide as societal life, even as wide as the new creation where righteousness will be the order of the day (2 Pet. 3:13; cf. Eph. 1:10; Col. 1:15-18). That righteousness which God asks us to emulate is an integral part of our life of faith and obedience.

The entire Mosaic legal system was instituted to provide redemption (therefore the continuity), and it was culturally conditioned (therefore the discontinuity); and so the redemption of Christ has as its aim, among other things, a reformed (redeemed?) state and statecraft.

Thus the dietary provisions (cf. Bahnsen p. 31) need no longer be observed (but see Acts 15:20), not because they are moral rather than redemptive, but because they are a part of God's plan of redemption that applied only to ancient Israel. Here the "moral" and "redemptive" blend. Trying to dissolve the amalgam violates God's design.

The Role of the Holy Spirit in Our Lives

The guidance of the Holy Spirit, strongly emphasized by our rich Calvinist tradition, helps us to determine our responsibilities to civil government. Unfortunately, Bahnsen makes only one minor reference to the Holy Spirit.

The supreme judge about all issues is the Holy Spirit speaking in the Scripture. As Jesus promised, the Holy Spirit leads us into all truth. The

Spirit does not simply provide a complete canonical revelation, but enables us to understand that revelation.

Conclusion

The Westminster Confession declares that the sundry judicial laws expired with the state of Israel "not obliging any other, now, further than the general equity thereof may require" (XIX, 4).[2] Bahnsen gives us a good example of the "general equity" of specific illustrations when he says we are to learn from regulations concerning rooftop railings the "broader, underlying principle" (p. 32) of safety precautions. If he applied the "civil provisions" of the Old Testament to our day in this same way, theonomists and principled pluralists could find major points of agreement.

All Reformed Christians are somewhat perplexed about what to do with some Old Testament laws. The classic distinction among moral, ceremonial, and civil laws may be helpful, but it is also misleading in several ways. These emerging aspects can be distinguished even in the Israelite community under Moses. But we must not superimpose on that undifferentiated society the contours of our complicated and specialized, differentiated society.

This distinction is also misleading if it gives the impression that some Old Testament laws may be wholly disregarded today whereas others must be rigorously observed. All the laws of the Old Testament are connected in some way to providing redemption. Even the regulations on dishonest weights and honest scales are related to God's deliverance of Israel from Egypt (Lev. 19:35-37). Moreover, all the Levitical laws are grounded on God's demand, "Be holy, because I the Lord your God, am holy" (Lev. 19:2, NIV).

Further, it is not immediately obvious why the Synod of Jerusalem (Acts 15) imposed on Gentile believers the Mosaic prohibitions on eating food offered to idols, sexual immorality, eating meat of strangled animals, and drinking blood (v. 20). How can we say we are free from the Old Testament dietary laws if the New Testament prescribes them for us Gentiles?

It is equally wrong to superimpose on our society the positive laws by which God adapted His abiding law of love and justice intended for ancient Israel. God does not intend us to do this. Distinctions were made even in the Old Testament; e.g., the Year of Jubilee was apparently intended only for farm areas, not for cities.

---

2. I wish the Westminster divines had stated as the primary clause of the sentence that these laws require us to observe their general equity. As it is, their stress on the discontinuity of the civil regulations tends to obscure the continuity of the general equity.

Yet this should be clear: the one all-comprehensive law that holds for all people in all times and places and transcends all human societies is the love commandment, and in civil affairs it should be expressed in terms of public justice.

The role of civil government is much broader, then, than enforcing God's criminal law, as Bahnsen contends. The duties of civil government are much broader than simply "delegated coercive power"; to safeguard social justice, it must also engage in educational tasks.

Justice is best achieved in our society with its many faith communities by according equal civil rights to all groups and to all individuals. This pluralist model seeks by all lawful means to translate the "general equity" of the Mosaic civil legislation into appropriate positive law. It is based upon the comprehensive commandment of love and various New Testament teachings about the responsibility of Christians to civil government (see, for example, Titus 2:2).

To adapt the principles of love and public justice to circumstances today we must understand how they were implemented in the Mosaic civil legislation. Today's civil magistrates are not "exempted" from God's law in its permanent form, but are still under the comprehensive love commandment as it applies to public justice. They are only exempt from the specific Mosaic statutes that were adaptations to Israel's unique and temporary position as the Old Testament people of God after He constituted them a theocracy. God's principal purpose was to use Israel to bring forth the Savior and sovereign ruler, Jesus Christ.

God demands that all rulers, regardless of their religion or ideology, promote public justice. To give one example: the law of restitution of land and of the ending of servitude, as encoded in the laws of manumission and the Year of Jubilee (Lev. 25), meant in essence that land, which was the means of production, would periodically be redistributed. In that undifferentiated, redemption-promising society, this practice reflected the inalienable right of all Israelites to an inheritance in the privileges of God's people, an inheritance of the Father.

The permanent principle in the Mosaic "civil legislation" with regard to land is that justice requires an equalization in ownership in order to insure freedom. The abiding norm is that land reform is a continual necessity and that people must be free to be personally and communally responsible before God. Land reform continues to be a crucial issue in many parts of the world (such as in El Salvador, where fourteen families own nearly all of the land).

Because Christ has come to fulfill all righteousness and has given us the Holy Spirit to lead us into the truth, our civil task today is to promote public justice with liberty and *shalom* for all.

3

The Christian America
Response to Theonomy

*Kevin L. Clauson**

Greg Bahnsen sets forth in his essay as well as in his books *Theonomy in Christian Ethics* and *By This Standard* the principle of theonomism. Theonomism asserts that the Bible itself commands civil magistrates to apply Old Testament law in its legal principle and in its penology to their societies, to the extent that it has not been explicitly altered by the New Covenant (Testament). From Matthew 5 and Romans 13 alone, this principle appears irrefutable. Any other interpretation of these passages (and of others cited in Bahnsen's essay) would appear to be contrived.[1]

In various forms, many have asked: What if a substantial majority of Americans were to become Christians? What if a real "revival" occurred, entailing full churches and a great demand for biblical teaching? Presumably some of these new converts will be civil government officials (elected or appointed). Certainly many of these converts will at least be potential voters. What would ministers teach new converts regarding their political and public policy duties? Would public policy change? Would ministers teach parishioners to obey biblical duties? If not, of what relevance is Scripture? Would pastors teach church members to adhere to Old Testament law (where not altered by the New Testament explicitly)? If not, where else inside or outside the Bible is there another detailed foundation for civil law? There is none. The "law of love," "law of Christ" (both New Testament phrases), and the concept of social justice

*Kevin L. Clauson, M.A., J.D., is currently Chairman of the Government Department and Associate Professor of Government and Economics at Liberty University, Lynchburg, VA. Previously he taught at Grove City College, PA. He has presented papers at several professional conferences and has published in *PS*, a journal of the American Political Science Association.

1. My comments do not necessarily represent or reflect the views of the institution at which I work or its well-known founder and chancellor, Dr. Jerry Falwell. I accept the *principle* of theonomy, and I will direct my comments to certain related subjects with that presupposition in mind.

are ethereal. Apart from the Old Testament law and the entire Bible, the "leading of the spirit" is ultimately heretical and therefore deadly evil— and potentially totalitarian. No scholar has ever been able to create a system of civil law based on "natural law" that is not arbitrary and constantly changing. Natural law cannot be based on nature because it is capricious and cruel, on human conscience because it is depraved, or on "reason" because it is vitiated by sin.

If there were a widespread revival in America, would crime and punishment change? Would abortionists be put to death, or would they be federally funded? Would those who practice homosexuality be punished, or would they be granted a special right to spread AIDS? Would thieves be forced to pay back ill-gotten gain, or would they be given a short tax-financed "vacation" in one of America's many "crime-training centers" (prisons)? Would public schools be abolished, or would legal theft to fund secular humanism and educational mediocrity continue? Would interest groups continue to "steal" from taxpayers for their own benefit (welfare programs, social security, business and industry subsidies, occupational licensing, antitrust laws, etc.)?[2] In short, would government change after a true (not simply emotional) revival? Disbelief in theonomism demonstrates a lack of confidence in real evangelism. If evangelism does not lead to changes (ultimately) in public policy, then something significant is missing—biblical Christianity. And if social change is not based upon detailed, God-revealed norms, then it will lead to revolution, anarchism, statism, and totalitarianism. If we believe in human depravity then we must follow explicit, thorough, biblical guidelines.

Nontheonomist Christians have many misunderstandings of theonomy. Bahnsen's essay does much to dispel many of the myths about theonomy. Nevertheless, a few others demand further consideration. Theonomists do call for a "theocracy," but by this they do not mean a fusion of institutional church and state or some kind of ecclesiastical establishment. Theonomists urge civil government to conform its laws and policies to God's laws as revealed in the Old Testament (except where there are "dis-

---

2. See Gordon Tullock, *Economics of Income Redistribution* (Boston: Kluwer-Nijhoff, 1983); Peter Ferrara, *Social Security: The Inherent Contradiction* (Washington, D.C.: Cato Institute, 1982); Richard McKenzie, *Plant Closings: Public or Private Choices* (Washington, D.C.: Cato Institute, 1983); S. David Young, *The Rule of Experts* (Washington, D.C.: Cato Institute, 1987); D. T. Armentano, *Antitrust and Monopoly* (New York: Wiley, 1982). On this general issue, see Herbert Schlossberg, *Idols for Destruction* (Nashville: Thomas Nelson, 1983), especially chap. 3; Thomas Sowell, *Knowledge and Decisions* (New York: Basic Books, 1982); and the writings of James Buchanan on "public choice" theory.

continuities"). Such a government would not be tyrannical; to say that it would is to call God a tyrant.[3]

Theonomists have denounced as lawlessness totalitarian revolutions in the French, Russian, and Cuban sense, which were very unlike the English and American "revolutions." Although theonomists advocate legitimate resistance to tyranny under some circumstances, they seek explicitly to change government through a type of "democratic process" (within "republican institutions" — not a mere semantic distinction).[4] That is, as increasing numbers of people accept Christianity and then biblical law (in greater consistency over time), eventually so many Americans will accept a theonomic view of civil law that it will change who gets elected, what policies they pursue, what kinds of institutional arrangements are established, and what is assigned to various levels of government.[5]

As Christianity expands and the Bible is followed more and more consistently, our government will become theonomic. Politics is an outgrowth of ethics, and ethics is an outgrowth of theology. Thus as hearts and minds are transformed and people seek the whole counsel of the Bible, ethics and politics will increasingly be based upon biblical norms (unless we fall into the dispensationalist trap and only accept part of the Bible as valid for our age).[6] Theonomists, in fact, maintain that a proper theological-ethical foundation must first be laid before political solutions

3. The theonomist proposal is not anything like Moslem "fundamentalism" (a misnomer); the Islamic State of Iran is a fusion of "church" and state, and furthermore, it is based on a religious system that is absolutely antithetical to God's Holy Bible. God hates the Islamic state as much as the Marxist state. Equating "Moslem fundamentalism" with American fundamentalism is inaccurate in two different ways. (1) Most of modern American fundamentalism (if not all) rejects any notion of a theocracy. Jerry Falwell, for instance, has no designs for establishing a Christian republic. (2) Theonomism is biblical Christianity and the Islamic movement in Iran is consistent Islam — two contrary religions. In superficial ways the two may appear *similar*, but in theology they are worlds apart.

4. The "democratic process" of which theonomists speak is simply the voting into office of more and more consistent (epistemologically) biblical Christians over time as more and more voters become Christians and apply their faith to politics (as well as to other institutions). As Christianity spreads, voters will want consistent Christians as civil representatives. "Republican institutions" means that decision-making arrangements will not involve direct popular voting or policy participation at the higher levels of government and that civil government will not be nationally centralized. Most civil government functions will be at the "local" level (towns, cities, counties, states, provinces).

5. Different functions belong to different institutions: national government, local government, the church, the family, and various private organizations and associations.

6. According to Dispensationalism only those Old Testament laws that the New Testament explicitly reiterates are to be applied today. In other words, dispensationalism assumes incorrectly that Old Testament civil laws were meant only for Israel in the Old Testament age.

to problems can be implemented. They want limited government, not totalitarian government, which is essentially the case in the Islamic State of Iran. As theonomic principles are progressively accepted, civil government will punish evil and "consolidate gains" made in the theological-ethical-conversion process,[7] encouraging further improvements in civil government.

Critics of theonomy often allege falsely that this system of government would produce Christian "ayatollahs" who would seize power and impose total change (as the early French revolutionaries did) immediately. Even if this were possible, it is biblically impermissible. Theonomists want government to have only limited powers.[8] (Ironically, some evangelical critics put an inordinate amount of trust in civil government to solve every social problem while complaining that theonomy is totalitarian.) The heart of the problem is that nontheonomists have no reliable basis for distinguishing between political and nonpolitical solutions to contemporary American problems. They fail to realize that government's functions are limited and other institutions (families, churches, schools, voluntary associations) are ordained by God to deal with certain areas of life.

Theonomists do need to differentiate more clearly between theonomism and utopianism (of various kinds). At least three main differences are apparent. (1) Theonomy repudiates the idea of earthly perfection — in terms of every individual becoming a sinless, regenerate person. Such an idea is heretical perfectionism. (2) Unlike secular utopians, theonomists insist that God's Holy Spirit, not human effort alone, will produce a progressive implementation of a theonomic regime. Man's ethical obedience to God's commandments is also essential to achieving a theonomic society. (3) Change will be based not upon autonomous human blueprints but upon God's inerrant, infallible, inspired written Word. This is neither utopian nor "unrealistic" (since God's Word is the basis of all reality).[9] To

---

7. Theonomy calls for the punishment of evil according to Old Testament-based standards. For example, all murderers would be executed. Crimes such as adultery could be punished by death (as a maximum permissible sentence). "Consolidating gains in theology and ethics" means that civil government would protect the religious freedom of the church, while punishing crimes in ways that are more and more consistent with biblical teaching.

8. Civil government would be responsible for national defense, a justice system (police force, courts, and punishment) and very little else. It would not be responsible for such things as "welfare" or "social security" programs, education, protecting businesses from "undue" competition, health care, or postal services.

9. See Thomas Molnar, *Utopia: The Perennial Heresy* (New York: Sheed and Ward, 1967) and James Billington, *Fire in the Minds of Men* (New York: Basic Books, 1980).

claim that God's law cannot or should not be applied because of the possibility of mistakes, as some critics do, incorrectly advocates perfectionism and denies God's law. Such a position would logically result in a totally impotent government, which would be no government at all.[10]

Critics often imply that theonomists believe this concept is the only important Christian doctrine. It is true that some write about theonomism almost exclusively, just as some authors write almost exclusively about the Holy Spirit or about marriage. Theonomists emphasize this doctrine because it has been forgotten. When Christians remember it again, then theonomists will give it proportionately less attention. Theonomists have never said that it is the only Christian issue or doctrine. Theonomy (as with all other doctrines) relates directly to many biblical doctrines including those of God, Christ, the Holy Spirit, salvation, apologetics, and evangelism.

Theonomists have even been accused of arguing that humans can achieve salvation by obeying the law. This is simply not true, and theonomist writers have repeatedly and flatly denied it. At the same time, the harshest critics of theonomy often imply that the laws of the messianic state will save sinners and society.[11] This belief is unmitigated legalism, or moralism.

Theonomists must continue their efforts to move beyond the principle of theonomy and to apply biblical law to specific situations. This may take decades or centuries in much the same way that the development of English and American common law did. The rewriting of today's American common law and the erosion of its biblical foundations invite legal positivism and anti-Christian rulings (in the name of a once Bible-based system).[12] Some have argued that the theonomic application of biblical laws to American society would require a vast army of "scribes" who would negate the "spirit of the law." Two problems arise here. (1) The "spirit of the law" (whatever that might be) must always be determined

10. God's law is not to be invalidated because of fallen human nature. Rather the fallenness of human nature necessitates God's revealed law.

11. See especially Ronald Sider, *Rich Christians in an Age of Hunger*, 2d ed. (Downers Grove, Ill.: Inter-Varsity Press, 1984). This belief is similar to liberation theology, except that instead of revolution bringing deliverance from "oppression," intervention of the state (in terms of pervasive regulations and laws) is the instrument of deliverance (social salvation). Significantly, this view has proliferated only in societies where biblical Christianity was waning or nonexistent.

12. For an analysis of the Christian roots of Western law and the grave intellectual crisis in the foundations of Western jurisprudence brought on by the erosion of its Christian roots, see Harold Berman, *Law and Revolution* (Cambridge, Mass.: Harvard University Press, 1983).

by someone based on some standard. (2) Equating theonomism with
Pharisaism is improper. The Pharisees stood on human traditions, while
theonomists stand on the Word of God, rather than tradition, natural
revelation, or conscience.

Theonomists must also deal in greater detail with specific "discontinuities" between the law of the Old and New Testaments. In this regard,
the redemptive-historical and cultural categories Bahnsen discusses are
very helpful. Clearly, the New Covenant is superior to the Old Covenant, but that does not mean the law was abrogated; nevertheless
changes have occurred.

A final major issue frequently discussed in relation to theonomy is
whether America ever was a Christian nation. My perspective as a Constitutional lawyer influences my analysis of this matter. The issue itself
involves several ambiguities. Are we talking about the Founding era (of
the Puritans and other Reformed-covenantal settlers) or the Revolutionary
era of the Constitutional Framers some 150 years later? Nevertheless,
there is nothing in the original U.S. Constitution (when not misinter-
preted by modern noninterpretivists),[13] the Bill of Rights, and the Constitution's subsequent amendments that is antithetical to the principle or
outworking of theonomy.[14] While some architects of the Constitution
were probably influenced by Enlightenment philosophy, their thinking
was also strongly shaped (perhaps in mediated form) by Puritan covenant theology (which existed before the writings of John Locke).[15] The
Constitutional era may not have been a utopian "golden age" (as some
political conservatives are prone to believe), but it was not a totally secularized age either.

The Constitution's provisions were shaped at least in part by biblical
ideas. The Framers understood the need for a limited central government, and they obviously saw little wrong with the laws of the states at
that time — laws based largely on biblical law as mediated by English

13. See Raoul Beger, *Government by Judiciary* (Cambridge, Mass.: Harvard University
Press, 1977). Noninterpretivism is a constitutional law doctrine that holds that the
Framers envisaged no definite meaning when drafting constitutional phrases. They left
words and phrases intentionally vague so that they could be cast in wholly new terms to
meet future exigencies.

14. A possible exception to this generalization are the several amendments passed during the years of the Populist and Progressive Movements in the late nineteenth and early
twentieth centuries.

15. For a discussion of these diverse strands, see M. E. Bradford, *A Worthy Company*
(Marlborough, N.H.: Plymouth Rock, 1982) and many of the works of historians Edmund
S. Morgan and Perry Miller.

common law. Separation of church and state as we have come to know it today (i.e., separation of civil government and political ethics) was largely foreign to them. The document they wrote is compatible with any attempt to build a theonomic society; that is to say, the Founders left most of civil government as they found it — at the local or state level. Very few restrictions were put on "local" governments.[16]

The question as to whether or not America has ever been a Christian nation, however, is not nearly so important as the question as to whether or not America (and any nation) can be a "Christian nation" in the future. America and other nations can be Christian if they adopt biblical laws in state, church, family, and all other entities and associations. We cannot trust man (individually or collectively); we must trust God and His immutable law. If civil magistrates will not apply the Old Testament law, then what will they apply? The law of man. If we will not be ruled by God, we will be ruled by tyrants.

16. Each state could establish its own grounds for execution; not even "procedural considerations" were considered a matter for the federal courts in this and many other areas.

4

The National Confessional
Response to Theonomy

H. B. Harrington*

I thank Greg Bahnsen for his excellent essay. As an
advocate of the national confession position, I agree with him in many
respects. It is my fervent desire that theonomists and national confessionalists will be able to consolidate their agreements and work out their
disagreements at least to the degree that we will be able to cooperate fully
with each other.

The first sentence of Bahnsen's essay is the key to the possibility of our
working together in the area of Christian civil government. "Any conception of the role of civil government that claims to be distinctively
Christian must be explicitly justified by the teaching of God's revealed
Word." The only word in the sentence with which I might have some
difficulty is "explicitly." It appears to me that, historically, Reformed
theologians have also considered doctrines established by good and necessary inference to be justified by the Bible.

Both national confessionalists and theonomists agree that the light of
God's special revelation must shine on every area of life; it must illuminate
every object of human knowledge if we are to see truthfully what is before us. Theonomy seems to be a logical extension of many Reformed
Christians' rejection of natural theology in apologetics and evangelism,
as the way to the knowledge of God. We believe that to know God correctly the light of Scripture is essential from the beginning. Therefore,
we must reject any personal or social ethic that is grounded on general
revelation rather than on biblically revealed principles of conduct.

Many national confessionists would disagree with me on this issue.
Some, perhaps a majority, accept some version of Thomas Aquinas's

*H. B. Harrington is currently president of the National Reform Association, pastor of
the Rose Point Reformed Presbyterian Church near New Castle, PA, and Professor of
Systematic Theology at Ottawa Theological Hall in Canada. He previously served pastorates in New Castle, Broomall, PA, and Glenwood, MN. He holds a B.A. from Geneva
College, is a graduate of Reformed Presbyterian Theological Seminary, and has done ad-
ditional study at New College, University of Edinburgh.

view of natural law. This position, however, undermines national confessionalism. Even if a formal profession of the lordship of Christ is retained, commitment to natural theology as the foundation for social ethics will result in some form of pluralism. Throughout the history of ethics whenever general revelation has been the starting point, the resulting ethical systems have not been reconcilable with biblical principles.[1]

It is true that throughout history people have often started with the Word of God in Scripture as their formal presupposition, but in Pharisaical fashion have ended up espousing the traditions of men. As Bahnsen points out, this takes place when some philosophic scheme intrudes so as to make the Scriptures teach the sinner's version of truth. People accept unbiblical assumptions that lead them to misinterpret the Bible and to constrict its application to only a few areas of human life. Interpretation is always an area of difficulty. We must always interpret the Scripture, and sin hinders everyone's effort to do so. Our only safeguard is continuously to reevaluate human conclusions in the light of Scripture, recognizing that the heart is deceitfully wicked; it is ever prone to seek independence from God.

Bahnsen clearly and correctly stresses the sovereignty of Jesus Christ over the world today. Theonomists have tended to emphasize the law of God while overlooking the Lawgiver. I have always preferred to refer to myself as a "Christian theocrat" rather than a theonomist. Of course, a lawgiver or king certainly implies a law, and a law certainly implies a sovereign. My preference for "Christian theocrat" stems from the need to oppose the dispensationalist interpretation of Scripture.

Within the Reformed camp we should be able to assume that when we speak of God's law we mean the law of the incarnate Son of God to whom the Father has committed all things. Nevertheless, it has not always been possible to make this assumption. Theonomists have boldly faced the question, If Christ is sovereign, what is His law?

General agreement within Reformed circles that Christ is Lord has little practical or ethical meaning so long as Reformed thinkers cannot agree on what Christ's law is. This is why the theonomic question divides the Reformed community today. It is regrettable that Reformed theologians frequently appear to have taken up common ground with atheistic secularism. Pluralistic social theory, proposed in Christ's name, inadvertently endorses polytheism at the national level. I agree with the direc-

---

1. In recent conversations several confessed theonomists expressed to me a willingness to move away from presuppositional apologetics. I believe that if such a move is made, they will cease to be theonomists in the contemporary sense of the term.

tion in which the theonomists generally have turned even when I have doubts about the conclusions they have reached.

My preference for the designation Christian theocrat is due to more than a reaction to dispensationalism or liberal humanism, however. It also reflects the fact that I am much more certain that Christ is presently Lord over the civil magistrate than I am as to what law Christ calls him to administer. It is certain that the Christian civil magistrate must administer some law that he regards as Christ's law, but I am not persuaded that the modern theonomist has correctly identified that law for us. The theonomic argument that the civil law of ancient Israel (with revisions) should become the basis of contemporary American civil law is thoughtful but not compelling. Difficulties arise over what laws Christ may or may not have changed in the New Covenant age. Moreover, various societal changes since the time of both Moses and Christ make many Israelite civil laws seem irrelevant.

If the Christian civil magistrate must look to Scripture in framing laws, where should he direct his attention? It is useless to argue the question of whether the Westminster Confession does or does not endorse or imply theonomy. However, the Westminster Standards, taken as a whole and including the Catechisms, do give us a direction. The moral law is summarized in the Ten Commandments. If we make it the duty of the civil magistrate to apply and enforce the moral law under modern conditions, we at least have a revealed basis for Christian civil law. This is not a theonomic solution, but neither is it a humanist or relativist solution.

One aspect of the theonomic reconstruction movement is especially frustrating: postmillennialism seems to be an integral part of reconstructionist thought. This doctrine is unnecessary for theonomic thinking, and yet it is tenaciously held by the theonomists whom I know as though their position would collapse if they did not strongly espouse this eschatological position. Bahnsen distinguishes two senses in which Christ is presently the "King of kings" (p. 28): the ethical and the eschatological. In the ethical sense, "all rulers ought to obey Him and stand under judgment, historical and eternal, for refusing to do so." In the eschatological sense, throughout history Christ's reign "which has been proclaimed in principle will see in practice more and more kings submit to it."

National confessionists agree without reservation that Christ is the "King of kings" in the ethical sense. All rulers ought to obey Him. However, the sense in which Christ is the eschatological "King of kings" constitutes a serious problem in biblical interpretation for myself and others who are in many respects sympathetic to the theonomic position. If, by the eschatological sense, it were meant that at the end of the age Christ would demonstrate His sovereignty, there would, of course, be no problem. This is not, however, what the postmillennialist means by the eschatological sense of Christ's kingship.

I would welcome the realization of the postmillennial hope that the nations will turn to Christ en masse and some golden age will result. But such a hope is not established beyond all reasonable doubt on the basis of Scripture. Thus, it appears that theonomists do what they say must not be done: they superimpose an extrabiblical program onto the Scripture. Millennialism of either pre- or post- variety is a philosophy of history. The Bible does express a philosophy of history in the doctrine of God's eternal plan to create and govern the world, with the goal of redeeming a people for Himself. Whether we can go much beyond this appears problematic to me.

Basing theonomy on postmillennialism is more than an academic or theoretical problem. It is a constant irritant that keeps apart people who might otherwise be working together. Those who are not postmillennialists, but who fervently believe in the ethical demands of Christ upon men and nations, are not happy when they are sneeringly referred to as "pessimillennialists" by a number of theonomists. It is an injustice to suggest that they cannot really be heart and soul for the ethical sovereignty of Christ unless they adopt postmillennialism. Theonomists, having rid themselves of natural theology and natural ethics, ought also to rid themselves of natural psychology. Christians are motivated by something other than an expectation of temporal success.

I trust I have indicated a desire to join with theonomists in constructing a political philosophy based upon special revelation. From that start we confidently proceed, knowing that we will not always come to the same conclusions, but believing that the Spirit will fruitfully guide us in our thinking. Also, I trust that I have made clear something of the pain a number of us in the national confession party feel when our intelligence, if not our sincerity, is derided because we remain neutral on the question of a millennium. For us this is a peripheral matter not relevant to the issue at hand.

Theonomist and national confessionist positions agree on the following points:

1. Jesus Christ is the Lord of all rulers on earth.
2. Moral law is constant throughout every age.
3. Special revelation is essential to correct personal and social morality.
4. Israelite civil law is profitable for instructing the law of nations.

5. God has ordained civil authority to be limited.

They disagree about the following issues:

1. Advocacy of biblical case law should be tied to an eschatological theory.

2. The moral foundation of civil law is the same in every time and place and does not necessarily include sanctions of Mosaic law.

3. Israelite case law is a practical starting point for determining Christian civil law.

Part Two
Principled Pluralism

During the past two decades principled pluralism has arisen as an identifiable and distinctive Reformed approach to culture and government. Advocates of the position trace its roots back to the teachings of John Calvin (1509-64) and the "consociational democracy" of Johannes Althusius (1557-1638). The basic premises of the position are more clearly delineated in the writings of Abraham Kuyper (1837-1920) and Herman Dooyeweerd (1894-1977). Kuyper, a theologian, professor, and statesman, and Dooyeweerd, a philosopher and professor of law, helped to inspire a resurgence of Reformed Christianity in the Netherlands in the late nineteenth and early twentieth centuries. They introduced and developed the concepts of *sphere sovereignty* and *sphere universality* which are foundational to principled pluralism.

This position rests upon several major tenets. God built basic structures or institutions into the world, each having separate authority and responsibilities. He established state, school, society, workplace, church, marriage, and family to carry out various roles in the world, and He commands human beings to serve as officeholders in these various spheres of life. Because of this *structural pluralism* no one institution can properly usurp the power or the functions of another. Structural pluralism is normative; it describes the way God has created the world. God has created each of these structures to be independent from the others; this sphere sovereignty means that no one sphere can properly usurp the function of or dominate others. These various structures, however, should work together (sphere universality) to promote righteousness and cooperation in society.

Many different communities of belief exist in today's world. This *confessional pluralism* is not normative; it has resulted from sin and is not what God desires. Nevertheless, the New Testament teaches that governments should accept the presence of conflicting faith communities within their borders and not discriminate against people because of the religious convictions they espouse. Therefore, the state should insure that all its citizens, whether they are Christians, Jews, Muslims, Hindus, Buddhists, or secular humanists, receive equal rights. Public justice must prevail; Christians should not have special privileges in society. All faith communities should have the legal right to worship, to evangelize, and to establish associations — schools, labor unions, political parties, benevolent societies, and the like — to promote their way of life.

Numerous articles and books advance the principled pluralist viewpoint. Three of the most influential books have been Gordon Spykman, et al., *Society, State, and Schools: A Case for Structural and Confessional Pluralism* (1981); Rockne McCarthy, James Skillen, and William Harper, *Disestablishment a Second Time: Genuine Pluralism for American Schools* (1982); and Mark Noll, Nathan Hatch, and George Marsden, *The Search for a Christian America* (1983). Spykman, who teaches theology at Calvin College, Skillen, the executive director of the Association for Public Justice in Washington, D.C., and George Marsden, who teaches history at Duke University, have been the leading spokesmen for this position.

Spykman's essay explains the biblical basis for this position. A biblical view of civil government must rest, he argues, not upon isolated prooftexts, but rather upon general principles taught throughout Scripture. Contrary to popular opinion, the Bible does not simply address narrowly religious matters or the issues of private life. Instead its teachings are relevant to all areas of life, including public policy. The central question is "not *whether* but *how* the Bible speaks to issues of society and the state" (p. 81). Matthew 13:24-30, 36-43 (the parable of the wheat and the tares), is foundational to the pluralist argument. Because the Lord of the harvest tolerates the tares, Spykman contends, the state should accept the existence of conflicting faith communities within its boundaries and safeguard the religious freedom of all its citizens.

Spykman argues that God's word comes in several forms: the original word of creation, the second redemptive Word in the Scriptures, and Jesus Christ, the incarnate Word. By His creational Word, God established government under His sovereign control to serve certain functions. Governments are subject to transcendent norms revealed in the Bible. Only by basing their social and political life on these divine norms can people experience peace, justice, and righteousness in their fullness.

The chief task of the state, Spykman contends, is to promote righteousness and justice in society and to treat the poor preferentially. He argues that the Bible, especially the Psalms, resounds with God's passionate plea to treat the poor and powerless fairly and compassionately.

Because God sides with the poor and defends their cause, civil government should do the same. God favors the poor and needy because societies often discriminate against and exploit them. When civil magistrates promote public justice and aid the poor and exploited, they please God.

Spykman urges Christians to work to create a genuinely pluralistic society as the only valid alternative to individualist and collectivist social orders. A pluralist society would provide equal justice for all in politics, education, religion, and society.

5

The Principled Pluralist Position
*Gordon J. Spykman**

My position rests upon certain hermeneutical, structural, and historical assumptions.

Working Assumptions

1. We cannot move directly from the text of the Bible to political theory. We need an in-between step, a framework for apprehending biblical teaching about statecraft, a world view. A world view attempts to provide a holistic understanding of scriptural teaching about all areas of life. It seeks to show the interrelationships among the various themes expounded in the Bible. Hermeneutically, our position is based upon biblical texts that teach that rulers are divinely ordained administrators of public justice. From these revelational pointers, we can then move on to the in-between step—the development of a reformational world view.

Rejecting the isolationist, accommodationist, dualist, and dialectical approaches to society delineated by H. Richard Niebuhr in his book, *Christ and Culture*, we contend that his fifth view, the transformational, reformational world view, most closely approximates the biblical approach. This paradigm of society, therefore, serves as our framework for evaluating the issues of state life. It directs our efforts to define and clarify the place and task of civil government within contemporary society.

2. Structurally, this reformational world view offers the societal context, with its various spheres and functions, for locating and understanding the role of the state as it relates to other aspects of our life together in God's world.

3. To understand the pluralist view of the state within society, we must contrast it to the individualism of the West and the collectivism of

*Gordon J. Spykman teaches theology at Calvin College. He has served a Christian Reformed Church pastorate in Canada and has been a guest lecturer at Dordt College, the Institute for Christian Studies, and Potchefstroum University. He was a member of two Calvin Center research projects, and is co-author of *Society, State, and Schools: A Case for Structural and Confessional Pluralism* (1981) and *Let My People Live: Faith and Struggle in Central America* (1988).

the East, the two dominant alternative views of society in our modern world. Most people assume that *rightist* and *leftist* social philosophies are the only choices we have today. Pluralism, however, is an authentic alternative to the two dominant models competing for the hearts and minds of our contemporaries. This essay will sketch the foundations and contours of principled pluralism and argue that it best expresses the biblical view of government and society.

Definitions

These three categories of society are described briefly below.

1. In the collectivist view, the basic unit in society is some all-embracing institution in society. This megastructure is the central bureaucratic seat of authority. It controls life in every other sphere of society. In ancient Greece, it was the city-state; in ancient Rome, the empire; in the medieval era, the Roman Catholic Church; in the modern period, various absolutist states. All other institutions are considered mere cogwheels in the machinery of some such societal megastructure. Thus, in our times the state is often ascribed a sovereignty and life of its own.

2. The individualist model makes free and sovereign individuals the fundamental building blocks of society. All societal institutions, such as marriage, church, and the workplace, have no status in and of themselves. They are mere artificial and functional creations of human beings and exist only for the benefit of people. Accordingly, autonomous people create the state to be a governing agency on the basis of popular sovereignty by means of a social contract.

3. Principled pluralism holds that all men live within a network of divinely ordained life-relationships. People do not find meaning and purpose either in their own individuality or as part of some collectivistic whole. Rather, people fulfill their callings within a plurality of communal associations, such as family, school, and state. God ordained each of these spheres of activity as part of the original order. Together they constitute community life.

Structural pluralism means that God has created the world with various structures — civil government, marriage, the family, the church, schools, the marketplace — which order life and coordinate human interaction. *Confessional pluralism* refers to the right of the various religious groups that make up a society to develop their own patterns of involvement in public life through their own associations — schools, political parties, labor unions, churches, and so on — to promote their views. The concept of *sphere sovereignty* teaches that each sphere in society has its own independent authority; no one sphere should dominate or usurp the role of the others. *Sphere universality* refers to the cooperative relationship among the various social spheres; they should work together to promote wholesome community life.

Today many astute commentators on world events announce the bankruptcy of both individualist and collectivist systems of society. Neither paradigm answers the needs of the hour. They create too many irresolvable problems, contradictions, and anomalies. The failures of both individualism and collectivism have led many to call for a renewed consideration of the only authentic alternative paradigm of society, namely, pluralism, with its accompanying view of the state.

Biblical Foundations

Many consider the effort to develop a biblical view of the societal order to be an exercise in futility and irrelevance. After all, what does the Bible have to do with society? Some assume that Scripture is concerned only with the way of salvation and therefore does not speak directly to any social issues. The case for principled pluralism is based neither on a pietist hermeneutic nor on a proof-texting approach to Scripture. Our view of society should not be derived from isolated passages scattered throughout the Bible. Such a piecemeal approach assumes that the Bible is a collection of timeless truths with built-in, ready-made applications for every situation. Rather, the Scriptures present principles and directives that hold for life as a whole in every age. We must therefore rely on the comprehensive meaning of the biblical message. Though couched in ancient *forms*, the Scriptures carry with them universal *norms* that should direct the lives of Christians and shape the societies they live in.

Principled pluralists reject the popular view evident in much public policy that the Bible is a religious book that deals only with narrowly religious matters. Such conventional wisdom assumes religion to be a personal and private affair, not integral to life as a whole. Public life is then assumed either to be nonreligious, operating on the secular principle of religious neutrality, or to be governed by a civil religion common to all. The right to "the free exercise of religion" is taken to mean no more than that each citizen is at liberty to accept as personal opinion whatever religious beliefs he chooses — or none at all. In this sectarian sense, to be or not to be religious, just as to be or not to be interested in art, is an option open to each individual. Thus both religion and the Bible are privatized.

Strangely, many evangelicals share this position with secularists. Evangelicals are quite willing to restrict the Bible to the privacy of inner religious experience and to regard it as irrelevant to public life and in no significant way normative for public policy. Consensus politics, they argue, demands such a stance. Thus secularists and many evangelicals acknowledge, tolerate, even extol America's religious diversity as long as it is confined to the church and excluded from the life of the state. The Bible, like other "holy books," deals with saving souls, not with reforming society. If we accept such a privatized Bible, it makes no sense whatsoever to speak of biblical principles for society and the state.

A very different understanding of Scripture lies behind the concept of principled pluralism. Its proponents contend that all of life is religion in the sense of an unbroken series of ongoing human responses — both just and unjust — to the Word of God, which holds for our entire life in God's world. Religion is therefore not a choice people make, but a given. As John Calvin taught, all men are by nature "incurably religious." Every societal issue is a human issue, and every human issue a religious issue. At bottom, all public policy is shaped, in the words of Paul Tillich, by some "ultimate concern." The dichotomy between "the-private-as-religious" idea and "the-public-as-secular" idea is wholly arbitrary and artificial. The public affairs of society and the state are no less religious than the so-called private affairs of individual, church, home, and school life.

Since all of life is religion, and since the Bible as a book of religion speaks to life as a whole, the question is not *whether* but *how* the Bible speaks to issues of society and the state. The question is not whether Scripture addresses matters of public justice, but *how* it addresses them. Clearly the Bible is neither a theoretical handbook on civil government nor a textbook on public policy. Yet no aspect of life is exempt from its norms, judgment, or call for renewal. God's revelation addresses all humans at all times in all situations. How then does it speak meaningfully and normatively to civil affairs?

As we analyze state life, we must first confess that the Bible confronts us as an urgent Word from beyond our own universe of experience. It is God's Word for a broken world, which comes as a message of renewal and reconciliation. It aims to reorder the life we live together in society. As Richard Mouw puts it, the Bible speaks "to human beings in their wholeness, including the entire network of relationships, institutions, and projects in which they participate."[1]

A right understanding of creation is therefore basic to a right understanding of re-creation. While Scripture is the Word of God, it is not

---

1. Richard Mouw, *Politics and the Biblical Drama* (Grand Rapids: Baker, 1983), p. 11.

God's only word for the world, nor is it His first word. God's original word created the world. To counteract the effects of the Fall and sin upon the world, however, God provided a second redemptive Word in the Scriptures. God's word therefore is broader than the Scripture. The Bible also witnesses to Jesus Christ as Word of God incarnate (John 1:14; Heb. 1:2; Rev. 19:13). It testifies to the cosmic significance of Christ's creating, sustaining, and redeeming work. John 1 is a redemptive rewriting of the Genesis 1 account. Christ is the mediator of creation as well as of redemption.

Thus, the word of God in its various manifestations speaks to all aspects of our world. To be a creature, therefore, of whatever kind, and to each after its own kind, is to be subject to God's creational and redemptive word in its abiding authority. Civil government, as the historically qualified, institutional unfolding of an original, divinely appointed governing task, is also a creature subject to God's sovereign claim. God expects all creatures to serve Him on behalf of His other creatures, to submit to His transcendent norms. God's word therefore holds for human beings in all their many ways of being human. Our life in society and the state is not self-explanatory or self-justifying. Civil government is not a self-sufficient and self-determining entity. Its origin, task, meaning, and purpose lie beyond itself. Therefore, the possibilities for, as well as the limitations upon, its historical-cultural development are given with creation. The political life of a community cannot unfold arbitrarily or capriciously. Its boundaries are circumscribed, and a community gives shape and form to its public life within them.

Thus understood, biblical religion offers the most practical way of living together in the world. For it alone conforms to God's established norms. As people seek consciously to base their life relationships upon these divinely ordained norms, they experience a certain affinity with the very nature of things. Anti-normative ways of structuring society produce anomalies, injustices, inequities, and resistance. They tend to become self-serving and, in the end, self-defeating and self-destructive, because they work at cross-purposes with the built-in meaning of life. Biblical religion aims rather to bring the structures of society in line with the God-given norms for society, and within this framework it aims to work out the structures and functions of a biblically directed view of the state.

When therefore the Reformers spoke of *sola Scriptura*, they did not mean that Scripture is God's only revelation. God also reveals His will in creation and providence. In fact, the creational word remains His fundamental and abiding revelation. When the distortion called sin entered our world, God gave the Scripture to correct and reinforce His original revelation upon our minds, redirecting our attention to its meaning, refocusing the intent and purpose of creation. God's message is always the same, but it comes in different modes. Its author does not contradict Himself. Though revelation comes in various forms, its norms are constant. The word holds, even when men do not discern or obey it.

In the historical order of all things, God's first word for creation remains basic; it is neither abrogated nor withdrawn (Rom. 2:14-15). By it God maintains His abiding claim on all persons and all societies, including the institutions of state, church, home, school, and all other associations in society. His word, first published in creation, then republished in Scripture, seeks to heal our life relationships in society and the state. The Bible can address these issues precisely because they have existed since the beginning. It does address them because, although biblical norms are still in force, man's response to them has become distorted. Scripture teaches that society and state can be reformed in and through the recreating work of Christ Jesus. He is working to counteract the destructive effects of human unrighteousness (Rom. 1:18-25). Human suppression of God's truth and distortion of His norms produce painful conflicts in society and cause the whole creation to groan expectantly as it awaits its final restoration (Rom. 8:18-25).

The case for principled pluralism rests on the conviction that the order of society points responsively to an ultimate normative order beyond itself as the source and criterion of its meaning. All communal tasks, including those of the state, must be measured against these creation ordinances, illumined by the Scriptures, as they continuously impinge upon us with an abiding authority. I contend that pluralism is more consistently obedient to the transcendent norm of God's word than any other view of society.

John Calvin and Pluralism

The roots of this pluralistic understanding of society are found in John Calvin. The sovereign rule of God in Jesus Christ over every part of life is the unifying theme in Calvin's world view. This conviction compelled Calvin to reject the Constantinian-medieval pattern of societal life, which had dominated Western Christianity for twelve hundred years. He attacked this longstanding paradigm of shared jurisdiction between church and state and the dualist assumptions upon which it rested. This paradigm drove a wedge into the religiously unified fabric of the societal order, compromised the integrity of the church, and fostered a secularized state.

Consequently, Calvin broke radically with the old order. He stressed that God's Word is as normative for the state as it is for the church. The nature of its claim is different for the two institutions. Yet both are divinely ordained and therefore are legitimate spheres of Christian service. Every institution in society—home, academy, marketplace, and industry, as well as church and state—offers an arena for Christians to fulfill their life callings.

While Calvin did not draw clear lines of demarcation among the various spheres in society (except for church and state), his thinking points unmistakably toward structural pluralism as the pattern for a just society. Calvin and his contemporaries, however, lived too much in the shadows of a society shaped by the ideal of an enforced universal Christendom to deal seriously with the growing realities of confessional pluralism.

Calvin's commentary on two New Testament passages clearly reveals his basic principles on society and the state. Expounding on Ephesians 5:21-6:9, Calvin declared:

> Society consists of groups, which are like yokes, in which there is mutual obligation of parties; . . . so in society there are six different classes, for each of which Paul lays down its peculiar duties.

Calvin strikes a similar note in his lecture on 1 Peter 2:12-17. There he focuses on the text, "Submit yourselves to every ordinance of man for the Lord's sake" (v. 13, KJV). These words prompt the following comment:

> The verb KTIZEIN in Greek, from which KTISIS comes, means to form or construct a building. It corresponds to the word "ordinance," by which Peter reminds us that God the Maker of the world has not left the human race in a state of confusion, so that we live after the manner of beasts, but has given them, as it were, a building regularly formed, and divided into several compartments. It is called a human ordinance, not because it has been invented by men, but because it is a mode of living well-arranged and clearly ordered, appropriate to man.

The various concepts—such as "groups," "classes," "parties," "gifts," "callings," "yokes," "offices," and "compartments," each with its own God-given "bounds," "operations," "mutual obligations," "peculiar duties," and "ordinances," which Calvin used here and in related passages—suggest the existence of structuring principles for the societal order. Johannes Althusius later formulated these ideas as associations-in-consociation, and Kuyper still later expressed them in the idea of sphere-sovereignty and sphere-universality.

Romans 13 and Revelation 8

Especially important to understanding biblical teaching on government, including the authority of the state and the responsibilities of citizenship, are Romans 13 and Revelation 8. From ancient times until today, these two chapters have generated long and heated debates among Christians. At first glance, they appear to make contrary claims upon us. Romans 13 (the ruler is a "minister of God," v. 4, KJV) seems to demand unswerving civil obedience. On the other hand, Revelation 8 (regarding the Babylonian whore) urges believers to "come out of her" (v. 4, NIV). Do not yield obedience to wicked civil authorities. How do we deal with this apparent contradiction?

Something deep inside us resists accepting any such discrepancies in the Bible. The Scriptures present an integrally unified message. We can best understand these two passages by realizing that while Romans 13 offers a normative picture of the state, Revelation 8 provides an anti-normative picture. In the former we meet civil government as it is meant to be, as it ought to be, as it is called to be. The latter confronts us with the horrible spectacle of the state as it all too often is, the state in its stark reality as an instrument of injustice and corruption. In short, Romans 13 presents the state at its best, Revelation 8 the state at its worst.

Thus Scripture describes both realities. Recognizing this biblical tension between normative and anti-normative alternatives, we must make our decisions regarding civil obedience and disobedience and participation in the political process. In the case of a "just war," we are called to obey the government's summons. When the state makes unjust demands, we may be called to resistance.

Eschatological Tolerance

Two interrelated passages in Matthew (13:24-30, 36-43) touch, obliquely at least, on the question of confessional pluralism. This parable of Jesus and His explanation indicate that a spiritual antithesis exists between two kingdoms radically at odds with each other. The work of the good "householder," "the Son of Man," is opposed by the evil deeds of the "enemy," "the devil." The growth of the "grain," springing from the "good seed," is threatened by the insidious presence of the "weeds." The "servant of the householder," the "sons of the kingdom," are keenly aware of the menace posed by the "sons of the evil one." Such apostasy rouses their indignation and impatience. They are moved by a holy intolerance. They wish to rid the world of the adherents of a false gospel and of false religions. The true church proposes to uproot the false church. But the Lord of the harvest says: "This is still the day of grace! Wait until the judgment!"

These passages do not refer directly to the role of the state in a religiously pluralistic country. They imply, however, that the state must also bear with the presence of conflicting faith-communities within its bounds. It must safeguard freedom of religion for all its citizens. The state should neither advance nor hinder one denomination at the expense of others. It should not establish a national church. The state has neither the calling nor the competence to evaluate such confessional issues. We should not long for a return to the Constantinian era with its *corpus Christianum*. For the coming kingdom advances, not by the enforcing power of the civil sword, but by the "sword of the Spirit," which is the persuasive power of the Word of God.

People who in principle hold to other perspectives often share some of these pluralist insights at a public policy level. Practical considerations prompt many who are basically individualist or collectivist in their outlook nevertheless to accept pluralist conclusions. This is so for a very fundamental reason—a reason rooted in the very nature of created reality. If this world is God's world, then the will of God for life in His world holds for all men and women. Because of this, people will often respond obediently, knowingly or unknowingly, to God's laws for human relationships.

The Task of Rulers: "Seek Righteousness" and "Do Justice" — a Preferential Option for the Poor

Principled pluralism teaches that the primary task of the state is to promote justice in society. Scripture literally resounds with the message of righteousness and justice. These biblical imperatives go hand in hand as two sides of a single truthful reality (Amos 5:24). Together they express the very heartbeat of the good news. It will not do, therefore, to separate them—as though righteousness relates us vertically to God as His free gift of grace, whereas justice relates us horizontally to our fellowman as a principle for public policy. The two biblical ideas are integrally one. Yahweh loves righteous dealings among men and nations, and His throne is established in justice (Ps. 89:14).

Psalm 82:1-4 accents God's sovereign insistence upon fundamental equity in the human community. He holds the "gods"—a symbolic title for rulers, judges, and all in positions of authority—accountable for avoiding partiality and dealing evenhandedly with His people. Seating

Himself in His ultimate court of appeals, God judges these "gods" by whether they have "maintained righteousness" and "given justice." And who are the special beneficiaries of this divine concern? Not the "wicked," but "the fatherless," "the afflicted," the "destitute." God defends their cause against the powerful who ruthlessly exploit them, and He castigates those "gods" (the so-called civil servants), who "judge unjustly" by showing "partiality to the wicked" and thereby neglect the rights of those who suffer oppression and exploitation. The state, as God's subservient administrator of public justice and righteousness, is called to follow His lead.

Psalm 72 echoes this same passionate summons. Listen to this divinely given "job description" for rulers:

> Give the king thy justice, O God, and thy righteousness to the royal son! May he judge thy people with righteousness, and thy poor with justice (vv. 1-2, RSV).

> For he delivers the needy when he calls, the poor and him who has no helper. He has pity on the weak and the needy, and saves the lives of the needy (vv. 12-14, RSV).

Psalm 2 reinforces God's demand that earthly rulers obey Him. It sternly warns rulers not to rebel against their divine anointing. For such rebellion is tantamount to rejecting the Anointed One, the coming Messiah.

If God thus takes the side of the poor and defends their cause, the civil government as the "public defender" of the powerless is called to do the same. Many Christians argue that government should "exercise a preferential option" for the poor. This position supports the hopes and aspirations both of many believing communities in Third World countries and of those who enter empathetically into their life experience. Other Christians, especially among those who live in affluent countries, however, balk at such ideas. Objections quickly arise. Does God offer His electing love only to the poor? Is poverty a condition for salvation? Are the rich excluded from entry into the kingdom of God?

Rich Christians, like ourselves, are inclined to appeal to both Scripture and personal experience to argue that wealth and poverty are not decisive criteria in settling a person's standing before God. Sometimes the self-evident teaching of Scripture regarding God's concern for the poor is even turned to self-serving ends. Riches are viewed, not as a hindrance to faith, but as a sign of divine favor. Biblical emphasis on the poor is spiritualized and thought to refer only to "the poor in spirit."

For surely the wealthy, it is argued, can also be spiritually poor. Whether people have or do not have an ample supply of this world's goods matters not at all to God. What matters to Him is only that we have a proper attitude of contentment toward riches and poverty, that we are "poor in spirit." Adopting this line of reasoning, many Christians do not see the Bible's insistent concern for the poor as substantially challenging the present status quo. They do not believe that Scripture directs them to end the oppression that causes a vast majority of our brothers and sisters in other parts of this world to live in abject poverty.

Such a reading of Scripture and reality misses the point of biblical teaching on this issue. It tends to misunderstand the basic nature of God's relationship to the poor and to ignore what ours ought to be. It blunts the force of the Bible's ringing affirmation of a divine predilection for the poor and the corresponding call for us to exercise a preferential option on their behalf. We must be clear on this point. God sides with the poor, not because they are "better" or holier than the rich. Poverty is not a means of grace any more than riches are. God's defense of the weak and needy is not based upon a spiritual value judgment. This divine predilection for the poor, which entails our preferential option for them, has nothing to do with election unto salvation. But it has everything to do with election unto service. We are indeed saved by grace alone. But it is no less true that we are saved to serve, especially to serve the helpless, the powerless, the defenseless who need our assistance sorely. And civil government is also called to render such service in the name of public justice.

God takes the side of the poor because He is the God of righteousness and justice. As such, He favors the poor and the needy because, as the Bible repeatedly declares, they are often the victims of injustice and unrighteous discrimination. They embody privation, oppression, powerlessness, and exploitation—all that God opposes in human relationships. Every human being has a divinely ordained right to a just and equitable share in the rich resources of God's creation—the right to life, liberty, and a responsible exercise of their offices in the family circle, in the workplace, in community associations, and in society at large. God's and our preferential option for the poor, therefore, rests upon a strategic decision rooted in a principled commitment to God's norms of righteousness and justice in society. God opts for the poor because they are poorly treated. And so must we. He calls us to oppose those "principalities and powers" which obstruct justice, those forms of institutionalized violence which dehumanize, disinherit, enslave, and rob the poor of their life and livelihood. Institutionally, this task belongs uniquely to the state.

When a rich and powerful minority inflicts suffering upon a poor and powerless majority, then inexorably God takes the side of the oppressed. For He champions righteousness and justice. And He looks to us His servants, and to the "gods" (civil leaders) to follow His lead. When those in positions of power and authority join in taking up the cause of public justice, when they too exercise a preferential option for the poor and exploited, then they find God on their side. When rich and poor join together to support the goals and advancement of the poor, then we can see signs of the coming of God's kingdom of justice, peace, and love.

The Origins and Basis of State Life

The basic plot of the biblical drama centers on three crucial turning points in history—the Creation, Fall, and Redemption—on the way to the consummation of all things. There are, accordingly, within the Christian tradition three major views on the historical origin of state life. Some locate it in the creation order, others in a divine intervention counteracting the effects of our fall into sin, and still others in salvation, rooted in the cross and resurrection of Jesus Christ. Each of these sharply contrasting views includes a very different outlook upon and attitude toward civil government and political life. Below is a brief overview of these three positions, taking them in reverse order.

1. The redemptionist view is clearly christological. It locates the origin of state life in the *order of redemption*. God's redemptive purposes in Christ are viewed as focused fully in the church, the Christian community, not in the state. This view does not, however, leave us with a completely secular view of the state. Its proponents argue that the light that shines in the church also radiates outward into the sphere of the state. Thus state life must reflect the life of the church. This dialectical view is characteristic of the thought of Karl Barth and Jacques Ellul.

2. Others locate the beginnings of the state within the *order of preservation*. In this view God ordained civil authority to counteract the effects of sin in human society (as described in Gen. 3). The task of the state is essentially negative: to preserve some semblance of order, decency, and humaneness in the world. This preservationist position finds its support largely in evangelical circles, but also in the Lutheran tradition with its dialectic of law and gospel (where the gospel of love and grace is the norm for life in the Christian community, while state life falls under the conditions of the law of justice). The Reformed tradition has also been influenced by this preservationist view.

Nevertheless, this Fall-oriented view offers a basically negative view of the state. The state's task is confined to curbing, hedging in, and restraining evil in society. Those holding this view expect very little from the state. Political life lies under the influence of sin. This position does not encourage a Christian presence and voice in civil affairs or the reformation of society.

3. Still others anchor state life in the original, foundational, and abidingly normative *order of creation*. By the dynamic power of His word, God created a cosmos, not a chaos, which He still continues to call to order. Built into the very fabric of our life in the world is both an integral unity and a richly variegated diversity. God assigns us a cultural mandate, which includes a wide spectrum of cultural mandates, among them a political mandate. God's creation involves not only the community as a whole, but within it a variety of communities, including the state, each having its own unique place and task within the larger community. Principled pluralism develops a view of the state rooted in the creation order, with all its unity and diversity.

Rejecting natural law theory, social contract theory, and the theory that the state is autonomous, principled pluralists argue that the biblical doctrine of the creation order provides a lasting basis for state life.[2] This

2. Natural law theories were "Christianized" by Thomas Aquinas. His synthesis of natural law for the state and canon law for the church has been preserved as the basis for traditional Western social philosophies, both Roman Catholic and Protestant, down to the present time.

At bottom, however, this Thomist view of society is a dualism seeking to become a synthesis. It presupposes a basic dichotomy between nature and grace. In this view, the church belongs to the supernatural realm of grace, while the state and other so-called secular institutions in society operate in the lower order of nature. There natural, not supernatural, law is the norm. Upon it the public sector of life is based. While the church directs eternal, spiritual matters, the state is in charge of the temporal affairs of life. Natural law functions there as a relatively independent, autonomous governing principle. Its demands are held to be accessible to and realizable by all reasonable men of good will, apart from divine revelation.

This view, when implemented consistently, tends to turn Christianity into "churchianity." That is, the church is considered the primary or even the sole source of Christian concern and influence in the world.

Social contract theory is a typically modern Western view of the basis of society, traceable to John Locke and other Enlightenment thinkers. At bottom, the idea of social contract is rooted in a commitment to popular sovereignty. Government is of the people, by the people, and for the people. The authority of government is dependent upon the consent of the governed. Free and sovereign people contract together to create a society with the state at its head. The will of the people is the ultimate court of appeal as expressed by majority rule in so-called free elections. God's transcendent norms are denied.

The view that the state is autonomous can be seen in the Greek city-state, Georg Hegel's notion of the state as the supreme incarnation of the spirit of a nation's people, Nazi Germany's "Third Reich," and the state socialism of many Marxist countries. In this view the state has a life of its own. It is autonomous—a law unto itself. It is self-justifying, needing no vindication beyond its own absolute existence. The state possesses inherent sovereignty. This understanding of the state's basis leads to a totalitarian regime.

view, though sometimes badly distorted and often obscured, is an intrinsic part of the Judeo-Christian tradition. Natural law theories are essentially secularized versions of the idea of creation ordinances, which have played a significant role in reformational thought and practice from Calvin in the sixteenth century, through Groen, Kuyper, and Bavinck during the nineteenth century, to our day. Proponents of this view maintain that societal life and the public order are not self-justifying or self-explanatory; they are dependent upon and responsible to a power beyond themselves. From the beginning, in and with and for the creation, God gave an abiding normative order, which should direct our life together in His world. Thus, we should seek to bring the actual structures of society into conformity with the divinely ordained structures for society.

The Norm for Public Justice in Society

Many assume, quite uncritically, that the concept of public justice has a universally accepted meaning that is self-evident to all thinking people. This is clearly not so. Different world views and different social philosophies bring with them different ideas of how public justice should be practically assured. As argued above, I believe that administering public justice evenhandedly and impartially is central to a biblical view of the task of the state. But various human communities have sought to achieve public justice in different ways. Let me briefly sketch four contrasting definitions of justice that have emerged in our Western world.

1. A classic view, going back to political thought in ancient Greece, and still in vogue today, holds that justice means giving every man his due. Each society pours its own content into this formal concept of "dueness" in keeping with its own world view and social philosophy.

2. A second view, intrinsic to individualist-capitalist societies, defines justice as that which gives to each man what he deserves. Justice is based on personal merit. Judged by private initiative and free enterprise, some people are deserving of more than others. Such societies provide poorly for underachievers.

3. A third view, prevalent among socialist societies, bases justice on human need. Its slogan is familiar: "From each according to his ability, to each according to his need." Once again, however, the various life-visions of different communities define quite differently what human need is.

All three of these definitions of justice are immanentistic and humanistic. None of them rests upon an absolute norm, a reference point beyond human wisdom and experience, that can claim the allegiance of people from different traditions. Each definition to a large degree is arbitrary. What these views seem to be groping after—justice—is illumined by revelational pointers presented in the Scriptures. This leads then to a fourth, more biblically directed understanding of public justice.

4. Pluralists define justice in terms of the biblical idea of office. As Scripture sheds its light upon our life in the creation, we come to recognize that people have been appointed as officeholders in God's world, clothed with a cluster of interrelated offices—a general office differentiated into a network of interacting offices. We are, for example, called to exercise our office as marriage partners, as parents, as citizens, as members or ministers in the church, as educators, as social workers, as operators of businesses, as government officials—in short, as "butcher, baker, candlestick maker," as "doctor, lawyer, merchant, chief."

But what does the biblical idea of office have to do with public justice? It means especially that the state should safeguard the freedom, rights, and responsibilities of citizens in the exercise of their offices within their various life-spheres according to their respective religious convictions. The government is obliged to respect, safeguard, preserve or, where lost, to restore, and to promote the free and responsible exercise of these other societal offices. That is what God commands the state to do to fulfill the biblical idea of public justice.

Pluralism: Our Last Best Hope?

Modern political theories, in the main, have oscillated between individualism and collectivism as though there were no intermediate social groups . . . that is, no plurally structured societies with free associations standing between individuals and the state.[3]

With these few words Robert Nisbet, an American social philosopher, sets in sharp focus the three major views of society that have shaped the course of events in Western history. The West has, of course, produced a veritable plethora of social theories. Yet, at bottom, these many modes of society fall into one or another of three fundamental types—individualism, collectivism, or pluralism. All other social models appear to be but variations on these three basic social themes, mostly at the pragmatic level of public policy.

Often our Western world is regarded rather uncritically as standing solidly within a Judeo-Christian tradition. Yet pluralism, that view of so-

3. Robert Nisbet, "The Politics of Social Pluralism," *The Journal of Politics* 10 (1978): 784.

ciety which most clearly reflects a biblical perspective, has generally come in as a distant third behind individualism and collectivism.

The social theories of the ancient and medieval world (prior to 1600) were overwhelmingly collectivist in outlook. Individual rights were severely curtailed. Even pluralist societal structures such as the medieval guilds, monastic orders, universities, and feudal domains were granted only limited independence under the general superintendence of church and state.

Only in the modern world period, as a result of the Renaissance and Enlightenment, do societal systems based explicitly upon individualist premises emerge. In principle, however, individualism lacks social substance. Institutions are "artificial" creations of individuals; they have only "fictional" reality; they have no constitutional standing in United States law. In its public policy individualism therefore tends inexorably toward a collectivist society, as is evident in Hobbes's *Leviathan*, Locke's "social contract," and Rousseau's "general will." In recent Western history a steadily growing convergence of individualist and collectivist ideologies has taken place. One result is a discernible erosion not only in the participatory rights, freedom rights, and benefit rights of certain groups, but also in the societal significance of such pluralist structures as marriage, family, school, church, business enterprise, and free associations. In our times it is becoming increasingly clear that traditional individualist-collectivist societal paradigms are incapable of accounting for the realities of daily experience. They create too many anomalies.

As an integral part of the creation order, as normative for our life together in the world, a pluralist view of society is the only valid alternative to collectivism and individualism. Though largely overlooked, it too has a history. Nisbet writes that at no time in Western philosophy has pluralism

> ever seriously rivaled other forms of community in general appeal,
> . . . and yet . . . the attraction of the plural community . . . has
> been a strongly persistent feature of western culture. Living as we do
> in a world grown increasingly more centralized and collectivized,
> . . . it is possible to see in the plural community man's last best
> hope.[4]

4. Robert Nisbet, *The Social Philosophers* (New York: Crowell, 1973), p. 7. Richard Neuhaus declares that contemporary Calvinism represents "an innovative approach to Christianity and the social order . . . viewed by some as a promising alternative to the tattered liberalisms, conservatisms, and radicalisms that have dominated religious social thought in recent years."

Nevertheless, our individualist-collectivist societies resist pluralism, which seeks to recognize the structural rights of plural associations within the public-legal order. Such a recognition, many fear, poses a serious threat to societal unity. The case is the same for confessional pluralism: granting official standing to the real religious differences among varying faith communities is viewed as divisive, a sectarian strategy, and a public menace. Therefore, religion is labeled private and only cautiously, if at all, accepted into public life. Often religion is declared to be incompatible with consensus politics because it is disruptive of societal harmony.

Mere tinkering with existing systems is not enough. Authentic reform demands the acceptance and implementation of the pluralist alternative. Only a fundamental reconstruction of society on pluralist premises can solve the problems produced by individualist-collectivist convergence.[5]

Contours of a Pluralist View of Society

Christian traditions have been shaped by various structuring principles. In Roman Catholicism the various spheres of life within both the Roman Catholic community and the society at large are regarded as subsidiaries of and subservient to either the church or the state. Typical of the Lutheran tradition is its two-kingdom theory. This Erastian view of church government placed the so-called spiritual aspects of life in the hands of church assemblies, while delegating the so-called secular tasks to the state. Historically, a similar pattern prevailed in Anglicanism. Anabaptists insisted that all societal life outside the church belonged to the kingdom of darkness and that Christians therefore should not participate in government.

Amid these conflicting traditions in Western Christianity, Calvinists developed their own biblically Reformed world view. They emphasized the sovereignty of God over all and held that the saving work of Jesus Christ liberates the Christian community for obedient discipleship and responsible stewardship in every sphere of life. No aspect of the world is alien terrain. Christian liberty is a gift of God in Jesus Christ, a freedom to be exercised in holiness. Such holy freedom impels Christians to reclaim every sphere of life for the King—home, school, state, university, labor, commerce, politics, science, art, journalism, and all the rest.

No limitations may be placed on the sovereignty of God, the kingship of Christ, or the renewing power of the Holy Spirit. Supreme sover-

5. As Herman Dooyeweerd says, "The point is not to find a suitable middle road between individualism and collectivism, but to recognize the false root from which both spring forth." "Individu, gemeenschap, eigendom," pp. 210-11.

eignty is God's alone. Everything creaturely has a dependent existence. All creatures derive their nature and worth from God. The sovereignty of each sphere, therefore, is God-given—a dependent, derived, delegated, and therefore limited sovereignty. It is limited by the supreme, overall sovereignty of God and by the sovereignty of other spheres of life, which coexist and work together. Sphere-sovereignty (with its related aspects of sphere-authority, sphere-responsibility, and sphere-stewardship) is always subservient to the sovereign rule of God. Through this means God makes His sovereign rule concrete in the affairs of men and exercises His absolute authority over the whole cosmos. The various differentiated spheres of our life-relationships give specific expression to His sovereignty: parental authority in the home, preaching authority in the church, pedagogical authority in the classroom, governing authority in the state's administration of public justice, and so on.

The various spheres in society are, therefore, not sovereign, but subservient in their relationships to God. They do, however, possess a certain sovereignty in their mutual relationships with each other. Each sphere has its own identity, its own unique task, its own God-given prerogatives. In each sphere man is called to exercise his threefold office as a prophet, priest, and king; but that office is focused differently from one sphere to another. In the exercise of these offices, man as steward is called to give an account. Each office must be made serviceable to God and fellow men. But the nature and extent of such sovereignty is defined by that sphere in life in which we are called to exercise it. Being a husband or father does not exhaust a man's life-relationships; neither does being a teacher nor a preacher nor a citizen. Biblical norms for living vary from sphere to sphere. God's Word lays its claim on our life as a whole. But obedience to that Word calls for a differentiated response in keeping with the nature of each sphere, since the various spheres involve varying sets of life-relationships.

In a highly differentiated society, like contemporary America, sphere-sovereignty offers safeguards against the many forms of worldly authoritarianism and totalitarianism that often beset us—especially in state life. For with it comes a recognition of proper limitations on the power of all earthly institutions. Sphere-sovereignty demands a rightful distribution of authority-centers in life.

This view of life helps to create a true sense of communality, not only by fostering a rich diversity of tasks, but also by engendering unity of purpose. As the many members constitute the one body, so the many spheres are integrated into the unified life of the community. For the corollary to the principle of sphere-sovereignty is the complementary principle of sphere-universality. When kept together, this twofold principle preserves communal life against both monotonous uniformity and tyranny, on the one hand, and fragmentation and polarization, on the other. Sphere-sovereignty (diversity of tasks) may not be sacrificed to sphere-universality (unity of life) or vice versa. Honoring both sides of this principle in their integral coherence and in their mutual and reciprocal interactions encourages the development of various coordinate spheres of activity in the human community, including civil government, which work together in numerous partnership arrangements.

Richard Neuhaus and Peter Berger in their work entitled *To Empower People: the Role of Mediating Structures in Public Policy*[6] argue persuasively for the restoration of what they call "the mediating structures" in society. They contend that modern life is largely "an ongoing migration between two spheres, the public and the private." The public sphere consists of such megastructures as the modern state, capitalist corporations, organized labor, and the massive bureaucracies that administer them. Private life is limited to the activities not directly controlled by these large institutions. Because of their size, power, and impersonalness these megastructures alienate people from their work, one another, and themselves. Personal identity, fulfillment, and meaning are realized only in the private life of the individual. The tension created by the conflicting influence of megastructures (alienating) and private life (meaning) is the crisis of our times.

To reform society, Berger and Neuhaus argue, we must rejuvenate and recognize in public policy those "mediating structures" which stand between people in their personal, private lives and the mammoth conglomerates which make up civil life. Mediating institutions such as family, neighborhood, church, and voluntary associations can help to connect private and public life. They can give private life a measure of stability and lend a measure of meaning and value to the megastructures of public life. If these mediating structures are safeguarded in law, people will feel more at home in society at large and have a more meaningful sense of involvement in the political order of the nation.

What Berger and Neuhaus advocate, the Calvinist tradition calls sphere-sovereignty and sphere-universality. This Calvinist approach offers a pluralist alternative to both individualist and collectivist models

6. Washington, D.C.: American Enterprise Institute for Public Policy Research, 1977.

of society. Waiting long as a readily available alternative, it is now begging for implementation.

Pluralism: Its Potential for Healing in Our Broken World

Pluralism is, therefore, not simply a synthesis of individualism and collectivism. It represents an authentic third way of viewing society. Whereas the other two views define the discrete individual or the collective whole as the ultimate locus of norms for society, pluralism holds that humans, being by nature social creatures, always stand in a plurality of life-relationships. Man can never be reduced to either a mere atomistic individual with no social responsibilities or a mere cog in a societal machine with no individual significance.

Accordingly, pluralism argues that the individual, standing apart from societal structures, is not ultimate. It posits instead a persons-in-associations model as the framework within which man's individuality finds meaning. Its proponents insist also that no large institution can properly claim to be the all-embracing societal structure, the one in which ultimate meaning is located. Pluralists hold instead that multiple societal structures such as family, school, church, business corporation, and state are real and meaningful. Sometimes called mediating structures, sometimes called societal spheres, these communal realities exist alongside the state, and each must be fully accorded its own unique right of existence.

In this view the state is not the single all-embracing structure. It has neither an ontological status higher than other societal institutions, as in collectivism, nor a purely artificial, fictional, derived, and contractual status, as in individualism. It has its own distinct God-given identity and sphere of influence. The state has a specifically limited scope, bounded and balanced by the rights of other societal groupings and spheres. Its specific function is to promote public justice, to balance the rights and responsibilities of the other societal spheres, to adjudicate differences between them as well as between individuals within them, and to promote and protect the rights of all. The state is the balance wheel that safeguards, regulates, and coordinates the work of the other wheels, ensuring a proper intermeshing of functions and, thus, facilitating cooperation in partnership. To this end, it is important to bear in mind that the case for pluralism involves the two basic dimensions repeatedly emphasized along the way, namely structural and confessional pluralism.

Life is fundamentally of one piece. It has a unifying focus. As life unfolds historically, taking on ever more complex and differentiated forms, this profound unity remains intact. The radically disruptive powers of evil are undeniably at work in the world, eroding human solidarity and societal unity. But reconciliation is also a present reality. Through redemption God is out to restore all of creation, including societal cohesion. This principle has been formulated in the idea of sphere-universality.

Created reality is not, however, a seamless garment. It also discloses a rich diversity of cultural tasks, sets of human relationships, and spheres of societal action. God has provided mandates in labor, marriage, government, church, education, and society, each of which demands our active response in its own sphere of endeavor. As a single ray of light passing through a prism is refracted into a multi-faceted rainbow of colors, so man's single societal calling opens up into a richly diversified spectrum of societal callings. This range of callings, given with creation, develops historically, taking on contemporary shape and form in a diverse but harmonious grouping of societal institutions. Each unit of the societal structure performs its own unique function like the cogs of a clockwork, thus contributing to the unified operation of the timepiece as a whole. These societal spheres are coordinate and cooperative, functioning for the good of all. No sphere may exercise its authority at the expense of another. Each has its own rightful area of jurisdiction. Each is entitled to full and equal standing before law. This principle is captured in the idea of sphere-sovereignty.

The concept of pluralism also includes confessional pluralism. We live in a religiously splintered world, surrounded by a wide range of contrasting faith communities. Pluralism, as an alternative way of living together in society, seeks to reckon seriously with these very real philosophical differences. It seeks to insure that the public as well as the private rights of all groups in society be safeguarded within a common democratic order.

Although this pluralist vision is expressed most clearly within the Calvinist tradition, it is neither sectarian nor parochial. Its perspective is cosmic; it embraces concerns common to all people. It disavows special pleading for the privileged status of established groups and vested interests. The rights that it affirms for one group in society it also advocates for others.

Case Study: Public Justice and Educational Equity

One area of American society where principled pluralism, if followed, would produce substantial change is in public education. It calls for disestablishing public schools.[7] Many of the early colonies granted certain

7. Cf. Rockne M. McCarthy, James W. Skillen, William A. Harper, *Disestablishment a Second Time: Genuine Pluralism for American Schools* (Grand Rapids: Eerdmans, 1982).

denominations official status. During the late eighteenth and early nineteenth centuries those state churches were disestablished. In the nineteenth and twentieth centuries an established public school system with its capstone in state universities replaced established churches as an official expression of the nation's convictions and values. As a result, government agencies today have a near-monopoly over the American educational system; they own, operate, and control it. As America previously disestablished its churches, it now needs to disestablish its school system. The present governmental school system violates the basic principles of a pluralist view of society and promotes injustice and partiality.

This is true in two ways. First, American public education is inconsistent with the idea of structural pluralism. It establishes a relationship between the state and a single school system that erases the lines of proper demarcation between the state and the schools of the nation. Disestablishment would liberate education from the political domination of the state and restore to the sphere of education its own unique sense of identity and integrity.

Second, the established educational system violates the idea of confessional pluralism. It refuses to recognize the religious plurality that is a fact of life in this country. Principled pluralism argues that every faith community should have the right to maintain schools consistent with its own religion and philosophy of education. A religiously diverse society demands a religiously plural school system. As the administrator of public justice, the state should relate evenhandedly to all schools, and all schools should be equal before the law. Then parents and students would have true freedom of choice in education without discrimination, "double taxation," or other undue forms of financial liability. In the field of education, as in other areas of society, principled pluralism calls for "liberty and justice for all."

One long half-step in the right direction would be a "tax credit" or "tax reduction" plan. Under such a legal arrangement a measure of tax relief would be granted to help cover tuition paid for nonpublic education. The most just and equitable plan, however, would be a voucher system. This idea, whose time may be coming, would involve giving to all parents of school-going children a certificate with a stated dollar value, which could be cashed in at the school of their choice, whether public, private, or church-sponsored. This would be a prime example of the convergence of the principles of structural and religious-confessional pluralism at work in education. Such a voucher plan would be the best guarantee of genuine freedom of choice in education without undue governmental and financial pressures.

6

The Theonomic Response
to Principled Pluralism

Carl W. Bogue*

M y response to Gordon Spykman's arguments is presented in four parts. The first part describes some areas of agreement between theonomists and principled pluralists. The second section presents methodological flaws apparent in Spykman's argument for pluralism. The third and most important section examines the substantive disagreement between the two groups. Part four analyzes contradictions inherent in the principled pluralism position.

Areas of Agreement

In an area as critical as the Christian's role in civil government, consensus among Christians is highly desirable. Thus we note with enthusiasm points of agreement. Theonomists agree with principled pluralists that "the Scriptures present principles and directives that hold for life as a whole in every age," and we, too, reject the contention of secularists and pietists that the Bible "deals only with narrowly religious matters" (p. 80). Since "all of life is religion," "the question is not *whether* but *how* the Bible speaks to issues of society and the state" (p. 81). The Bible "is God's Word for a broken world" (p. 81).

More specific to our theme, theonomists agree with principled pluralists that "civil government . . . is . . . subject to God's sovereign claim" (p. 82). Thus, Christians should "seek to bring the actual structures of society into conformity with the divinely ordained structures for society" (p. 91). Our task is "to reclaim every sphere of life for the King" (p. 94). "God's Word is as normative for the state as it is for the church" (p. 84).

*Carl W. Bogue received a B.A. from Muskingum College, a B.D. from Pittsburgh Theological Seminary, and a Th.D. from the Free University of Amsterdam. He presently pastors the Faith Presbyterian Church (PCA) in Akron, OH. His published works include *Jonathan Edwards and the Covenant of Grace* (1975), *Hole in the Dike: Critical Aspects of Berkouwer's Theology* (1977), and *The Scriptural Law of Worship* (1988).

There is, however, an anomaly about this agreement. It is precisely these above premises, consistently applied, that lead to the theonomic conclusion that "all civil magistrates today are under moral obligation to be guided and regulated by the law of God (throughout the Bible) *where and when* it speaks to political matters" (Bahnsen, "The Theonomic Position," p. 42). Spykman's premises, therefore, conflict with his pluralist position rather than support it.

Methodological Criticism

Several stylistic and methodological aspects of Spykman's argument make it very difficult to understand the pluralist position on the biblical role of civil government. Our discussion would be greatly enhanced by a clearer definition of *pluralism*, especially of *confessional pluralism*. Spykman also fails to present any rationale for the adjective *principled*, which is especially important considering that pragmatic arguments are often used to support the position.

Spykman's threefold division of individualism, collectivism, and pluralism as the only alternatives for structuring society is very questionable. Collectivism and individualism may easily be defined as rejecting God, implying pluralism as the godly alternative. However, since pluralism cannot be sustained exegetically, this threefold division is, at the very least, begging the question. Many thinkers, in fact, reject all three of those alternatives. Even Spykman cannot keep the alternatives distinct and cites collectivists and individualists with "pluralist conclusions."

Much of Spykman's argument consists of historical surveys that are oversimplified and irrelevant. Simply because we are at a critical juncture in our history does not mean we must accept sociology over biblical exegesis. Spykman criticizes the Reformed tradition as a "Fall-oriented view" that leaves us with "a basically negative view of the state" whose task is confined to "restraining evil in society" (pp. 89-90). This critique misses the immense positive benefits that accrue to any society that restricts the state's sphere to that defined in Scripture. This position may or may not seem to "expect very little from the state," as Spykman alleges, but the issue is what Scripture commands and permits. Spykman's assertion that "traditional individualist-collectivist societal paradigms are incapable of accounting for the realities of daily experience" (p. 93) tells us nothing about what Scripture requires. In another section (pp. 83-85) Calvin is set forth as a forerunner of confessional pluralism, while evidence to the contrary is simply set aside by asserting that Calvin lived "too much in the shadows" of medieval society. This may be convenient for his argument, but it is not accurate.

Moreover, Spykman's argument rests upon many slogans that are emotive rather than denotative. If all "proof-texting" (p. 80) is wrong, as he alleges, then our confessions of faith are hermeneutically untrustworthy. Theonomists are concerned about using proof-texting out of context, but we are even more concerned about a position that has no proof-texts! Despite his critique of proof-texts, Spykman uses some anyway (see pp. 82-85), but they do not actually support his argument. The debate, then, is not about the use of proof-texts as such, but whether they are properly used.

Spykman's claim that "the Bible is neither a theoretical handbook on civil government nor a textbook on public policy" (p. 81) is reminiscent of the evolutionists' contention that the Bible is not a science textbook. The use of such a slogan does not prove pluralism. Is not the real question whether the Bible is true when it does speak to civil government and public policy? Simply put, is Scripture to be trusted when it says that justice means defending the oppressed, requiring restitution for theft, and executing murderers?

Another methodological weakness is evident in Spykman's assertion (pp. 80, 83) that the Bible has "constant" and "universal" norms, which hold for life as a whole in every age, that are couched in variable forms. It all depends! Does Spykman simply mean what all Reformed Christians would affirm, that the parable of the Good Samaritan, for example, while still obliging us to neighborliness, is set in the ancient Near East? Or is he urging us (as some neo-evangelicals have done by making a distinction between form and content) to alter the unchanging content by calling it changeable form? Is Exodus 20:13 (the sixth commandment) a norm or a form? Which is Deuteronomy 19:5 (man-slaughter)? Is Exodus 21:12 (the death penalty for murder) a norm or a form? Is murder ever to be tolerated, even if it is in accord with people's respective religious convictions? What about sodomy? Is the requirement for kings to "kiss the Son" (Ps. 2:12) obligatory today, or is it a "changing form"?

Pluralism: the Real Issues

Spykman argues for two types of pluralism: structural and confessional. Does one lead to the other, and are they supported biblically? Most of his essay argues for structural pluralism, which in principle does not divide pluralists and theonomists. The problem is that Spykman infers confessional pluralism from the premise of structural pluralism.

God has created structures to order the world, of which civil government is one. In simplest terms this sphere-sovereignty means that the state should not administer the sacraments (the church's sphere) or educate children (the family's sphere), and neither the church nor the family should execute criminals (the state's sphere). Theonomists agree, therefore, that the scope of the state is specifically limited. We maintain, however, that the state and all other social structures are obligated to do all that God commands them — no more and no less.

While theonomists believe that structural pluralism is biblical, we contend that confessional pluralism is not. Unfortunately, Spykman does not clearly explain this important concept. He does say that the state must "safeguard the freedom, rights, and responsibilities of citizens in the exercise of their offices within their various life-spheres according to their respective religious convictions" (p. 92). Note, it is "the freedom, rights, and responsibilities of citizens" to do what is dictated by their religious convictions, not by God's law or revelation, which Spykman argues, God requires the state to guard. And he defines *confessional pluralism* as "granting official standing to the real religious differences among varying faith communities" (p. 94).

This confessional pluralism, which theonomists repudiate, is set forth as though it followed logically from structural pluralism. As a creation ordinance, civil government, Spykman asserts, is subservient to a transcendent norm. That transcendent authority (God) ordains the family, the church, and the state, but God does not permit rebellious children, idolatrous worship, or elevating Caesar as Lord. Spykman says that one sphere may not "exercise its authority at the expense of another" (p. 98). The Bible teaches, however, that the church may excommunicate families. Moreover, the Scriptures declare that the state may prevent child abuse and may even exercise its authority by executing an adulterous member of a family.

It is simply a non sequitur to infer confessional pluralism from structural pluralism. While the Scripture teaches that the state and the church have different spheres of authority, it does not direct states to protect the practice of Islamic jihad or of Marxist revolution. The non sequitur spills over into Spykman's historical survey as well. To demonstrate that Calvin's rejection of confessional pluralism (his endorsement of the death of Servetus) is not his true position, Spykman quotes Calvin's commentary on Ephesians 5:21-6:9 and 1 Peter 1:12-17 (p. 84). Neither, however, even obliquely supports confessional pluralism. Structural pluralism is not equivalent to, nor does it imply, confessional pluralism.

Pluralism in the only distinctive sense, namely, confessional pluralism, must be in view when Spykman asserts that "pluralism is more consistently obedient to the transcendent norm of God's word than any other view of society" (p. 83). However, he offers absolutely no support from the Bible for this crucial assertion. If some "natural law" premise should be implied in support of confessional pluralism, however, we would surely agree that the influence of sin necessitates our judging it by the standard of God's written revelation. Because it lacks scriptural support, confessional pluralism contradicts the Reformed confession of *sola Scriptura*.

Spykman contends (pp. 91ff.) that administering "public justice" is "central to a biblical view of the task of the state." Although acknowledging the existence of differing views of public justice, he does not provide a biblically supported rationale for the view he alleges to be correct, which defines "justice in terms of the biblical idea of office" (p. 92). Nor does he explain what the biblical idea of office is. Spykman moves illegitimately from this view of "office," which alludes only to structural pluralism, to confessional pluralism. The biblical role of civil government, he argues, is to enable citizens to exercise their various offices in various areas of life as their religious convictions direct (see p. 92). Nowhere does Spykman give exegetical support for such a definition of public justice. In fact, confessional pluralism promotes what Scripture defines as injustice and lawlessness and denies that magistrates are ministers of God.

Interestingly, Spykman admits that his one explicit attempt to provide a scriptural basis for confessional pluralism is not a biblical argument at all. The parable of the wheat and tares in Matthew 13 is briefly set forth (pp. 85-86). Having said that "these passages do not refer directly to the role of the state in a religiously pluralistic country," Spykman does exactly that, concluding from this parable "that the state also must bear with the presence of conflicting faith-communities within its bounds." He is forced to appeal to admittedly unwarranted eisegesis because he can find no exegesis that supports his conclusion. Spykman seems to be using Matthew 13 as a proof-text (an approach he has denounced) to argue that civil government is not obliged to punish rapists, murderers, or homosexuals, since some may affirm these acts because of their own religious convictions. In point of fact, pluralists do believe the state should punish some offenses, but in so doing they violate the "principle" of their "pluralism." And if they will not in fact be consistent in their pluralism, should they not agree with theonomy that the definition of crime and the equitable punishment thereof is to be obtained solely from the just and authoritative Word of God?

Public justice, by definition, is evenhanded and shows no partiality. God does not have a double standard for political ethics. God's law, reflecting His immutable moral character, does not allow different people to adopt differing standards in political ethics. His law applies to all people regardless of their religious faith.

Internal Contradictions

Since "every societal issue is . . . a religious issue" (p. 81), and since pluralists do draw lines and refuse to tolerate certain acts, they must not hold to pluralism consistently. In fact, Spykman's argument illustrates this point.

Confessional pluralism seeks to safeguard the exercise of different religious world views and to grant "official standing to the real religious differences" among people (p. 94). Yet, Spykman argues also that rulers should show preference for the poor (pp. 86ff.). Despite acknowledging that Psalm 82 teaches the state to avoid "partiality" (p. 87), he concludes that civil government is called to "exercise a preferential option for the poor" (p. 89).

Treating the poor preferentially logically requires civil government to provide extensive programs for the poorer segment of society (welfarism). This choice is grounded in "a divinely ordained [human] right to a just and equitable share in the rich resources of God's creation" (p. 88). There is, however, no scriptural evidence for such a redistribution of wealth. Moreover, it contradicts the pluralist premise, preferentially embracing a form of Marxism rather than a pluralistic tolerance of conflicting views.

To be consistent, confessional pluralism must protect equally the rights of the poor as well as those who are economically selfish. Some worship money; others discriminate because of racist convictions or religious beliefs. While individual Christians may renounce such belief, the state may not prefer the poor over these other groups if confessional pluralism is consistent with its own premise.

Leviticus 19:15 is one of many biblical passages that teach that we are to favor neither the rich nor the poor but, rather, be impartial in administering justice. The traditional Reformed view of the civil magistrate encourages governments to use biblical civil law to define and restrain the lawless practices of false religions. The pluralist, if consistent, must instead instruct the government to protect the right of some to act lawlessly. Whether pluralism safeguards the practice of lawlessness or gives preferential treatment to the poor, it is diametrically opposed to Scripture.

Conclusion

To argue for confessional pluralism in politics — where "every societal issue is . . . a religious issue" — is to advocate a "political polytheism," thus violating the first commandment. Pluralists argue from the teaching of John Calvin and the concept of God's sovereignty that Christians should reclaim "every sphere of life for the King." However, their approach promotes instead a plurality of conflicting kings.

"Righteousness exalts a nation" (Prov. 14:34, NIV), but what is righteousness? Pluralism advocates civil government as "the balance wheel" (p. 97) that safeguards the belief in and exercise of a plurality of conceptions of righteousness. According to pluralism, "our last best hope" (pp. 92ff.) is thus not righteousness, but righteousness and unrighteousness coexisting, with both equally condoned and protected by civil government.

Theonomists believe it is *impossible*, even if it were desirable, for a state to balance such conflicting world views. The moral chaos of the past twenty years in our nation testifies to this. Despite the good intentions of its advocates, pluralism can only be the last best hope for rulers who "take counsel together, against the Lord and against His Anointed" (Ps. 2:2, NKJV). By contrast, theonomists insist that our best and only hope is for all civil magistrates to be regulated by the law of God where and when it speaks to political matters, lest the Son "be angry" and they "perish in the way" (Ps. 2:12, NKJV).

7

The Christian America Response to Principled Pluralism

*T. M. Moore**

This seems to be a most opportune time for Christians to be investigating the biblical teachings on the role of government. The bicentennial celebration of the United States Constitution provides a historic backdrop for such an undertaking; and what many are beginning to recognize as an impending crisis in the American political system lends a note of urgency.[1]

This response seeks to accomplish three ends. First, I will identify aspects of Gordon Spykman's presentation with which all Reformed Christians can heartily agree. Next, I will examine problems inherent in Spykman's pluralist approach and present some conclusions that seem to follow from those criticisms. Finally, I will discuss briefly the Christian America alternative and suggest how it could be implemented in the American political experience.

Areas of Agreement

All Reformed Christians can enthusiastically endorse at least five aspects of Spykman's position. Especially important is his effort to understand how Scripture speaks to the larger issues of life in society and to apply its teachings to all spheres and activities. Spykman contends correctly that "the question is not *whether* but *how* the Bible speaks to issues of society and the state" (p. 81). All meaningful Christian contributions to the role of civil government begin with this fundamental principle.

*T. M. Moore is president of Chesapeake Theological Seminary, a nontraditional graduate institution for training in ministry in Baltimore. He has written three books, *Genesis: Studies in God and Man* (1981), *Making God's Good News Known* (1985), and *Chain Reaction!* (1985) with D. James Kennedy — and has contributed chapters to four other books. He has done graduate study in theology and educational leadership and has served as a Visiting Assistant Professor of Philosophy at the University of Delaware.

1. Cf. Terry Eastland, "Party Poopers," *The American Spectator*, May 1987, pp. 33ff.; Peter Brimelow, "Judicial Imperialism," *Forbes*, June 1, 1987, pp. 109ff.

Equally important is Spykman's call for Christians to understand Scripture holistically. This approach prevents us from using a proof-texting method to develop a biblical perspective on government. Recognizing the organic nature of Scripture gives us access, through the analogy of faith, to the whole counsel of God on our subject.[2]

Further, Spykman rightly sees that the nature of the state and the tasks of government are religious issues. Because human beings are made in the image of God, "the public affairs of society and the state are no less religious than the so-called private affairs of individual, church, home, and school life" (p. 81).

We should also recognize, as Spykman argues, that such disciplines as history, sociology, political science, psychology, and economics can contribute greatly to our understanding of political issues. Because of God's common grace, the findings of scholars in the social sciences, even if these scholars are not Christians, can shed much light on our deliberations.

Finally, Spykman is to be applauded for his forthright acknowledgment that civil government is a "creature subject to God's sovereign claim" and, therefore, should serve God "on behalf of His other creatures" (p. 82). The tendency of civil governments to arrogate unto themselves final authority in all matters is a great evil. Only recognition of and acquiescence in the sovereign rulership of God can deliver a nation and its government from what Augustine referred to as the "deadly corrosive" of the desire for autonomy.[3]

While Spykman's development of those biblical themes is commendable and helpful, his general perspective on the biblical role of government and the practical implications he develops involve several areas of difficulty.

Problem Areas

To start with, numerous parts of Spykman's argument lack clarity.[4] For example, Spykman does not clarify what he means when he says that Scripture opens up "principles and directives" for us, or that the Scriptures "carry with them universal *norms*." How precisely does Scripture unfold or "carry" with it these principles, directives, and norms (see p. 80)? Perhaps he means that the Scriptures declare them or set them

2. Louis Berkhof, *Principles of Biblical Interpretation* (Grand Rapids: Baker, 1971), p. 53.

3. Augustine, *The City of God*, vol. I, III. xiv, trans. John Healey, ed. R. V. G. Tasker (London: Everyman's Library, 1967).

4. Cf. John Frame and Leonard J. Coppes, *The Amsterdam Philosophy: A Preliminary Critique* (Phillipsburg, N.J.: Harmony Press, n.d.), p. 5. I am particularly indebted throughout this paper to the insights presented by Frame.

forth. This does not seem to be the meaning he intends, however, because he claims that these norms exist in a realm beyond the creation; this realm is also beyond the Scriptures themselves, which are an aspect of the creation given to "correct" our sin-distorted experience.

Further, and in a similar vein, what does Spykman mean when he says that the word of God "speaks to all aspects of our world," or that this word, in the form of "creation ordinances," "impinge[s]" upon us "continuously" and "with an abiding authority?" (pp. 82, 83). How do we encounter this word from beyond? How do the Scriptures open this word to us so as to cause it to impinge and bear upon us?

In addition, Spykman's argument seems to hinge at times on unfounded assertions. For example, his claim that pluralism is "the only authentic alternative paradigm of society" (p. 80) only makes sense if one first accepts the basic dialectical premise of Spykman's historical argument, that is, the notion that pluralism is the only viable mediating position between two unacceptable extremes. Pluralism, however, is not the only other way of conceptualizing society's organization. Another alternative is the federal system of government which the Founding Fathers devised. It established a balance between a strong central government and decentralized, more local governments operating with unique authority in their own realms. This "balance of powers" approach can serve as a paradigm for other areas of authority, such as the church, home, marketplace, and school.

Similarly, the only support Spykman offers for his assertion that God has issued a "creational word" that "remains His fundamental and abiding revelation" is his own observation of the creation. Certainly Scripture does not speak of a "creational word." God reveals Himself through the creation, but the nature of this revelation, according to the Scriptures, is of a qualitatively different nature from the Word-revelation He has inspired in the Scriptures. This point is expanded upon below.

Unfortunately, Spykman's pluralistic perspective on the biblical role for governments seems to rest primarily upon such unsupported assumptions as these. He has failed to provide a strong, clear scriptural basis for his position.

Spykman's lack of clarity and unsubstantiated claims are related to, and perhaps derive from, a third problem—a faulty hermeneutic. His improper method for understanding Scripture is evidenced in two ways.

First, Spykman confuses the Word of God as revealed in the Scriptures with the revelation which God discloses through creation. When he says that Scripture "is not God's only word for the world, nor is it His first word" (pp. 81-82), he begins to tread on thin ice. Certainly the Bible talks about a word from God which is declared through the things He has made (cf. Ps. 19:1-6), but this is not intended to indicate a revelation of the same significance as that which He has given through the Scriptures (cf. Ps. 19:7-11). Ultimately, Spykman exalts God's revelation in nature above the Bible. He insists that the meaning of Scripture can only be unlocked by first understanding the meaning of God's word inherent in the creational norms around us. We must, therefore, first examine the creation to discern the norms and directives we will then use to inform and guide our understanding of the Scriptures.

Second, how can we discover and access that realm above the creation — and even above the Bible — which, according to Spykman, contains the creational norms that are the keys to our understanding of everything else? He never directly explains how we are to recognize or identify these norms (which, he argues, are the very word of God, superior to the Bible and to the created order) or how we are to use them to guide our understanding of the other avenues of God's revelation.

Spykman implies, however, that these norms are to be discovered scientifically, through reasoned analysis and study. For example, Spykman's frequent use of historical analysis[5] reveals his belief that history provides ultimate norms — creational norms — which should direct our interpretation of the Bible. Yet such an approach exalts the analytical powers of man's mind above the plain words of the text of Scripture and ignores the supremacy of God's revelation over mere human interpretations (cf. Isa. 55:8-9; 2 Pet. 1:20-21).

This confusion over what the word of God is and how it is to be discerned is a major shortcoming of Spykman's pluralistic approach. It also explains why his perspective offers little clear or consistent biblical basis for his claims about the role of government. Granted, he cites a number of passages to argue that civil government should promote justice throughout society, especially on behalf of the poor. But he does this in a proof-texting manner, an approach he himself denounces and one that, in this case, yields fruits that others have thoroughly exposed for their incorrectness.[6]

5. Cf. Gordon J. Spykman, "Pluralism: Our Last Best Hope?" *Christian Scholar's Review* X, 2 (1981): 99ff.; Rockne McCarthy, Donald Oppewal, Walfred Peterson, and Gordon Spykman, coordinator, *Society, State, and Schools* (Grand Rapids: Eerdmans, 1982).

6. Cf. David Chilton, *Productive Christians in an Age of Guilt-Manipulators* (Tyler, Tex.: Institute for Christian Economics, 1985); Ronald H. Nash, *Social Justice and the Christian Church* (Milford, Mich.: Mott Media, 1985). Both men argue cogently, for example, that the redistributionist ends that Spykman's view supports violate both the free will of man and the eighth commandment.

Much of Spykman's chapter provides historical analyses designed to support his pluralist presuppositions about the role of government. Moreover, his exegesis of history is based upon a highly selective perspective. Others as diverse as Karl Marx, Arnold Toynbee, Barbara Tuchman, and Fernand Braudel might argue with equal force for their own understandings of history. Then he uses the results of his historical studies as a framework for interpreting the Scriptures, without sufficiently considering the plain teaching of the Bible in all its comprehensiveness and simplicity. Can such an approach possibly yield a truly and fully biblical perspective on any matter, including politics?

In the light of the preceding, certain of the pluralist claims that Spykman sets forth are unworkable. His idea that various "mediating structures" must be "fully accorded" their "own unique right of existence," regulated and safeguarded by the civil government, is either altogether utopian or hopelessly naive (p. 97). Could any democratic society of any form safeguard "the public as well as the private rights of all groups in society" (p. 98)?

Spykman's view fails to take into account the absolutist claims of such "mediating structures" as Marxist political factions and such fringe religiopolitical groups as the Ku Klux Klan, not to mention the Christian world view itself. Even if the state could effectively regulate and coordinate the work of the other institutions and groups, it would have to limit the rights of certain groups to make room for the rights of others. By so doing it would redefine the spheres of each group according to its own absolutist perspective on what constitutes the public weal at any given time. The state would be the final arbiter as to what kind of balancing of the social spheres represents "a proper intermeshing of functions" or true "cooperation in partnership" (p. 97). This would make the state the source of truth, which contradicts the clearly revealed Word of God in the Bible.

Implications

Based upon my above argument, I draw four conclusions about Spykman's principled pluralistic position.

First, because of his lack of clarity, his misleading and faulty hermeneutical method, and his failure to explain specifically how Christians can work to achieve the ideal he sets forth, Spykman's case for pluralism is not likely to play in Peoria. Christians have enough difficulty committing themselves to those things which the Scriptures clearly teach, such as witnessing to the risen Christ, diligently studying the Word of God, and resisting daily temptations to sin. It is not likely they will rally behind so arcane and dubious a position as Spykman presents here. Second, Spykman's pluralistic proposal is unrealistic. In *Society, State, and Schools* Spykman and associates describe what the state must do to establish their pluralistic perspective:

> We are asking this: that the state acknowledge its own deeply entrenched world-view; that it also acknowledge the resultant social paradigm that shapes its public policy; that it further acknowledge that its prevailing world-view and social paradigm is not neutral; that it then cease to impose its world-view and social paradigm upon society as a whole as its test of public orthodoxy and its standard for public funding; that it recognize the fundamental rights of confessional communities holding to other world-views and social paradigms to give structural form to their commitments publicly in the social order. . . .[7]

It is very unlikely that our increasingly secular state will ever adopt an ideological neutrality. Moreover, doing so would require giving every crackpot sect, cult, and interest group a share of the federal subsidy pie.

Third, Spykman's approach militates against the very possibility of discerning a biblical view of government. Using Spykman's academic and intellectual categories as the glasses through which we examine and analyze the Bible will severely limit our understanding of its full meaning. His approach will cause us to neglect the analogy of faith and the illuminating presence of the Holy Spirit.

Finally, Spykman hardly mentions the role of the finished work of Jesus Christ in establishing a civil government based on biblical principles. He seems to assume that reconciliation among institutions and confessional communities in any society can be achieved through the mediating work of the state. This approach narrows the focus of Christ's work to redemption and the life of the church. In his essay, however, Spykman denounces limiting the gospel to only a few spheres of human existence.

The Christian America Alternative

As an alternative to the principled pluralist perspective on civil government, let us consider the Christian America approach.

By this term we do not mean that the republican form of government as embodied in the Constitution of the United States most closely ap-

---

7. Spykman et al., *Society, State, and Schools*, pp. 165-66.

proximates a biblical view of government. God is not bound by forms of government in accomplishing His will. Indeed, the Bible reveals that, at various times, God has served His people and blessed the nations through such varied political forms as autocracy, military dictatorship, confederation, monarchy, oligarchy, protectorate, and republican empire. In each case, the unique circumstances of a nation—the level of its spiritual experience, the security of its borders, the degree of its economic stability, the intensity of its national identity, and so forth—seem to have been the primary factors involved in determining which form of government God used.

Nor do we mean by "Christian America" a mythical golden age of Christian pervasiveness and prominence in America. Such an age has never been. Wheat and tares will continue to grow together until the harvest; yet the mere presence of the wheat makes concern for the well-being of the field a crucial matter.

Nevertheless, the United States Constitution clearly was drafted at a time in America's history when a largely Christian consensus still prevailed throughout the colonies. Even the "enlightened" efforts of such men as Thomas Jefferson could not overcome the informing and guiding presence of Christian concepts in society—concepts that served to stave off wave after wave of Enlightenment thinking and influenced the Framers' understanding of the nature of law, of man, and even of the structure of the national government.[8]

The Christian consensus in the last decades of the eighteenth century strongly influenced the political thinking of that time. Through the exertions of a renewed Christian consensus, our civil government can, in whatever form is required, realize the ideals of a biblical view of government.

But what are those ideals? The Bible indicates that God has determined the legitimate bounds of governmental functioning in society. These include the restraint of evil and, thus, the promotion of righteous-

---

8. On this a variety of sources can be cited. Among the primary sources, one might cite selections from "The Federalist Papers," e.g., nos. 2, 6, and 10, in Michael Kammen, ed., *The Origins of the American Constitution: A Documentary History* (New York: Penguin Books, 1986). Even aspects of the constitutional debates themselves reveal a conversational awareness and ready acceptance of biblical images and ideals. See, for example, the debates as recorded in Ralph Ketcham, ed., *The Anti-Federalist Papers and the Constitutional Convention Debates* (New York: Mentor Books, 1986). Secondary sources for this argument include Henry F. May, *The Enlightenment in America* (New York: Oxford University Press, 1976); James Turner, *Without God, Without Creed* (Baltimore: The Johns Hopkins University Press, 1985); Leonard W. Levy, *The Establishment Clause: Religion and the First Amendment* (New York: Macmillan, 1986); Forrest McDonald, *Novus Ordo Seclorum* (Lawrence: University Press of Kansas, 1985).

ness according to the standards of God's law (Rom. 13:1-4; 1 Pet. 2:13-14); the preservation of peace and the promotion of human dignity (1 Tim. 2:1-3); the execution of judgment and justice against unrighteousness (Deut. 17; Jer. 25:8-11); and the promotion of a social, cultural, and moral climate conducive to the furthering of God's kingdom (Isa. 44:28; 45:1-3). Yet such ideals cannot be achieved without the governing powers self-consciously recognizing the supremacy of God and of His Son, Jesus Christ (Ps. 2). Therefore, Christians have the unique challenge to convince our government to adopt a more biblical approach. Strengthening and enlarging Christian congregations is especially important to accomplishing this task.

Specifically, we challenge Christians to use an "inside-out" strategy to prod our civil government to adopt a biblical approach. We call believers to a deep conversion of their hearts; to a complete transformation of their minds; to a comprehensive reformation of their lives; to express their renewed perspectives and powers through a living example of godliness and divine love and an effective proclamation of the eternal truths of the gospel. We urge Christians to press ahead to penetrate, occupy, and take charge of every sphere of influence and every aspect of human life and interest, to refashion those spheres — including that of the civil government — according to the clear and explicit precepts and teachings of the Bible, by the power of the Holy Spirit, and at a level appropriate to each believer's experience in the world (cf. John 3:1-16; Rom. 12:1, 2; Eph. 4:20-24; Matt. 5:16; Acts 1:8; 2 Cor. 10:3-5; Eph. 5:15-17).

When renewal, growth, and blessed unity in Christ occur, the nations and their governments will marvel (Deut. 4:5-8). They will exhort one another to emulate the example of the people of God (Mic. 4:1-5) and, like old Nebuchadnezzar coming to his senses, will give glory to God for His wisdom, power, and grace (Dan. 4:36, 37). Then and only then will the ideal of a biblical role for the civil government begin to be realized.

8

The National Confessional
Response to Principled Pluralism

David M. Carson*

The original purpose of our consultation was to provide a forum for Reformed Christians who hold diverse views on civil government to dialogue informally and privately enough so that there could be interaction as well as confrontation, understanding as well as argument. Because so many people expressed interest in attending the consultation it became more public, and our original purpose has had to be modified. But it is in that original spirit that I have tried to think and write.

All of us, whatever our views, have to come to terms with confessional pluralism. We live in a state constitutionally committed to this position. Christians may sometimes feel constricted and discriminated against because of the faulty implementation of that pluralism, especially when it seems that secularism has achieved the status of an established religion. Nevertheless, the First Amendment forbids Congress to establish a religion and to interfere with the free exercise of religion, and thus, there is a constitutional basis for confessional pluralism.

Of course, we live in a society that is in fact pluralist, with many different "confessions" of belief and commitment. Not only do we have the three traditional faiths—Protestantism, Catholicism, Judaism, with their own internal divisions—but also an almost tropical growth of "cults" and, more significantly, an increasing belief that all traditional religions are irrelevant. Barring a dramatic intervention of God in His sovereignty, these trends will continue during our lifetime.

At this point, then, we are not free to choose among the options presented at this conference. Whatever our goals and hopes for the future, we cannot now simply elect to have a national confession, a Christian America, or a theonomic society.

*David M. Carson holds a B.A. from Yale University and a Ph.D. from the University of Pennsylvania. He is presently Professor of Political Science at Geneva College (PA).

Our nation's ideological (or religious) pluralism needs to be taken more seriously than many evangelicals appear to be taking it. It seems to me that many Christians consider the United States to be a "Christian" country. They assume that if the majority were not so silent, or if it were not for the conspiracy of a group of secular humanists, that if the true majority had its way, then public schools would again begin their days with Bible reading and Christian prayer and the strongly biblical content of the McGuffey Readers, widely used in the nineteenth century, would once more dominate our textbooks.

Some time ago I came across a typology that has influenced my own thinking greatly. It runs as follows:

> The United States could once have been called a Protestant country, in the sense that the majority of Americans were at least nominally Protestant. With the large migration from Ireland and southern Europe in the nineteenth century, our nation could be called Christian. After the flight of Jews from the Russian pogroms late in the nineteenth century it could be called religious. With the spread of Enlightenment ideas and the growing acceptance of secular humanism in the twentieth century, America can no longer be called even that.[1]

Any serious discussion of public policy has to start by taking that typology seriously. Any public policy that is democratic, or representative of our culture, will not be Christian—not only in such matters as school prayer, but in many other dimensions as well. We need to think through strategies that come to terms with that reality.

Given this context, what Gordon Spykman calls confessional pluralism is an attractive strategy for a variety of reasons. I appreciate the tone of pluralism. Os Guinness has made a convincing case for what he calls principled persuasion.[2] He argues that pluralism demands persuasion as opposed to scorn, arrogance, or the kind of confrontation that provides ammunition for secularists. There is a shrillness in many Christian utterances that seems to me to grow out of defensiveness rather than confidence in God—and that is usually counterproductive. We need reasoned speech backed by living out the views we profess. Guinness argues that the more serious problem for Christians at the moment is not the

---

1. I have not been able to find its source.
2. Os Guinness, "Reappraisal and Realignment," an address given at Geneva College, February 22, 1985.

attacks from the outside but the weakness of the inside, the "sapped vitality," "the anemia in Christian discipleship." Pluralism calls us to the persuasion of word and deed.[3]

Confessional pluralism also has its theological attractions. God Himself did not choose to coerce us into believing in Him or to accepting His salvation provided through Jesus Christ. Instead, He woos us, as Hosea vividly describes. He "speaks" to us through the prophets, but especially through the Logos, His Son. Is that a model for us? Surely Christians should surpass non-Christians in respecting the created freedom and dignity of human beings.

Finally, confessional pluralism is attractive for historical reasons. The results of the exercise of political power by Christians have often been frightening. The reign of "King Covenant" in seventeenth-century Scotland was unenviable. (Even a friendly historian comments, "Thus did the Covenanters take upon themselves the power which they had denied to the Crown." He says, "This was an age of extremes; however courageous and reasonable an objection, it was unfashionable, even dangerous, to go against the tide in that time of turmoil and intense patriotism, and temperate men suffered accordingly.")[4] The current South African regime, which oppresses a whole race of people in the name of the Scriptures, is also repulsive.

But pluralism seems to me to involve its own difficulties. Spykman presents structural pluralism as an alternative to both the individualism and the collectivism of the twentieth century. How much we need alternatives to both—and how much the gospel has to say on that issue! The concept of structural pluralism does not solve all problems, however. The relationship between sphere sovereignty and sphere universality is easier to state than to apply to specific situations. Nevertheless, I am grateful for Spykman's efforts to move these concepts beyond their Dutch origins in Abraham Kuyper and Herman Dooyeweerd in order to influence evangelical thought more broadly.

Part of the reason why principled pluralism seems a persuasive option is that it does not deal with the hard cases. This can be illustrated by discussing a central contradiction in Spykman's argument between the implications of structural pluralism and those of confessional pluralism. In describing structural pluralism he says (pp. 94-95):

---

3. Ibid.
4. J. D. Douglas, *Light in the North* (Grand Rapids: Eerdmans, 1964), pp. 30-31.

Such holy freedom impels Christians to reclaim every sphere of life for the King—home, school, state, university, labor, commerce, politics, science, art, journalism, and all the rest. No limitations may be placed on the sovereignty of God, the kingship of Christ, or the renewing power of the Holy Spirit. Supreme sovereignty is God's alone.

This description of the relation of the state to God and to Jesus Christ seems to support the national confession position. However, in explaining confessional pluralism, Spykman declares (p. 98):

It disavows special pleading for the privileged status of established groups and vested interests. The rights that it affirms for one group in society it also advocates for others.

How can one reclaim all of life for Christ and still recognize the rights of all faiths? Take, for example, the task of the state in its sphere, which is to provide public justice. *Justice*, as Spykman points out, is a very slippery word. It is always defined in terms of the religious presuppositions of those defining it. Can there then be a genuinely pluralist definition of justice? Can the state therefore be pluralist in reality? Or will it always define *justice* in terms of one specific world-and-life view, Christian or otherwise?

A second problem with pluralism as a goal for our society concerns the need for social cohesion. Sociologists widely agree that a common religion is necessary to hold a society together. When the religious base of a society is undermined, or its unifying vision is lost, the fragmentation of life and the polarization of society is likely to occur. Our society's confessional pluralism, however, prevents foundational biblical principles from being the basis for social cohesion. And, thus, the issues of public policy are becoming increasingly intractable.

The formal pluralist model originated and worked well in the Netherlands. But the Netherlands is a special case. The country is geographically small. It has a long and dramatic national history of struggle against the Spanish and against the sea; this has produced a strong sense of nationalism, which, in turn, provides the cohesion within which pluralism can exist.

Can a pluralist model handle the wide differences in a heterogeneous society like our own? In our society the answer to this problem of competing religious differences has been to create a "civil religion"—neither Protestant nor Catholic nor Jewish (as Will Herberg points out)—with its own symbols, holy days, saints, holy places, rituals, and theology.[5] This civil religion is a significant rival to faith in Jesus Christ. Daniel Poling, a noted Protestant minister and former editor of the *Christian Herald*, wrote: "I formed a habit that I have never broken. I began saying in the morning two words, 'I believe.' Those two words *with nothing added* . . . give me a running start for my day."[6] Richard DeVos, a well-known Christian layman and founder of Amway, produced a film distributed by Gospel Films, which he entitled *Believe*. It urged on its viewers six objects of belief with no apparent priority: ourselves, our families, our country, God, the free enterprise system, and our fellow man. The American Tract Society distributed a tract urging us to see in the red stripes of our flag a symbol of the blood of Jesus Christ. Many sociologists would argue that such a civil religion is inevitable in an otherwise religiously pluralist society in order to maintain social cohesion, to keep the society from flying apart.[7] Does accepting pluralist society as the model, therefore, require us to support a civil religion that is in some degree idolatrous?

The third and most serious problem with pluralism is that it is not biblical. Although pluralism is a very attractive option, the Scriptures do not teach that it is the proper goal for society. The Bible instructs nations to confess our Lord Jesus to be what in fact He is: King of kings and Lord of lords.

Christ's lordship is especially taught in the Psalms. The Psalter contains two sorts of references to God as ruler of the nations. One is the frequent reference to God's special relationship as the ruler of His covenant people, Israel. It is inappropriate to apply those references to civil government, our own included. America is not the new Israel. Carefully excluding those, however, there are still many clear references to God as the God of *all* nations. Let me quote Spykman again, with reference to Psalm 2 (p. 87):

> Psalm 2 reinforces God's demand that earthly rulers obey Him. It sternly warns rulers not to rebel against their divine anointing. For such rebellion is tantamount to rejecting the Anointed One, the coming Messiah.

5. Will Herberg, *Protestant, Catholic, Jew*, rev. ed. (Garden City, N.Y.: Anchor Books, 1960), chap. 5.
6. Quoted in Herberg, p. 89, from an article by Poling in *Parade*, September 19, 1954. Herberg adds the emphasis.
7. E.g., Robin M. Williams, Jr., *American Society: A Sociological Interpretation* (New York: Knopf, 1951), p. 312, quoted in Herberg, p. 74.

Spykman is right. I would not say it differently. (Pss. 7; 9; 10; 22; 24; 33; 46; 47; 66; 67; 68; 76; 82; 83; 86; 96; 98; 99; 117; and 148 also emphasize this point.)

Many years ago I heard Nicholas Wolterstorff deliver a paper on the christological view of the state, which built upon his extensive study of the phrase "principalities and powers" in the New Testament.[8] In one sense, I have never recovered from hearing that paper. The state is one of the principalities and powers created by Christ (Col. 1:16). It fell in the Fall of man and, therefore, tries to separate us from the love of God. It is redeemed by the death of Christ on the cross (Col. 2), and eventually it will be totally reconciled or destroyed (1 Cor. 15).

> The day of total reconciliation has not yet arrived . . . the mopping-up operation and the skirmishes go on, though the battle has been essentially won. In Christ [and here Wolterstorff quotes from Karl Barth] the angelic powers are called to order and, so far as they need it, are restored to their original order.[9]

Urging states to recognize the reality of their submission to Christ would seem to be part of our task in the present age.

To what then are we called?

First, to understand the nature of the pluralist society in which we live.

Second, to principled persuasion. We need to know what we believe as Christians, and we need to learn how to participate with civility in public discussion in order to persuade others.

Third, to persuade Americans to submit to the sovereignty of Jesus Christ over our nation and to the kingdom of God as righteousness, peace, and joy in the Holy Spirit.

Why do we stand when we sing the "Hallelujah Chorus"? Because, according to the legend, King George II stood when he, the most powerful sovereign in Europe, heard the words,

> For the Lord God Omnipotent reigneth,
> King of kings and Lord of lords.

---

8. "Contemporary Christian Views of the State: Some Major Issues," *Christian Scholars' Review* (1974): 311-32.

9. Ibid., p. 330. His quotation of Karl Barth is from *Church and State* (London: SCM, 1939), pp. 28-29.

Part Three
Christian America

As compared to theonomy, principled pluralism, and national confessionalism, the Christian America position is more difficult to define and enjoys less agreement among its proponents. In broadest outline, this view asserts that the United States has a substantial Christian heritage, which we should seek to revitalize. Christian principles and values were present in many colonial charters, the Declaration of Independence, state constitutions, actions of the national government (employing chaplains, opening legislative sessions with prayer, and calling national days of prayer and thanksgiving), and even in the federal Constitution. Most of the Founding Fathers were church members who diligently studied the Scriptures and affirmed most major Christian tenets. Christianity was granted special status in American law. An underlying Christian consensus helped to shape the structure of the new nation's government and to insure the freedom its citizens enjoyed. Biblical principles especially influenced America's decision to limit, separate, and balance the powers of government. In the twentieth century secularization and relativistic humanism have combined to erode America's Christian commitment and to remove biblical values from most areas of our public life. Vigorous efforts should be made to restore explicitly Christian convictions in our government and to devise laws that reflect specific biblical norms.

That America has a strongly Christian base has been enthusiastically and widely asserted by many evangelical Christians. The late Francis Schaeffer defended this position, especially in his *A Christian Manifesto* (1981). Its leading advocates today are John A. Whitehead and Harold O. J. Brown. Whitehead, a practicing attorney, has written many articles and books, most significantly, *The Second American Revolution* (1982). He also founded The Rutherford Institute, a nonprofit organization located in Manassas, Virginia, that seeks to help Americans understand how our legal and political systems are built upon the Judeo-Christian heritage. Brown has recently returned from pastoring a Reformed church in Switzerland to resume his teaching duties in theology and ethics at Trinity Evangelical Divinity School. His book *The Reconstruction of the Republic* (1987) advances a longer argument than space permits in this volume as to why America must be rebuilt upon Christian foundations. Peter Marshall, Jr.'s *The Light and the Glory* (1977), Greg Singer's *A Theological Interpretation of American History* (1981), and John Eidsmoe's *Christianity and the Constitution* (1987) also present the case for a Christian America.

In the chapter that follows, Brown contends that the United States can survive only by reestablishing a fundamentally Christian approach and system of values. Such a goal is appropriate, he argues, because the Bible commands Christians to create a society where biblical norms are enforced by law. A Christian America would have laws based upon the Ten Commandments, church-state collaboration to promote justice and righteousness, a public school system with "Christian coloration," and a voucher system to support private education.

Brown maintains that the United States should end its long-standing complete separation of church and state and direct these two institutions to work together to promote the temporal welfare of all citizens. He points to Switzerland as an example of a democratic nation where church-state collaboration has produced a prosperous and just society. The Holy Roman Empire offers an even better model than Switzerland does for a Christian America. Roman rulers tried to refashion society in harmony with Christian teaching and, thereby, bequeathed to Europe "a rich heritage of Christian law." To survive, America should officially and enthusiastically adopt Christianity as its spiritual center and moral foundation.

While Christian Rome had its faults, it demonstrated the great good that results when Christian values inform a nation's political life. America's "wall of separation" between church and state, however, makes it almost impossible for Christian politicians to base our nation's laws upon God's norms and prevents biblical teachings from guiding our moral reasoning. Christian politicians should be allowed, encouraged, and expected to act upon biblical principles. It is possible to make America Christian because Christianity is still "deeply rooted in the heart and experience" of many Americans, and the nation's "strongest and most persistent ethical impulses remain Christian" (p. 136). Only the gospel can provide a unifying vision and commitment powerful enough to hold the American people together.

Brown insists that the fundamental principles of both tables of the Ten Commandments can and should be "incorporated into public law even in a religiously mixed society" (p. 140). His Christian America approach differs most sharply with theonomy in its argument that public law, instead of conforming to biblical teaching in all its details, should be informed or directed by the Scriptures. The Bible does not provide all the specific laws needed by a complex, technological society, but its general principles should serve as the basis for all of America's laws.

9

The Christian America Position
Harold O. J. Brown *

W̄e are now entering the last eighth of our twentieth century, a century that may properly be called the most bloodstained since the world began. As we look to the dawn of the twenty-first century, even those of us who consider ourselves bound to heed the words of Jesus find it hard not to be anxious and troubled (see Matt. 6:34). Indeed, the more we know and understand about the world today, the harder it is to be anything other than pessimistic. The Austrian systems analyst Hans Millendorfer has observed,

> Whoever follows the discussion about the future, as it is carried on above all by agnostics and atheists, is shaken at the hopelessness expressed, and at the deep longing for hope, which is seen as possible only if there is a transformation of values.[1]

Millendorfer implies that hope *is* possible—but only if a certain condition is fulfilled: "The future will be Christian, or it will not take place."[2] Similarly, I believe that the future of the United States as a society will be Christian, or it will not take place—and if in some sense it *does* take place, that future will not be ours.

*Harold O. J. Brown is Professor of Biblical and Systematic Theology at Trinity Evangelical Divinity School near Chicago. He received a B.A. from Harvard, a B.D. and Th.M. from Harvard Divinity School, and a Ph.D. in History from Harvard. Between teaching stints at Trinity he pastored the Evangelical Reformed Church of Klosters, Switzerland, for four years. Among his many published works are *Christianity and the Class Struggle* (1970), *Evangelium und Gewalt* (1971), *Death Before Birth* (1977), *Heresies: the Image of Christ in the Mirror of Heresy and Orthodoxy* (1984), and *The Reconstruction of the Republic* (revised 1987).
    1. Millendorfer-Gaspari, *Konturen einer Wende*, p. 342.
    2. Expressed in an oral presentation: "Die Zukunft wird Christlich sein, oder sie findet nicht statt."

Introductory Remarks: Lessons From History

This chapter will first examine the fundamental nature of the United States today. America is neither a nation nor an empire, as I shall define the terms. It can instead become a Christian commonwealth: a society structured to provide for the general welfare (common weal), taking Christian principles as its standard for what constitutes welfare and as its guide for attaining such welfare.

Second, I wish to show that it is in accordance with Scripture and, therefore, natural for Christians to try to establish central biblical, Christian values *by law* in our one large corner of this fallen world. The current American doctrine that our society must be pluralistic in the sense that all values and value judgments are equally acceptable, is self-contradictory and destructive.

Third, I will examine a few practical implications of this approach as it affects specific laws, the relationship between denominations and the state, the legitimacy and scope of civil government, and public and private education.

America Today: An Appreciation

The United States of America recently celebrated two bicentennials: one of the Declaration of Independence and the other of its national Constitution. Will there be any such tricentennials? Despite its inauspicious beginning the United States of America enjoyed a rapid rise to power and wealth. Our country emerged from the greatest conflict the world has yet seen — World War II — as the most powerful state on earth — militarily, scientifically, industrially, and financially. Forty-odd years later, we have not entirely lost those advantages; but, frankly speaking, we find ourselves in some danger of being compared to the Ottoman Empire at the close of the nineteenth century: the power that had caused the nations of Europe to tremble with fear was ridiculed as the "sick man of Europe."

America's situation in the opening years of the third century of our independent existence is uncertain. We can look back on a meteoric rise, but we find ourselves in a troubled present and look forward to an uncertain future. The frantic anxieties of those who opposed Robert Bork's confirmation as an associate justice of the United States Supreme Court, if sincere, reveal an awareness that the future of the United States indeed hangs by a thread. It hangs thus not only, but not least, because as a people and a society we do not recognize, and certainly do not understand, some of the most important things that have made us great.

A Lesson From History: The Democratic Parallel
   The United States of America ought to break with the long disputed, but increasingly dominant, tradition of total "separation of church and state." This doctrine, historically speaking, is neither constitutional nor a necessary implication of the nonestablishment clause of the First Amendment. Moreover, whereas in earlier decades it was merely not beneficial, as presently understood, this separation has become an increasingly important factor contributing to social disintegration. The United States should now consciously adopt a view of society in which church and state collaborate — work together — for the temporal welfare of the public: Christian, non-Christian, and even anti-Christian. The non- and anti-Christian public, and even a part of the Christian public, will oppose such a contention. The experience of a small but sturdy democratic society, Switzerland, indicates however that the collaboration of church and state can produce a prosperous and just society for Christians and non-Christians alike.
   It may seem somewhat paradoxical for an American residing overseas to argue *in absentia* that America needs to return to its spiritual roots. An explanation may be in order. My country of residence, Switzerland, is the oldest and to many the most successful democracy in the world. It does not practice the separation of church and state. Officially, Switzerland is much more Christian than the United States. Despite many outward signs of church-state collaboration, the practical reality, I have to acknowledge, looks different. In most cantons, either the Roman Catholic or the Reformed church is state-supported; sometimes both are. Religious instruction is a regular part of the curriculum in public schools.[3] The forms are there; unfortunately the daily life of the Swiss people reveals that the faith is not there. Some will argue that government support for the forms has eroded the people's support for the faith, and indeed this is an argument which contenders for a Christian America must face. To establish Christian forms while losing Christian faith is not something that any Christian can support.

   3. In my town of Klosters the Protestant children march out of school en masse every other week to attend a children's service in the town's Protestant church. The *Bsatzig*, a biennial event at which *Kreis* (county) officials are elected and sworn in, involves an open-air service at which the (nonreligious) men's chorus sings, the three local marching bands (also nonreligious) play, and I, as the town's Protestant minister (religious), preach. Thus, in Switzerland, church and state cooperate. Even our church edifice is a joint project of church and state. The body of the chuch belongs to the congregation. The tower with the clock and the bells, however, belongs to the town; the time is of interest to everyone, and the bells are used to call people in from the fields and warn of fires, floods, and military mobilization, as well as to call people to worship.

The Swiss federal constitution was written with a definite Christian orientation; two major confessions and the local congregation play an active if controversial role in political debate. Sunday closing remains the general rule, and the major national holidays are all church holidays: Christmas, Good Friday, Easter, Ascension, Pentecost, and the national Day of Prayer.

Beneath this veneer of Christian tradition, the substance of daily living is far more secularized than in the United States. Due to the political structure, officials who may or may not be — and generally are not — active Christians make many important church decisions. Sunday is a holiday, but at best 8 percent of the people use their holiday freedom to attend church. Infant baptism is the all but universal rule, and almost all schoolchildren are confirmed at the age of fifteen or sixteen. For many of those involved, however, these formal services represent the only times they darken a church's doorstep before the virtually obligatory church wedding; we might say, an average attendance of once in eight years.

In short, in Switzerland, as in other European countries with state-related churches (England, Scotland, West Germany, Scandinavia), the church is endorsed by the government and largely ignored by the people. In modern Europe officially supported Christianity, both Catholic and Protestant, seems rather like the official cult of emperor worship in ancient Rome: everyone is obliged to give lip service, but hardly anyone takes it seriously.

If this were what a "Christian America" would mean for America's people, it would be better to let the proposal die. Unless it is possible to have a Christian society that is more deeply Christian in practice than formally (or formerly!) Christian Switzerland, it is vain to pursue this argument. It is possible, however, to profit from certain Swiss examples and avoid other Swiss mistakes.

Comparing Switzerland with the United States seems justified because Switzerland, although small, is a successful democracy. It has effectively blended several ethnic groups who speak a total of four languages and a variety of dialects, thus reflecting some of America's fundamental challenges in miniature. It has created an island of unmatched security and prosperity; Switzerland's per capita gross national product is currently the highest in the world. Can we learn anything from Switzerland without repeating its mistakes?

Another Lesson From History: The Imperial Parallel

Major differences do exist, of course, between Switzerland and America. Switzerland is a small society and the United States an immense one. Switzerland has four different languages, but all of its people are from similar western European stock. (The United States has only one national language, but scores of ethnic groups are present in America.) The best parallel to America, where diverse peoples and languages mingle across thousands of miles, is the greatest civic enterprise the world has ever known — the Roman Empire.

Irate preachers and other moralists often warn that late twentieth-century America is becoming another pagan Rome. What many people fail to realize is that many of our Founding Fathers intentionally sought to make the United States resemble certain aspects of pagan Rome. In emulating features of ancient Roman life that seemed praiseworthy, however, the Founding Fathers overlooked the fact that pagan Rome's early republican virtues offered no protection against civil war, corruption, the rise of the Caesars, and the decadence for which ancient Rome is now known.

Our Founding Fathers took much that was Roman — and pagan — as their pattern for the American republic. Their mistake was not in looking to Rome — from which we can indeed learn much — but in ignoring the lessons the empire itself learned in its transition from paganism to Christianity. Centered on Rome in Italy, the empire lasted in the West for almost seven hundred years — over three times as long as the history of the United States to date. In the fourth century this empire became Christian. Though Italian Rome fell in A.D. 410, the empire in its Christian phase did not die. Christianized and transplanted to Constantinople, it endured for an entire millennium (until 1453).

There was a time when the United States was a naively Christian nation. The vast majority of our people were northern European Protestant Christians. Our governmental institutions were religiously neutral — not hostile, as they have subsequently become. Even as substantial non-Protestant groups entered the country, the United States remained "a Protestant nation" in sentiment for decades. Except for the distinctly religious foundation of New England, America's Christians never consciously tried to "make America Christian," nor were they really aware that its Christian values were being rejected and replaced. Now, as we discover that this is so, serious Christians do not think of re-Christianizing America, because we, too, have come to consider ourselves a minority.

At the time of the conversion of Constantine the Great, Roman emperor from 306 to 339, Christians made up no more than 10 percent of the population of the Roman Empire. The conversion of Constantine inaugurated Christian Europe. The civilization that subsequently developed is in disrepute now, for a variety of reasons. In my opinion, however, it compares favorably with pre-Christian paganism — and with post-Christian degeneracy.

American secular tradition sneers at Constantine, because he began the process of creating a Christian state. The American evangelical tradition disdains him, because he established *Catholicism* as the empire's official faith (a Catholicism not yet Roman, of course). In the United States, our dominant religious heritage is Protestant independency: Reformed, Baptist, Methodist, fundamentalist, and even Unitarian, all of which are suspicious of "state churches." This has produced general disrespect for the achievements of Constantine and his successors. Americans speak with relief rather than with regret of being post-Constantinian[4] and sometimes even of being post-Christian. Although Americans in large numbers are indeed Christian, America is still pre-Christian — and it is time for a change. It is important for Americans to consider Constantine's Christian empire seriously, because as Cicero's pagan republic fails this Christian model could work in the United States.

Several aspects of this Christian empire are noteworthy. It covered a large territory and embraced diverse races, languages, and cultures. It was militarily successful for centuries, but it was not a militarized society. It was not based on race, but on an ecumenical idea. As its rulers took Christianity seriously, they tried to remake society in harmony with Christian teaching. There was no Roman Civil Liberties Union to hamper them. Christian emperors such as Theodosius I, Justinian I, and Leo III quite naturally worked to bring Roman law into conformity with the biblically revealed law of God. The Christian empire thus bequeathed to Europe a rich heritage of Christian law.

Many modern Christians, including Reformed thinkers such as the late Francis Schaeffer, want to renew American society on the basis of the Bible or of biblical law alone. They tend to ignore the Roman and medieval past except to point to it as a bad example. Those who oppose the idea of a Christian America warn of the dangers of following the Constantinian precedent. A contemporary Christian republic would not, however, be the same as the Roman empire, although it would not be totally different, either. Christians living during the last fifteen centuries were never once able to come close to creating a Christian society,

---

4. By "post-Constantinian" we mean an era in which the state no longer establishes an official church. Post-Constantinian society will be worse than pre-Constantinian society, however, because during the Middle Ages the Catholic Church served as the custodian of much that was valuable in pagan Roman governmental tradition.

opponents continue, but only made matters worse than they were under paganism or Islam; how then, can Christians today do any better? Constantine, Justinian, and even Charlemagne, however, produced societies built largely on Christian principles. The monarch, at least formally, was subject to God and sometimes to the church. God was honored, at least outwardly, and His commandments were enacted into public laws. Large vestiges of this heritage remain throughout Europe today. Sunday closing is the rule even in Communist Eastern Europe.

A major reason that Christianity supplanted paganism in Rome was that society knew it needed a spiritual center. Our society, like third-century Rome, cannot long survive without a spiritual center. We now face a worldwide movement that has a center—Marxism; Charles deGaulle called it "the most odious of all the tyrannies known to man." Meanwhile, Islam again threatens the existence of a jaded, post-Christian West, as it did in the seventh and seventeenth centuries. Christian Rome, though hardly perfect, was far better than pagan Rome. This fact ought to inspire American Christians to dare to inject more Christianity into our own "repaganized" society.

America's Revolutionary Dream: The New Order of the Ages

America made a mistake in the year 1787. Officially, government (the federal government first, later all the states) broke with Christianity. Initially, this development had little influence on the life of the people, largely Protestant Christians, simply because the government was so limited in scope and so much of life was guided by traditional associations in family and church. The most innovative feature of the new American federation was not its independence from Britain, its republican government, its preindustrial capitalism, or its more egalitarian social order. Rather, it was the conviction that the United States was making a new departure in human history, expressed by the motto on its Great Seal: *Novus Ordo Seclorum* (The New Order of the Ages). Where other societies—for example, Hapsburgian Austria—stressed continuity, the United States claimed to be a new order. America really does not represent a new order in the sense of supporting revolutionary change, and, even if it did, such change would not work. We ought therefore once again to try the "old order" that served us so well—the law of God and the gospel of Christ.

In the past, the majority of America's population was composed of Christians, largely Calvinistic Protestants. Christianity inspired personal and family morality, but it did not give America its national symbols. It was the symbolism of Rome—not of Vatican Rome with its papacy, but pagan Rome—that gave us the Capitol, the Senate, and even, although uncrowned, our own American Caesars, democratic leaders to whom we ascribed semidivine honors.

Our federal symbols reveal this clearly. Our flag is an arrangement of stars and stripes, symbolizing nothing more spiritual than the number of states in 1776 and today. Examples can be multiplied. The Roman fasces (the bundle of rods enclosing a headsman's axe) flank the speaker's rostrum in the House of Representatives; the cross has never been an American symbol. The Capitol dome illustrates the imagined apotheosis (deification) of our first "Caesar," George Washington (the structure was commissioned after his death). The only government-built "temples" in Washington are dedicated to human beings ("divine Caesars")—Thomas Jefferson and Abraham Lincoln. Those shrines certainly are the scene of a kind of quasi-religious adoration of our great presidents, like that of the Roman emperors. It is possible to exaggerate the significance of all this. Nevertheless, these features symbolically express the essentially humanistic spirit of American government, which runs counter to the generally Christian sentiments of the majority of America's people. As the government assumes a greater and greater role in regulating values, this man-centered bent, which once was insignificant, becomes more and more influential.[5] Although the American people are largely Christian in their orientation, America's real federal religion is a kind of unconsciously humanistic Caesar-worship.

Our American dogma of the "wall of separation" between church and state virtually requires schizophrenia of Christian politicians and cuts the body politic off from the only realistic source of moral reasoning for a people still predominantly Christian. In contrast, by working to bring the structure of Roman law into conformity with the biblically revealed law of God, many Christian emperors bequeathed to Europe a legacy of Christian law.

In America, it was not the rulers, but the people, who gave society its Christian character. We neither need nor want an American Constantine, but we do need to accept the principle that Christian political leaders, in a democracy as well as in an empire, can properly be expected to act on Christian principles. Such action is not a fault; failure to act on Christian precepts is the fault.

5. Of course, no one worships Washington, Jefferson, or Lincoln—but then probably almost no Romans really believed the emperor to be divine. In the Soviet Union, which is officially atheistic, Lenin's Tomb is a quasi-religious place of pilgrimage.

There are two reasons for suggesting that America follow the imperial precedent. First, the United States, as it now exists, is closer to the imperial model than to the national: a multitude of diverse races, cultures, and languages with no ethnic unity, but with the possibility of a common ideal. Second, simply because neither Constantine nor his successors achieved a Christian empire, it does not follow that no one else should try. What they did achieve was better than what had preceded them, and better than a good deal of what has succeeded them.

The Revolution That Was Not One

Many historians and sociologists contend that the American Revolution of 1776 was no revolution at all, since it left virtually all of the social, economic, and even religious structures of colonial America intact. What was revolutionary was not what the Founding Fathers did, but what they thought that they were doing: establishing the New Order of the Ages. We stand in the rubble of this *novus ordo* and can see the impending bankruptcy of secular utopianism.

Because Constantine's empire was far from perfect, voices inside and outside of Christianity warn, "Don't try it again!" Perhaps we can learn from Constantine, as from the Swiss, and avoid some of his mistakes.

The most revolutionary aspect of the founding of the United States was neither independence nor democracy, but the new government's official neutrality on religion, which has gradually turned into a mild to severe antagonism toward religion. Lamentably, this antagonism is now helping to undermine all the foundations of a humane America.

Naively or deliberately, America's Founders may have endorsed a neo-classical, non-Christian symbolism: the eagle, the obelisk, the pyramid on the Great Seal, and the Roman fasces in the House of Representatives. Nevertheless, the people as a whole remained Christian in a cultural, if not a committed religious, sense. Public prayers were offered to the God of Abraham, Isaac, and Jacob in the name of Jesus, festivals were Christian, and chaplains were provided for those in crisis situations in the armed forces, hospitals, and prisons. Furthermore, pre- and post-independence awakenings, revivals, and renewals gave a sense of vitality to American religion.

Waves of nineteenth- and twentieth-century immigrants brought religious diversity, but also fresh intensity. For a while each of the major religious traditions of Europe, including Judaism, became stronger and more vital in America than in the old country—and most still are. So many of America's people are rooted in Christianity, at least sentimentally, that the eradication of Christianity from public life creates widespread rootlessness and disorientation. My argument here for restoring and extending America's Christian foundations is not primarily theological but practical. A Christian America in which most people are sentimentally Christian will be far less dangerous to all religious minorities than an America in which religious inhibitions have been banished.

There can be no doubt that American Christianity is still vital despite its somewhat bewildering and eccentric character. There can be no doubt that revival and renewal are underway in the United States, despite the moral failings of, and battles among, some of the celebrities of the electronic church. Consequently, Christianity in America has the potential to affect society — for better or for worse.

The minimal amount of religious culture that we still have is a last bulwark against modern barbarism. One of the unmistakable signs of trouble is the increasing hostility of our governmental bureaucracy and much of the communications media to the vestiges of Christian culture in America. At the same time, the evangelical revival and the charismatic renewal movement have inspired countless numbers of American Christians to labor to reverse secularizing trends and to repossess the society of which they constitute the strongest and most stable component.

Which trend will win out?

Restoration or Temporary Reaction?

Will our efforts to "restore" a Christian America produce something enduring, or will they be only a temporary swing of the pendulum away from secular humanism? The answer depends on the Christians in America. The question really has two parts: (1) Is it possible to make America Christian? (2) If it is possible, will it be bearable for the large numbers of Americans who are not Christian or only nominally so? The Christian America answer is based on what some theologians call *triumphalism* — a belief that the church must triumph visibly. We can create a society that is fundamentally Christian, yet it would promote the welfare of both the distinctively non-Christian minorities and the many nominal Christians who live in it.

Restoration is possible. Historical trends can be reversed, as several examples show. The monarchy was restored in England following Oliver Cromwell (in the seventeenth century), and it has been secure ever since. Christianity in the United States, like the monarchy in England, is deeply rooted in the hearts and experience of the people.

As I have argued elsewhere,[6] if Americans are to have a fundamental, widely shared world-and-life view, it has to be Christian; nothing else commands the loyalty of more than a small minority of Americans. In late twentieth-century America, the strongest and most persistent ethical impulses remain Christian—not necessarily clearly, articulately, or wisely Christian, but Christian nonetheless. In other words, if a Christian America could be restored, it would have a chance, like the restored British monarchy, of surviving. Nothing else will permit America to survive with a vital purpose and a set of shared values—and without these the survival of America is not worthwhile.

America: The Generic State

When discussing a Christian America we must consider precisely, what is America? Is it a nation? A republic? An empire? A commercial venture?

The United States of America is a generic name and strangely non-revealing. America basically does not know what it is. The United States is not a nation in the traditional sense, because it lacks a common ethnic heritage and spiritual tradition. A viable alternative to nationhood is an empire, but to constitute an empire a society must have a sense of mission that transcends differences of race, language, and culture. The United States currently seems to be a kind of political "limited liability holding company," and that is not enough to sustain its existence.

A nation (from Latin *natus*: born) is a people with common roots, ethnic and spiritual. A state structure can exist without a nation, but a nation can hardly exist without a state. A nation needs a state structure to survive. The alternative to the nation is the empire, which can embrace a multitude of ethnic groups united by a shared vision and by their desire to share that vision with the whole world. They have since lost their empires and have never really found themselves again as nations.

Rome, our second history lesson, was never a nation. It passed from being a city-state to an empire without ever becoming a nation. It was immensely successful as a *res publica* (the public interest), an empire that diverse nations, races, and cultures could recognize and with which they could identify without considering themselves forced to submit to a foreign nation. Rome believed that it had a mission to its world.

America—the United States—is clearly not a nation now, and it is hardly likely ever to become one. Our present ethnic mix is multina-

---

6. *The Reconstruction of the Republic* (Milford, Mich: Mott Media, 1981).

tional, and our immigration patterns seem to guarantee that the United States will never again have ethnic homogeneity (as we did before 1850). We therefore need the spiritual unity that Christianity could give us. Otherwise we remain nothing but a generic state, like the mule "without pride of ancestry or hope of progeny."

Various critics have argued that America is in fact already an empire. It has to be an empire, that is, a many-faceted society held together by a common vision; the only other viable alternative would be some kind of police state. My contention is that the common vision for America ought to be the Christian one. From a pragmatic perspective, no other vision will work given the people that we are; from a principled perspective, the Christian nation is based on truth and will secure more justice in this fallen world than any other.

Biblical Principles

America's future will be Christian or it will not take place. Using two historical parallels—democratic Switzerland and imperial Rome—the preceding section has tried to show that societies with a fundamentally Christian orientation can do very well in this fallen world, particularly in comparison with the other possible alternatives. I hope that it is possible to convince non-Christians in America, not only that a Christian society is preferable to the dialectical materialism and dictatorial tyranny of the communists, but also that it is preferable to what America's pluralistic society is becoming. Nevertheless, I speak chiefly to Christians and, so, shall try to deal with two questions. (1) Is there solid biblical justification for seeking to establish Christian principles in a mixed society that is not a theocratic unity as ancient Israel supposedly was? (2) Do we have the right to seek to "impose" our principles on others who do not share them?

The Justness of Justice

Biblical ethics are a form of metaphysical moralism or divine command ethics.[7] It is important to recognize, however, that biblical ethics

7. This system insists that moral principles are given to us from an "Archimedean point" outside the temporal universe, in other words, by divine revelation. God's commands tell us what is good and what is evil. Biblical ethics differ significantly from four alternatives:
   1. Ethical relativism teaches that no action is right or wrong in itself, but only better or worse than the alternatives.
   2. Utilitarianism declares that the right action is that which brings the greatest utility, defined as the greatest good for the greatest number.
   3. Hedonism maintains that the basis for making moral choices is in attaining pleasure and avoiding pain.
   4. Deontological ethics argue that the basic question to ask when making moral choices is whether one could wish all people at all times to act on the same principle. This is called universifiability.

are not simply a series of arbitrary commands. They come from the Author of the universe and of life, who has made us in His image. For this reason, biblical commands, although they often frustrate us in our designs and desires, nevertheless generally strike us as right (see Rom. 8:22; 2:15). Human beings do know, not with total accuracy and reliability, but in a general way what is right in God's sight and, therefore, right in an absolute sense. This does not prevent them from performing evil deeds or from taking pleasure in them (see Rom. 1:31). Because man is made in the image of God and has the law written in his heart, he is able to understand the justness of God's justice, even though he is fallen and his will is in conflict with that justice.

If non-Christian, unregenerate men and women can intuitively sense the rightness of God's justice, the Christian with the light of Scripture should readily understand that God's Word is our adequate and reliable teacher about justice. Inasmuch as it is the purpose of civil government to establish and promote justice in society, Christians have no real alternative other than to try to promote biblical standards and principles in legislation and law enforcement.

Refusal to try to establish biblical standards in the laws of society may have one of two causes. (1) Some Christians may not be convinced that God's laws are just. (2) Other Christians may doubt that they can ever convince non-Christians to legislate in harmony with biblical law.

Two biblical principles contained in 1 Corinthians 5:11, however, seem to me to authorize every Christian to make the effort. "Knowing therefore the terror of the Lord," Paul continues, "we persuade men." There should be no doubt in the mind of any Christian that God will ultimately and harshly judge injustice. We do not have the power in the United States to impose principles, biblical or otherwise, on an unwilling majority. But we do have the right, and the ability, to seek to persuade our fellow citizens to implement God's justice in our society. And if our interpretation of Romans 1 and 2 is correct, we have a head start in our task, because the law of God is written in people's hearts, and to some extent their minds are aware of what it requires.

Imposing Morality

The argument that "we must not seek to impose morality" is essentially false for two reasons. (1) All legislation imposes morality. Social security and medicare, for example, impose certain social values and compel us to pay for them. (2) We are not seeking to *impose* morality. We seek to *persuade* the majority of our people that certain standards are moral and just. If persuaded, the people will impose this morality on themselves, just as they do in other cases.

If we do recognize that God's justice is just, should we not apply it in every situation in which we are involved? It should be entirely natural for Christians in a democratic society to seek to bring the laws of their society into harmony with God's law — and we need make no apology to others for our effort.

The Legitimacy of Government

In Romans 13, Paul states that the powers that be, the government authorities, are ordained of God. Although God warns the people of Israel to expect government (that is, the king) to abuse its power (1 Sam. 8:10-18), He does declare that civil government is legitimate. Its power is legitimate but limited; whenever the laws of God conflict with those of human government, we must obey God and not men (Acts 4:19; 5:29). Romans 13:4 (a New Testament verse that authorizes capital punishment) states that government, as God's servant, brings judgment upon evil. Paul presumes that government will seek to reward the good and to punish the evil.

In the contrary case, where government punishes the good and rewards the evil, it cannot be considered God's servant and so, may be opposed or even deposed by Christians. If civil government is legitimate when and only when it seeks to promote justice, then those who know what true justice is, namely, Christians who know the standards of God's Word, should seek to persuade their rulers to follow those standards. In the case of a republic such as the United States, this means promoting biblical values through the democratic process.

Implications

Specific Laws of the Old Testament

The statement "Biblical precepts should shape civil laws" confronts us with two kinds of problems. The first is a problem of principle: Is it valid? The second is a problem of application: Can we do it? For detailed guidance we must turn, not to the New Testament, which emphasizes faith and love rather than conduct, but to the Old Testament, which has a much fuller and more detailed set of laws, extending even to case law. The bulk of Old Testament legislation is intended to enable the people of God to live holy lives dedicated to Him.

The Goal: Formation of a Holy People. The goal of Old Testament law was to train the people of Israel in justice and purity to make them a "holy people" (Exod. 19:6; Deut. 7:6). The heart of Old Testament law though, known as the Ten Commandments, is universally applicable, embodying general principles of justice to all mankind. The Ten Commandments are not in themselves detailed enough to produce a distinctively holy people; the ceremonial and dietary laws are suited to accomplish that. The ceremonial and dietary laws, therefore, are not intended to secure public justice and so should *not* be seen as applicable to all people generally.

Which regulations are necessary to secure public justice for all, and which relate only to God's people, to Christian believers (in New Testament terms)? These questions must be examined.[8]

A Further Goal: Public Justice. The four commandments of the first table forbid worship of other gods, worship of images, and profanation of God's name and require sabbath-keeping. The commandments of the second table require respect for parents and forbid murder, adultery, stealing, false witness, and coveting. Until recently, the second table was considered more or less normative for secular law in Europe and America (although it is admittedly difficult to regulate the sin of covetousness by civil law). Because the Ten Commandments, especially the second table, are reflected in a general way in the public laws of almost every nation, they cannot, taken alone, shape a holy people. This means, then, that the fundamental principles of Old Testament law in the Decalogue can be applied to all human beings, regardless of whether they want to belong to the people of God (see 1 Tim. 1:9). The restoration of the Ten Commandments to a place of honor in our society could have great symbolic significance; public posting of these commandments in courtrooms, schools, and other public buildings would proclaim God's standards to be the foundation of public justice.

The fundamental principles of the Decalogue, both tables, can and ought to be incorporated into public law even in a religiously mixed society. A few examples of their implications are given below. Just as the Decalogue itself does not specify penalties, our concern here is not to establish particular penalties but to see that public laws endorse and embody the principles of the biblical commandments.

1. The commandment "Thou shalt have no other gods before me" sets the tone for a Christian society. Practically speaking, this commandment

---

8. A problem arises when the moral law, summarized but not exhaustively contained in the second table of the Ten Commandments, seems to overlap with the laws of ceremonial purity, as frequently happens with laws relating to sexual behavior.

would refer to public ceremonial recognition of only the God of Scripture. This public recognition should also extend to Jewish worship, as is generally the case in the United States, but there the interconfessionalism would have to end. Other religions would be completely tolerated and permitted to worship freely, but their views would not be recognized on public occasions.

2. The commandment not to make graven images for worship prohibits public veneration of created images or objects. Inasmuch as public worship itself is limited in modern America, this commandment calls for no particular change in our common practice.

3. The commandment not to misuse the name of God is already respected in laws relating to perjury. Public blasphemy as well as false swearing should also be punishable by law. It would be logical to accord protection from insults to all religious groups, forbidding the mockery of things that people hold sacred.

4. The law concerning Sabbath day rest is largely respected in terms of the five-day work week. However, buying and selling on Sunday, as though it were a normal business day, is now widespread in the United States. Sunday closing laws should once again be made the rule, as they are throughout Europe and even in the East Communist bloc; those who keep another Sabbath could possibly be excused from Sunday closing provided they close on another day.

5. Respect for parents means that the state should enhance their authority over, and acknowledge their primary responsibility for, their children. Current practices that allow schools and clinics to provide contraceptives and abortions to minors without even notifying their parents (the so-called squeal laws) would be changed. Regulations to prevent child abuse would still be required; in addition, abuse of parents by their children would be punishable by law.

6. Current laws against killing would be supplemented by explicit prohibitions against abortion and euthanasia. Capital punishment for murder (although not required in the Decalogue itself) could be reinstated when there are eyewitnesses.

7. The prohibition of adultery could be reaffirmed in civil law and again enforced. Laws against rape must be retained and enforced; other sexual offenses, such as homosexual acts, prostitution, and fornication should once again be prohibited, or existing prohibitions retained.[9]

---

9. This is a touchy area, where abusive enforcement is a constant danger. Investigation and prosecution should be limited to flagrant offenses.

8. The prohibition of stealing generally in effect in state laws might be extended to prevent various forms of white-collar theft, including prevention of theft by government through excessive taxation and planned inflation (a practice that used to be called "debasing the coinage").

9. The prohibition of false witness should bring increased protection for individuals and institutions against slander and libel.

10. The commandment against coveting, inasmuch as it involves no overt act, can only be implemented by public law insofar as it encourages respect for the sanctity of the home and for the right of individuals to enjoy security in their possessions against excessive taxation, abusive collection laws, and the like.

Specific Regulations and Case Laws. The principles of the Decalogue are not detailed enough to provide a comprehensive guide for public law. What sort of traffic regulations, for example, ought to be enforced? What level of taxation is morally justifiable? To what extent may a government conscript citizens for military duty and for public works? Under what circumstances should a specific killing be considered murder, manslaughter, or self-defense? Should the penalty for theft be imprisonment, corporal punishment, or restitution? What principles should govern interest-taking?

When its general principles are taken into account and translated from the simpler agrarian society in which they were revealed to our more complex society, the Bible to a large extent does answer these and other questions. In his monumental *Institutes of Biblical Law*, [10] Rousas J. Rushdoony has shown in much detail that it is indeed practical to make this application, although he applies biblical law much more thoroughly than I find proper or feasible. His intention is to create a fully theocratic society, not merely a society based on general biblical principles.

Public law should always be *informed* (given its basic inner structure) by the Bible, although not necessarily *conformed* in all its details to the Bible. Conformity is not required in those areas where the purpose of biblical legislation is to enhance the purity and holiness of God's people, because the general population in a secular society is not the people of God. God's laws provide an essential guide to establishing the justice that such societies need to practice, but, again, we must not try to enforce purity and holiness for the general public.

If informed by biblical law, public law will help to secure justice for human beings even in a fallen world. Such law will constantly remind

10. Nutley, N.J.: Craig Press, 1973; reissued by Presbyterian and Reformed.

them that their dignity and worth result from their creation in God's image and that He holds them accountable for their actions.

Freedom and License. Laws relating to freedom of expression and to sexual conduct will be difficult to write and to apply in the light of biblical principles. The third commandment forbids blasphemy; it seems quite proper to punish blasphemous misuse of the name of God and of His Son as a matter of principle and to prohibit mocking and insulting that which other religions hold sacred as well. Freedom of speech was not intended to apply to slander or to gross affronts against personal honor.

Enforcing Old Testament legislation with regard to sexual offenses creates a difficult problem today. The Old Testament prescribes the death penalty for both parties guilty of adultery, for rapists, and for those committing acts of homosexuality and bestiality, and lesser penalties for fornication. In general, however, Old Testament law mandates the death penalty without exception or pardon only for premeditated murder with eyewitnesses present. Therefore, a society seeking to base its law on biblical precepts could punish other offenses by exile, corporal punishment, or fines which in general should be paid to the injured party, not to the government.

A Christian society ought to have legislation against flagrant offenses to sexual morality. The Old Testament seems to display a certain ambivalence in this area, despite its frequent severity regarding sexual matters. Prostitution is condemned for both daughters and sons of Israel; yet its existence is recognized, and prostitutes seem to be tolerated, as in the famous judgment of Solomon (1 Kings 3:16-28). The contemporary concepts of *consenting adults* and *victimless crime* are foreign to the Bible.

Widespread public acceptance of sexual offenses previously considered detestable by most societies makes it very difficult to apply biblical standards today in the area of sexual conduct. For example, because AIDS is incurable and invariably fatal, it would be logical for the state to require stringent reporting of cases, the quarantine of patients, and perhaps even mandatory AIDS testing, as some "extremists" have demanded. Instead, there is a special "right of privacy" for AIDS patients. Today, some academicians and journalists are recommending incestuous acts as a positive good. Many countries, including the United States and Switzerland, penalize lawful marriages and promote concubinage (living together without marriage) by provisions of their tax laws.

Given the condition of public moral sensibility today, new laws on sexual profligacy will have to be introduced gradually. Theonomists advocate close obedience to biblical principles of sexual morality. Such a position could not be enforced without a tremendous expansion of police surveillance and court action. Can we not advocate government support for fundamental principles of biblical sexual morality without requiring government to enforce all of the provisions of the Old Testament with their drastic sanctions? [11]

Laws themselves cannot prevent crime, but the educational and inhibiting value of laws should not be underestimated. Although biblical laws cannot prevent all sin, they should teach men what is right and wrong. And although public laws cannot prevent all crime, they too should teach men what is right and wrong. Anti-discrimination laws, for example, do not prevent prejudice, but they do suppress some of its most harmful expressions.

Conclusions. It is entirely appropriate for Bible-believing Christians to attempt to persuade society as a whole to adopt laws that are consistent with basic biblical principles. Biblical principles are the best guide to promoting justice — the proper goal of any civil order, Christian or not. The most general biblical principles, enshrined in the Decalogue, are clearly intended, not simply for God's covenant people, but for mankind in general. More specific biblical principles, contained in Old Testament moral legislation and case law, are generally valuable guides to proper, publicly desirable civic law. Properly presented, they should appeal to a sufficient portion of the public to be enacted into public law. Ceremonial and dietary regulations are not applicable to the general public, indeed, not even to the believing Christian community. The Old Testament holiness legislation provides many principles for moral conduct that would be useful to society as a whole, but they generally cannot be applied in detail. We should not seek to impose on society specific Old Testament penalties such as death for a variety of transgressions that most contemporary civil codes do not consider capital crimes. Old Testament principles, such as requiring restitution, rather than imprisonment, in the case of robbery, are valid and will appeal to the democratic public.

---

11. The negative reaction of the general public to charges of adultery against presidential candidate Gary Hart and televangelist Jim Bakker makes it clear that society in general still considers adultery to be wrong. Perhaps the existence of legislation and sanctions against adultery might have helped these two men resist the temptations that brought them disgrace.

Church and State

I support a limited collaboration of church and state. The term *church* even in a society with two churches (Protestant and Roman Catholic) such as Switzerland, does not describe an organizational entity but a somewhat amorphous constituency. This is all the more so in the United States with its many major denominational families, a host of small and tiny denominations, and thousands of independent local congregations. Consequently, "collaboration" between church and state will require creativity and flexibility. The state, a highly visible structured entity, will have to try to take seriously the reality of the church as an invisible but real body of believers, a body with rights that in many areas stand above those of government. In Calvinistic thought, there is a measure of visibility to the church—consisting of those who confess Christ, participate in the sacraments according to the Scripture, and submit to church order and discipline.

What Do We Mean by Church? In proposing church-state collaboration we must first identify what the church is. In many European societies there is only one church, sometimes two (Catholic and/or Protestant). All other religious bodies are *sects*. Free church bodies with an orthodox biblical faith, such as the Evangelical Free Churches, are often placed on a par with non-Christian cults of Christian origin, such as the Mormons and the Jehovah's Witnesses, or even with totally non-Christian cults, such as Theosophy and Anthroposophy. We should, by contrast, only define *church* to be Christian.

The state should give the status of *church* only to those bodies which satisfy a scholarly, descriptive definition of orthodoxy. This requirement will be considered legislating "respecting an establishment of religion" and is unconstitutional according to the current interpretation of the First Amendment. But we need not view it that way.

The present interpretation of the amendment—that the government must remain totally agnostic with regard to religion and the church—is incorrect. When the First Amendment was adopted, there was a general consensus among Americans as to what constituted a Christian church. Episcopalians, Congregationalists, Presbyterians, Methodists, Roman Catholics, and even Baptists constituted churches. Jews, Muslims, and the scattered freethinkers did not. To the Founding Fathers the phrase "establishment of religion" did not refer to establishing a religious organization of any kind but, rather, setting up a national church by law. The amendment does not mean that Congress may make no determination regarding any religious organization but, rather, that Congress may not establish a church by law.

In a Christian America it will be necessary to distinguish between churches on the one hand and other religious bodies, groups, and organizations on the other. Both categories may receive public recognition and a certain amount of public encouragement through tax deductibility and other benefits, although not necessarily in the same measure. Traditional non-Christian bodies such as Judaism and Islam could be accorded rights similar to those of Christians, but they would not be defined as churches.[12]

Recognized churches should enjoy certain privileges. For example, contributions made to them ought to be tax deductible (as they presently are), and church income should not be subject to taxation. At the present time, churches are treated somewhat more leniently than other non-profit institutions. All those bodies recognized by the civil government as legitimate churches would continue to enjoy favorable treatment. Traditional non-Christian religions should receive similarly favorable treatment. This would not substantially change the present situation, except to provide a basis for rejecting the claims of spurious organizations to be legitimate churches.[13]

Specific Aspects of Church-State Relationships. In Mark 12:17 Jesus says, "Render to Caesar the things that are Caesar's, and to God the things that are God's." Later in the same chapter He restates the greatest commandment to love the Lord our God with all our heart, soul, mind, and strength (v. 30, citing Deut. 6:5). Because some things are due to God alone, the state's claim upon human existence is limited. The greatest commandment tells us that our highest personal commitment is due to God, and to no one and nothing else.

Most Western governments have given a measure of symbolic and practical recognition to the principle that the kingdom belongs to God,

12. This proposal involves a governmental agency, charged with the task of determining precisely what constitutes a church — a "religious entanglement" such as the Supreme Court and the ACLU dread. If civil government is not permitted to make such a distinction in good faith, however, then an absurd situation will arise. All sorts of strange societies will be created claiming to be churches in order to take advantage of the privileges that government affords them.

13. Fly-by-night religious operations without Christian legitimacy would be evaluated as are other institutions that claim to operate for the benefit of society and seek to merit nonprofit, tax-deductible status, such as hospitals and colleges. So-called para-church religious organizations, such as campus and youth ministries, and evangelistic associations would continue to have to meet the same scrutiny as at present. Money-making operations such as Christian television networks may properly be subjected to even closer scrutiny.

as David states in 1 Chronicles 29:11. This recognition is in part verbal and visual — crosses on flags, legends on coins — and this acknowledgment of God's sovereignty is good and desirable. Furthermore, governments have allowed certain things to be set apart and reserved for God's purposes, or, more practically, for church purposes. For example, servants of the church (clergy) have generally been exempted from military service, and contributions made to churches are generally tax deductible.[14]

Implications for Education. In effect, we have been arguing for a kind of "mixed economy." Church and state would negotiate to some extent the areas where they share responsibility and the ways they work together. The symbolic priority would rest with the church as God's household, but the bulk of practical duties would lie with the state.

Both church and state have a stake in the future. The church is concerned with eternal matters, the state with temporal ones. The state does have a necessary interest in both the health and the education of its citizens.[15] Parents have the primary authority over, and responsibility for, their children before God, yet the civil government cannot reasonably leave everything to parents. In circumstances where traditional values are strong enough to secure the desired educational goals without state involvement, state action is not necessary. Unfortunately, however, such circumstances generally do not exist in modern America.

In a pluralistic society the state experiences considerable difficulty in trying to teach values in government schools, because no matter what values it teaches, someone is sure to disagree. In a Christian society it would be reasonable and possible to expect a measure of Christian education in government schools.

14. In most Western countries the prevailing social theory is that tax exemption and/or deductibility is granted to churches because they are nonprofit institutions with social value such as schools and hospitals. This has, in turn, led to the criticism that churches and other nonprofit institutions are supported by the tax revenue the government loses by permitting taxpayers to deduct their contributions from their taxable income. Obviously, a problem could arise for governments if substantial numbers of people began contributing huge portions of their income to churches and other tax-deductible charities. Under American tax laws, there is a limit to the percentage of one's income that can be made tax-deductible by contributing to a recognized charity. This concept is reasonable, as long as government does recognize the right for at least a certain percentage (traditionally, a tithe or 10 percent) of one's gross income to be given to the church before taxes.

15. In order to encourage good health the state has to make regulations that may impose on the privacy and restrict the personal liberty of its citizens, such as drug control and anti-smoking laws. Logically, this interest would also justify the state's legislating against abortion, rather than in favor of it, as the abortion of large numbers of children means aborting the future.

If America were officially Christian, public school education would have a Christian coloration. This used to be the case; that coloration was vaguely Protestant, but Roman Catholics protested against it and established their own schools in large numbers. For decades Catholics protested against being forced to pay school taxes to support "Protestant" public schools while contributing their own funds to support Catholic parochial schools. While Protestants argued that this "democratic public education" was essential to America's future, they certainly understood that government schools inculcated a general Protestant outlook. Beginning in the 1800s, and rapidly since the 1960s, the Protestant outlook has been expelled from public schools, which today vary from mildly to militantly secularistic in spirit. Consequently, Protestants in increasing numbers, including independent evangelicals and fundamentalists, have established Christian schools, none of which receive government financial support.

In recent years, the school voucher proposal has met with increasing favor. This would require the government to give parents a voucher for a certain amount of school tax money; the voucher would then be presented to the school chosen by the parents and their children, whether it be a public, church-related, or independent private school. The voucher program would be a tremendous boon to independent education. Unfortunately, government educational authorities regard it as a threat to their present virtual monopoly. Nevertheless, a voucher system is constitutionally permissible and philosophically justifiable, and it ought to be introduced now. Even if a measure of Christian perspective were introduced in public schools, it would still be desirable to have vouchers to permit independent schools to flourish.[16]

Concluding Observation

The proposal made here for a Christian America takes both divine and human realities into account. It acknowledges the following: (1) the sovereignty of God and the primacy of His claim on us; (2) the legitimacy of the state and of its interest in its people; (3) the predominantly Christian coloration of American society; and (4) the existence of sub-

---

16. The voucher proposal, like several others, would again require a measure of government "entanglement" in the affairs of nonpublic schools to establish that they are indeed bona fide schools and maintain acceptable standards. In the case of Christian schools, this would require a measure of government supervision, which, in turn, could produce abuses such as government control. However, the present situation produces other abuses in both public and private schools.

stantial non-Christian minorities whose rights must be respected. The example of modern Switzerland shows that a mixed society can establish a strong measure of Christian values without injuring its non-Christian minorities. The example of ancient Christian Rome shows both that it is natural for Christians in leadership positions to attempt to influence their societies and that their influence need not be harmful but can be very good.

In effect, ours is a realistic appeal for a *civitas permixta*, a society in which Christian values permeate but do not dominate institutional life with the result that non-Christians need not feel out of place, at least no more than any minority in any society, even the most tolerant one. A society needs "overarching values" to provide a basis for civilized discourse and even for dissent. Democracy can function only when and where certain basic areas of agreement and a common perspective on values exist.

We began this essay by introducing the phrase *Christian commonwealth*, and we end with it. A commonwealth is a social organization that seeks the common good (weal). Christians logically believe that the teachings of Scripture will promote the common good and, therefore, may properly strive to make their commonwealth Christian. If it is true that Christian values really do promote the common good, it ought to be possible to convince enough people, Christian and non-Christian, to establish a Christian commonwealth in a way that safeguards the spirit or the rights of all of its citizens.

10

The Theonomic Response to Christian America

Joseph N. Kickasola*

Harold O. J. Brown's essential outline is tripartite: historical (models), biblical (principles), and practical (implications, procedures, specifics). I will respond successively to Brown's three divisions, describing, first, areas of agreement and, second, areas of disagreement. We largely agree about biblical principles, but we disagree substantially about historical and practical matters.

Areas of Agreement
Historical
Brown is correct in stating that the United States must reestablish a fundamentally Christian approach and set of values for practical reasons. We must re-lay the biblical foundations on which our society is based. Pluralism in the ethical sense is "self-contradictory and destructive." It is both scriptural and natural for the Christian instead "to try to establish central biblical, Christian values *by law*" (p. 127, Brown's emphasis).

We agree that the Christian emperors from Constantine onward have given us a rich heritage of Christian law. Christian Europe need not be ashamed when compared with "pre-Christian paganism" or with "post-Christian degeneracy" (p. 131). Government and media hostility are increasing against the residual presence of Christianity in America at the same time that the evangelical revival and the charismatic renewal movement are increasing in their efforts to reverse secular trends.

Biblical
Brown's section on biblical principles (pp. 137-39) is highly commendable. Especially important are his points that the purpose of civil govern-

*Joseph N. Kickasola, Ph.D., is Professor of Public Policy at CBN University in Virginia Beach, VA, where he teaches international studies, biblical law, Hebrew and Aramaic. He previously was Professor of Old Testament at Ashland Theological Seminary. Among his numerous writings is "The Bible, Ethics and Public Policy" published in the *Journal of Christian Reconstruction*.

ment is to provide justice, that law by definition is enforced morality (or enforced immorality), and that Christians should "seek to bring the laws of their society into harmony with God's law" (p. 139). The authority God has assigned to civil government "is legitimate but limited" (p. 139). God does not give to His civil minister, the state, any power that is contrary to His Word.

Practical

Brown argues correctly that, while law cannot prevent crime, its role in justice and deterrence and its educational value are very important. The law of God is binding on "all human beings," regardless of whether they want to belong to the people of God" (p. 140). But this does not mean, we agree, that the laws regarding the purity and holiness of God's people should be enforced on the general public. The state is also limited in what it is permitted to do within traditional civil areas, such as taxation. Nevertheless, Brown is correct in stating that some areas of sexual behavior — such as adultery, rape, homosexual acts, prostitution, and fornication — are not merely matters of personal purity, but are also public sexual offenses that biblically could be recriminalized.

Finally, while theonomists disagree over how to enforce biblical Sabbath laws, I applaud Brown's argument that Sunday closing laws should be reinstituted in the United States. The Sabbath principle, along with labor and marriage, is at least a creation ordinance "made for men."

Areas of Disagreement
Historical

The question about how America is a "Christian" nation raises issues of jurisdiction, especially that of church and state. Brown argues that America, neither a nation nor an empire, can be "a Christian commonwealth" (pp. 127, 149). He maintains that a society organized to seek the common good can be based upon Christian principles of organization. His biblical and practical sections reveal what some of those Christian values are — and most of them are laudable — but what are his Christian principles of organization? What is "Christian" organizationally about his commendable desire for an America with Christian values remains undefined. He wants an America that is fundamentally Christian in orientation, yet livable for all. What does that mean, especially in terms of church and state jurisdictions for the basic operation of that America? He informs us, well enough, that America ought to end the total separation of church and state and that these two institutions should "collaborate —

work together—for the temporal welfare of the public" (p. 128). Although Brown envisions a "limited collaboration," he also contends that the collaboration of church and state in Switzerland has thus far served well (pp. 128-29). He argues further that Switzerland, which does not practice separation of church and state, is, officially speaking, "much more Christian than the United States" (p. 128).

As Brown acknowledges, however, the effect of state-endorsed churches in modern Europe is stultifying. As he declares, in "European countries with state-related churches . . . the church is endorsed by the government and largely ignored by the people." Everyone is "obliged to give [officially supported Christianity] lip service, but hardly anyone takes it seriously" (p. 129). Instead of seeing such organization as fundamentally flawed, though, Brown sees it as fundamentally Christian and insists that "it is possible . . . to profit from certain Swiss examples and avoid other Swiss mistakes" (p. 129). On the normative side, he explains that simply because neither Constantine nor his successors achieved a "Christian" empire, "it does not follow that no one else should try" (p. 134).

My basic concern is with the normative side of these jurisdictional questions and with Brown's analysis of the American experience. While describing both Switzerland with its established-church tradition and America with its free-church tradition (two contrasting church-and-state jurisdictional examples), he fails to tell what a Christian America *ought* to be. In more specifically jurisdictional terms, normatively and biblically speaking, what is Christian or biblical about an established Christian America? Is Brown advocating establishmentarianism or disestablishmentarianism as the proper Christian understanding of the Bible?

To save space and gain clarity, I have numbered my responses, both generally to the normative jurisdictional issue and specifically to Brown's description of the American experience.

1. In my judgment, the Old Testament teaches that Israel ought to have been (and Israel was) a Yahwistic nation with a disestablished church, that is, every jurisdiction as a matter of principle should have been under the law of Jehovah. Moreover, the New Testament teaches that the United States (and Switzerland, and every nation) ought to be a Christian nation with a disestablished church and with every jurisdiction as a matter of principle under the law of Jehovah-Jesus. This biblical and normative—by law, but not yet present in actual fact—and jurisdictional assumption, which has not been mentioned in Brown's chapter, is crucial to the remainder of my response.

Space permits only one illustration to defend my assumption. There was jurisdictional and institutional separation of church and state in the

Old Testament, as is illustrated by priest (Levi through Aaron) and temple in contrast to king (Judah through David) and palace. The church even then was disestablished (not state-sponsored), as is illustrated by the tithe. The tithe was not a tax (not state-coerced), but a contribution (voluntary, by church persuasion). Voluntarism (as in America), rather than establishmentarianism (as in the tax-financed state-church of Germany, for example), is the biblical pattern.

2. The biblical concept of jurisdiction (literally, "the speaking of the law" by each sphere for its own sphere) is grounded in the sovereignty-responsibility perspective of biblical covenantalism. God determines what His law is for each created sphere. God initiates a covenant with all men, a bond or relationship initiated by (either common or redemptive) grace and circumscribed by law. Man should respond personally and corporately as a dependent creature, not as if he were the autonomous Creator.

Biblically, God's covenants divide into two categories: the covenant of creation (e.g., Jer. 33:20, 25) and the covenants of redemption (e.g., Eph. 2:12; Heb. 13:20). The covenant of creation pertains to all men and all nonecclesiastical spheres as regulative law (moral and civil). The covenants of redemption in succession have pertained to believers and the ecclesiastical sphere (the church) as restorative law (ceremonial) — God's retrieval system for sinners. This covenantal redemptive-nonredemptive distinction is not clearly present in Brown's chapter. This vital distinction helps us not to secularize the church or sacralize the world.

The church is given the sword of the Spirit and of mercy (restoration), and the state is given the sword of steel and of justice (restitution); both are God's ministers, respectively, of persuasion and coercion. All of the jurisdictions, whether of the self (e.g., controlling anger), the church (confessing anger), the state (punishing acts of anger), or the family, business, etc., are multiple authorities, separate yet interdependent, directly (not hierarchically) subordinate to God's authority. A state-church, and a church-state, join together what God, for our protection and liberty, has put asunder.

3. I believe the Founders of America largely understood and accepted items *1* and *2* as a vital part of Christianity. They did not break, as Brown claims, with Christianity in 1787 (the date for the drafting of the Constitution), officially or unofficially. They formally disestablished the church at the federal level. The *Novus Ordo Seclorum* was the New Order of the Ages, not because it was a "secular utopianism," but because it was the first time a Christian nation had been founded with a disestablished church. This is not neutral but nonecclesiastical; it is not secular but nonsectarian.

I have similar objections to Brown's assessment of our national symbols. The Founders deliberately chose symbols of authority that were clearly nonecclesiastical. A cross is marvelously redemptive and ecclesiastical. This symbol is very inappropriate, therefore, for the nonredemptive and nonecclesiastical civil sphere of coercion. But the fasces, with its rods of the scourger and its axe of the headsman, is universally understood under the covenant of creation as a symbol of corporal punishment. All the other universal symbols were understood in a Christian, not anti-Christian, sense.

4. Brown disapproves of the "total separation of church and state." Again, there is need to use cautious language here for readers. We undoubtedly agree that "separation of church and state" has in our day, unfortunately, come to mean separation of Christianity and state or, worse, separation of God and state or, even still worse, separation of morality and state. But, in my view, the separation should be "total" in the institutional-jurisdictional sense. Brown advocates a "limited collaboration" of state and church, which is always fundamentally flawed in principle and, as Brown himself argues, erosive of faith in its effect. No wonder those in the free-church tradition are suspicious of this proposal. Further, Brown is correct that the First Amendment renders any federal denomination or state-sponsored church(es) unconstitutional, and that the states one by one followed this lead. This is the biblical pattern, for establishmentarianism is no more proper (though less embracive) on the state level than it is on the federal.

5. Brown has a faulty understanding of who should have jurisdiction in education. He supports "a measure of Christian education in government schools" (p. 147). In my judgment, a Christian America should have no government schools, since action, rather than thought, is the only lawful sphere of jurisdiction given by God to the state. Education belongs to the family sphere, and, therefore, all schools should be privately owned and controlled. Brown's proposed voucher system would lead to government interference with Christian education. The state wants to get God out of education, and God wants to get the state out of education. Furthermore, the current system of *mandatory* funding for the state school system (euphemistically called the "public" school system) makes it a state religion, even makes it the humanistic state-church; such a system, therefore, violates both the First Amendment and the biblical principles mentioned above.

Biblical

As explained above, I agree almost completely with Brown's excellent biblical section.

Practical

Brown's essay concludes with implications, procedures, and specific proposals for implementation. He attempts to explain specific ways that modern Christians can properly use the old Yahwistic law. This is the classic question of how the New Testament uses the Old Testament, plus the perennial casuistic question of how to make cross-cultural applications. Brown's specific goal is to describe how Christian public justice can be achieved. This goal is made more difficult by the fact that the Old Testament has a dual goal: formation of a holy people and accomplishment of public justice. Given Brown's aim of applying justice in society, he needs to discover a principle that will allow him biblically to discriminate between the twin goals of holiness and justice. He does not, however, present a clear principle of discrimination. Just as Brown is unclear in his historical section on questions of jurisdiction (what spheres?), so now he is unclear in his practical section on questions of authority (what laws?). His attempt to articulate a principle of discrimination seems related most directly to two of his terms: "theocratic" and "holy."

Brown uses the word "theocratic" twice without definition. In his biblical section he asks, Are we biblically justified in "seeking to establish Christian principles in a mixed society that is not a theocratic unity as ancient Israel supposedly was?" (p. 137). His answer seems to be affirmative, in that these principles are eternally binding whether or not everyone believes in them. They are inherent in the natural order of men and things by God's creative design. In his practical section Brown uses the word once more when he declares that Rousas J. Rushdoony "applies biblical law much more thoroughly than I find proper or feasible. His intention is to create a fully theocratic society, not merely a society based on general biblical principles" (p. 142). Both of these quotes counterpose "principles" and "theocratic." *Theocracy* literally denotes "God's rule." In these contexts "theocratic" probably means "God ruling through the principles and particulars of His law." "Theocratic unity" probably means a theocratic society as opposed to a (religiously) mixed society. A "fully theocratic society," then, means a religiously homogeneous society bound by all the principles and particulars of God's law. By this definition Brown is not a theocrat, for he finds such particularity improper and unfeasible.

Many Christians (not Brown) argue that "the Old Testament was a theocracy, but the New Testament teaches separation of church and state." This is not true. Both the Old and New Testaments teach institutional and jurisdictional separation of church (a disestablished church, no less) and state and family, each directly under God, to be guided by those portions of the Bible which speak explicitly to its particular sphere. The separate powers — judicial, legislative, and executive — all reflect the power of God (cf. Isa. 33:22). Even according to the popular definition of *theocracy* (God ruling through a church-state), Brown is not a theocrat, because he seems to advocate, in principle at least, the opposite (a state-church). By either definition, by authority or by jurisdiction, Brown does not present a principle of discrimination. The term *theocratic* does not discriminate between holy people and public justice. It merely describes (in the Old Testament) when both holiness and justice are required, or (in the New Testament) those holiness elements unique to Old Testament Israel. So, we search on.

Theonomists argue that the *nontheocratic* nations surrounding Israel were bound by God's law. Israel's uniqueness did not exempt its neighboring nations from obeying God's holy standards of personal and civil righteousness for His creatures. The moral-civil (nonceremonial) law, which was not limited to the theocratic *nation*, is not limited to the theocratic *age*. In general, what was binding *outside* Israel is binding *since* Israel. Covenant theology fully appreciates those Scriptures which teach that the continuities of the Testaments are far greater than their discontinuities. Theonomy, specifically, holds to a maintained-unless-modified approach, that is, the Old Testament is presumed to be maintained in the New Testament unless the New Testament modifies some feature of it.[1]

Jesus Christ is prophet, priest, and king, offices that correspond, respectively, to moral law, ceremonial law, and civil (judicial) law. Jesus Christ wields both the sword of the Spirit and the sword of justice in their delegated spheres. He is Lord of heaven and of all nations, of which America is one. When the American Framers, fleeing established religions, rightly founded this Christian nation without an established church, they in principle founded a Christocracy of Jehovah-Jesus. In my judgment, they erred in strategy, but not in principle, when they decided to omit the name of Jesus from their founding documents. We should do what they failed to do: put His name on our founding civil documents in nonredemptive and nonecclesiastical language. Such could be done in this jurisdiction (the civil sphere) by referring to Him, not in His role as Savior and Redeemer, but as King of kings and Lord

---

1. This is in marked contrast to dispensational theology, which employs a repealed-unless-repeated approach, a discontinuity model that asserts that the Old Testament has been repealed by the New Testament unless the New Testament repeats some feature of it.

of lords, the Creator and Lawgiver of men. Such wording would not have established, nor shall it establish, Christianity or any church; none would have been, nor shall be, by that act state-related, state-supported, or state-endorsed. Everyone is bound by Christ's nonecclesiastical law, whether or not one believes in His civil lordship. By entering His name we would avoid both pluralism and establishment of religion with one stroke. He and His civil law-word would officially become Lord in American civil government — a Christocracy of Jehovah-Jesus.

Brown's term "holy," like his word "theocratic," describes but does not discriminate. We learn (pp. 139-40) that the Old Testament law trained the people of Israel "in justice and purity to make them a 'holy people.' " Brown contends that the Ten Commandments are applicable to all man-kind. But the Decalogue, which makes people holy, cannot make them "distinctively holy," Brown asserts. "The ceremonial and dietary laws are suited to accomplish that." He observes (p. 140) that moral law "seems to overlap with the laws of ceremonial purity, as frequently happens with laws relating to sexual behavior." Brown then correctly asks, "Which regulations are necessary to secure public justice for all, and which relate only to God's people, to Christian believers (in New Testament terms)?" In my view, a redemptive-nonredemptive discriminator is painfully absent here.

The absence of a principle of discrimination becomes more problematic when Brown discusses sanctions. Because the Decalogue itself does not specify penalties, public law is not relieved from setting a table of specific penalties. Yes, it is possible to advocate that government separate sexual crimes from the Old Testament's "drastic sanctions" (p. 144). But is it permissible, lawful, scriptural?

Finally, Brown goes from nonscriptural thinking to unscriptural methodology, even if the conclusion be correct, when he argues that "specific Old Testament penalties, such as death for a variety of transgressions that most civil codes do not consider capital crimes," should not be imposed (p. 144). The renewed mind must move from Christ to culture, not from culture to Christ (Rom. 12:2; Heb. 2:2).[2]

2. I urge readers to consult Brown's *The Reconstruction of the Republic* (Milford, Mich.: Mott Media, 1981), which is very helpful and inspiring. However, this book still does not clarify the problematic areas of Brown's chapter. If, on the other hand, readers want to pursue some of the biblical reasoning for my responses, they could see my article, "The Bible, Ethics and Public Policy," *Journal of Christian Reconstruction* (1985): 111-27. Lastly, but pertinent only to Brown's historical section and my responses to it, readers could examine the *Journal of Christian Jurisprudence: A Publication of the CBN University College of Law and Government*, the three bicentennial issues: 1986, 1987, and 1988.

11

The Principled Pluralist Response to Christian America

James W. Skillen*

Harold O. J. Brown's appeal for a Christianized American imperium implies a fundamental misunderstanding of God's revelation culminating in Jesus Christ. His argument, in fact, has disturbing parallels with the one made by Greg Bahnsen.

At the height of the Roman imperial order, the emperor was understood to be the mediator between God (or the gods) and the world. Even though the Roman Empire was not integrally totalitarian as are some modern states, it nonetheless claimed supreme and overarching authority such that all lower authorities were considered subservient or subject to the imperium.

Although Roman law and order had many positive and constructive characteristics, the empire's basic organizing principle stood in direct conflict with the claims of Christ. Jesus maintained that all authority in heaven and on earth had been given to Him. He is the only mediator between God and men. Understanding Christ's claim, the early Christians refused to bow before the emperor; they had given allegiance to another mediator — Jesus Christ.

When Constantine and subsequent Christian emperors began to make the Roman Empire "Christian," they did not fundamentally challenge the structure of the Roman political order. They gave a privileged place to Christianity instead of to other religions. In essence, they said that Christianity could now exist by the grace of the emperor under his authority as God's chief earthly mediator. The Bible says just the opposite,

---

*James W. Skillen holds a B.A. from Wheaton College, a B.D. from Westminster Theological Seminary, and a Ph.D. from Duke University. After teaching at Messiah, Gordon, and Dordt Colleges, he has served since 1981 as the Executive Director of the Association for Public Justice in Washington, D.C. His extensive publications include numerous articles, contributions to several books, editing *Confessing Christ and Doing Politics* (1982), and coauthoring *Disestablishment a Second Time: Genuine Pluralism for American Schools* (1982).

namely, that any political authority (emperor included) exists by the grace of God under Christ, the only mediator between God and humanity. Christ's revelation teaches that no earthly authority should be recognized as solely competent to make all law. The battle between pope and emperor throughout the medieval period led to the legal recognition of at least two authorities as competent to make law under God. Today throughout much of the world, families, churches, universities, and many other institutions are recognized as having independent status; the state cannot simply pass any laws it wishes to regulate and control these associations.

For these reasons and many more, we may not draw an analogy between "God's people," defined as the body of Jesus Christ, and a state or nation or empire. To even consider this conception opens up the possibility of misunderstanding who God's people are under the lordship of Jesus Christ. Jesus has, in His death and resurrection, disqualified all other mediators. Political leaders have an important, but limited, office as ministers of justice and, therefore, cannot claim unlimited or total control over human life.

Given the earth-changing historical fact of God's incarnation in Christ, Christians must look at political life through different glasses than those used by early Greeks, or later Romans, or even the Jews under Mosaic law. If Christ is the sole and supreme mediator and lawgiver, then every human authority must be recognized as a limited authority in a particular field of competence. This means we must accept the ongoing differentiation of God's creation order as intended from the beginning of time.

This also means, consequently, that a general appeal to God's law and moral authority is an inadequate basis for any human authority seeking sanction for his or her actions. Without doubt, God's law holds for us; it is binding on us in this world. But no earthly authority has been given the right or obligation by Christ to enforce all of God's law everywhere as if he or she were God or Christ. Only Christ is the judge of all the earth. Only God will bring about the final judgment and assess the faithfulness of every parent, teacher, scientist, artist, church elder, and political authority. To appeal to the Decalogue or to God's commandments as a basis for political life, as Brown does, is insufficient for showing what in particular is binding on political authorities. God's laws hold for all those in authority, but no authority possesses competence to enforce *all* of God's laws *everywhere*. What is necessary is to show what the specific competence of the state ought to be, which Brown does not do.

All earthly authorities who appeal to God's law must show how and why that law holds for the particular area of responsibility they have.

Moreover, they must demonstrate that the means they propose to use to enforce the law are biblically justified. Simply because God's law is opposed to a certain kind of evil does not allow rulers to act in any and all ways they choose in order to punish or stop that evil. Parents, elders, civil governors, business owners, teachers, and many other authorities have different kinds of limited responsibility; none has unqualified or undifferentiated authority.

In his discussion of "imposing morality," Brown asks, "If we do recognize that God's justice is just, should we not apply it in every situation in which we are involved?" (p. 139). Elsewhere he declares that "Christian emperors such as Theodosius I, Justinian I, and Leo III quite naturally worked to bring Roman laws into conformity with the biblically revealed law of God" (p. 131). He argues further that "it should be entirely natural for Christians in a democratic society to seek to bring the laws of their society into harmony with God's law—and we need make no apology to others for our effort" (p. 139).

My argument above sought to show why Brown's statements are a dangerous half truth. What must be clarified are the limitations of the various offices God appoints. In the offices of parents, teachers, governors, or elders, Christians should seek to heed and apply God's law as appropriate for each of those areas of life. But their authority in these offices is not undifferentiated or unlimited. Parents should not have the right to put their children to death if they sin. Civil authorities should not have the right to determine when my children should go to bed. School teachers should not run churches, not should church elders govern the state. Thus, the way in which one should "seek to bring the laws of his society into harmony with God's law" all depends on the particular authority and competence God has given that person—what "say" he has given to a particular office of authority.

It may well have been "entirely natural," as Brown suggests, for one of the emperors to try to bring Roman laws into conformity with the laws of God, since emperors assumed mediatorial authority over everything in the empire. But the "naturalness" of that act derived from Roman imperial claims, not from Christ's teaching. Thus, no matter how "natural" it may have seemed to a Roman emperor, he was at least partially in error.

That is precisely what scares me about Brown's argument that a "Christian imperial" framework would work well in America. From a biblical point of view, the United States should seek continually to define more clearly its constitutional or lawfully limited political character as a republic—as a limited state. It should more carefully differentiate its public laws from the kinds of laws that parents have the authority to make in their homes, that teachers should make in the school, that business people should make in their enterprises, and that elders should make in the church. Conceiving of America as some kind of undifferentiated moral "whole" or something analogous to God's kingdom of Israel prevents this kind of differentiation.

Only after we understand the contextual whole of the Old and New Covenants on their own terms, and only after we comprehend the character of American society after two thousand years of history following the incarnation of Christ—only then can we carefully extract and apply particular moral teachings and laws to our families, schools, churches, businesses, and states today. And only then can we determine what is biblically legitimate and illegitimate in contemporary American public law and government. Brown's approach does not help us very much to do this because of his rather casual, loose, and often romantic reading of Western history.

This is where Brown's Christian America and Bahnsen's theonomy, however different, present us with the same problem. Both want to organize modern political life on the basis of God's law. But what does that mean for our differentiated society? All Christians should be theonomists in the sense that they ought to believe that God's law is binding on His creatures. *Theonomy* means the rule of God's law, and to be a theonomist is to believe that God's law ought to be obeyed in all of life. But the real debate is over *who* should enforce *what* part of God's law in *which* institutions and situations.

The Scriptures clearly teach that the true and ultimate enforcer of God's law is God Himself, not human beings. The Scriptures also teach that the strict enforcement of God's law can only bring death to lawbreakers. When God sent His Son to earth to fulfill His law and to redeem His creation, Jesus Christ went to the cross of death to do His Father's will—suffering judgment against sin and thereby making possible the restoration of the creation.

Those who live by faith in Christ under the blood of His redemptive sacrifice may now live lives of thankful stewardship, seeking to obey God's law, not as the means to salvation, but out of thankfulness for their restoration by His grace. Christians now live in anticipation of the coming great day of the Lord. Then Christ will complete the judgment against all unrighteousness, and God's glory will be unveiled fully, so that His people will obey all of His law without fault because it will be written in their hearts.

The kings of Israel and Judah have shown us that human beings, even God's chosen people, cannot create a just and perfectly obedient society on earth. Such a society cannot be created—not because God's law is inadequate or faulty, but because the response of sinful human creatures, even God's chosen ones, is never sufficient. When the true King of Israel, Jesus Christ, appeared, He did not try to regather Israel into one corner of the world to reestablish a little theocracy among the nations. Rather, He announced through word and deed that His kingdom embraces the entire world and can never be confined within any human imperium. He will be satisfied with nothing less than total dominion over the whole earth. That is why Jesus gave His followers no reason for political hope short of the full realization of His global kingdom. That is why He sent them out to the four corners of the world to proclaim to everyone the nature of His kingdom. That is why Gentiles as well as Jews must hear the Word, since His kingdom embraces people from every nation and from every race.

The reason why Jesus and His disciples rejected the Zealot option is that they were not seeking to restore old Israel to a place of independence. They were not seeking to overthrow Roman authority by force. They were not seeking simply to displace non-Christian religions with Christianity within the Roman Empire.

God's people would henceforth be a global people, a worldwide people, living among all the nations with no higher authority than Christ, their Lord. They would have political offices just as Joseph and Daniel did, but none of the states or kingdoms in which they would live and serve would be like ancient Israel. No state could legitimately claim to be God's theocracy or imperium on earth. Christian nationalism or statism should be anathema to the people of God.

Theocracy, in the sense of the rule of God, or theonomy as the rule of God's law, must now be understood on the terms that God has revealed in Christ. Jesus Christ reveals how God is choosing to rule. Christ shows us how God's law binds us today. Christ did not ask His people to develop duplicates of ancient Israel or to try to create "Christian" states or empires. Rather, He asked them to go forth into the whole world, living in obedience to His commands, to teach and preach to everyone about the kingdom of God. Among other things, this meant a renewed emphasis on discerning all the responsibilities, and developing all the gifts, that God has given His people—as parents and children in homes; employers and employees in their work places; elders, deacons, and members in congregations; rulers and "subjects" in political society, and so forth.

Governments must, indeed, enforce laws for the sake of the public well-being of everyone in their territories. Civil governments, as Paul explains, are ministers of God. But no government may legitimately seek universal moral authority over life, since the range of its authority is limited.

Two passages of Scripture illustrate how the coming of Christ has led to a radical change in the way we should view the use of force, and consequently, how we should evaluate the nature and practices of any modern political order.

In Exodus 23:20-24, 31-33 (NIV), God speaks this way:

> See, I am sending an angel ahead of you to guard you along the way and to bring you to the place I have prepared. Pay attention to him and listen to what he says. Do not rebel against him; he will not forgive your rebellion, since my Name is in him. If you listen carefully to what he says and do all that I say, I will be an enemy to your enemies and will oppose those who oppose you. My angel will go ahead of you and bring you into the land of the Amorites, Hittites, Perizzites, Canaanites, Hivites and Jebusites, and I will wipe them out. Do not bow down before their gods or worship them or follow their practices. You must demolish them and break their sacred stones to pieces. . . . I will establish your borders from the Red Sea to the Sea of the Philistines, and from the desert to the River. I will hand over to you the people who live in the land and you will drive them out before you. Do not make a covenant with them or with their gods. Do not let them live in your land, or they will cause you to sin against me, because the worship of their gods will certainly be a snare to you.

By way of contrast, Jesus declared to those who would be disciples:

> You have heard that it is said, "Love your neighbor and hate your enemy." But I tell you: Love your enemies and pray for those who persecute you, that you may be sons of your Father in heaven. He causes his sun to rise on the evil and the good, and sends rain on the righteous and the unrighteous. If you love those who love you, what reward will you get? Are not even the tax collectors doing that? And if you greet only your brothers, what are you doing more than others? Do not even pagans do that? Be perfect, therefore, as your heavenly Father is perfect (Matt. 5:43-48, NIV).

Under the Old Covenant, God had a particular purpose in separating Israel as a nation from others. Because of the sin of these various nations, God ordered Israel to wipe them out. They were not to live with them in the same land. But now that God's "schooling" of Israel is past (as Paul explains it in Galatians), and now that the judge of all the earth has been revealed in Christ, it is not only unnecessary for God's people to live in an exclusive state as did Israel, it is actually illegitimate for them to try to do so. Christ wants us to express His universal lordship precisely by living fairly with everyone—even enemies—in the field of the world (see the parable of the wheat and the tares, Matt. 13:24-30, 36-42). Instead of driving people out, we must recognize that God gives rain and sunshine to the unjust as well as to the just. Thus, the Israelite theocracy is no longer legitimate for the Christian era.

This response does not, of course, answer the question of what does constitute a God-honoring, limited, and legitimate political order today. That we must work out in accord with the hermeneutical and historical suggestions outlined above. But what it does is to alert us to the fact that a Christian America, as envisioned by Brown, may be closer to the kingdom of Antichrist than to something befitting the honor and glory of Jesus Christ, Lord of all the nations.

12

The National Confessional Response to Christian America
*D. Howard Elliott**

Harold O. J. Brown contends that the United States can survive as a vital society into the twenty-first century and beyond only in reestablishing a fundamentally Christian approach and values.

Most Christians will agree that America's future is at stake, threatened from many sides. But the future is in the hands of God who loves the world and has sent His Son to redeem His chosen ones from destruction. "For dominion belongs to the Lord, and He rules over the nations" (Ps. 22:28).[1] As the ruler of the earth, God decrees ruin for those who refuse to follow His lead. "The nations have fallen into the pit they have dug . . . the wicked are ensnared by the work of their hands. The wicked return to the grave, all nations that forget God" (Ps. 9:15-17). On the other hand, however, God blesses those individuals or nations which love Him and keep His commandments. "Blessed is the man who makes the Lord his trust" (Ps. 40:4). "Blessed is the nation whose God is the Lord . . ." (Ps. 33:12-19).

The history of the world reveals how God has dealt with nations: "For the nation or kingdom that will not serve you will perish; it will be utterly ruined" (Isa. 60:12). The United States is no exception to the rule, God will treat America in the same way.

Brown assumes that if America would go back to its original standards, supposedly Christian, then it has a chance of continuing into the twenty-first century. Granted, reestablishing the Christian features of the colonial governments would be better than what we have now. Yet it

*A graduate of Geneva College and Reformed Presbyterian Theological Seminary, D. Howard Elliott has held pastorates in RPCNA congregations in Winchester, KS, Beaver Falls, PA, and Topeka, KS. He has served as Clerk and Moderator of the Synod of the RPCNA and has edited *The Christian Statesman*, the official periodical of the National Reform Association.
1. Scripture quotations in this chapter are from the New International Version, copyright 1973, 1978, 1984 by International Bible Society.

is questionable whether even this would put America into proper relationship with God.

Switzerland is presented as an example of a democracy that is officially Christian. While Switzerland might be formally Christian, it appears to give only lip service without the heart, form without substance. The apostle Paul urges Timothy to have nothing to do with those who display "a form of godliness" but deny its power (2 Tim. 3:5). Switzerland as a so-called Christian democracy falls far short of the ideal; therefore, America should reject that pattern of government, even though its traditional forms appear to be Christian.

Brown cites the Roman Empire after Constantine (fourth century A.D.) as a good example of a Christian establishment. The culture of Europe for the following twelve centuries was strongly influenced by Christianity, but many of its values and practices were challenged and changed by the Reformation. Much of this "Christian" history is very undesirable; it displays a corrupted Christianity, which is not a proper ideal for America.

Because these two "Christian societies" have failed, should we conclude that a truly Christian society can never exist? Certainly the failures of the past should not be accepted as the standard for the future. The American ideal and challenge, whether it be secular or Christian, is to develop a better society than has ever existed before. America has been striving to create a better world for itself and other countries economically, politically, socially, industrially. Even though our nation constantly fails to attain its goals, we must not give up the effort or reject all ideals. Christians believe that all such failures result from not relying upon that supreme power, God, who has brought everything into existence and sustains it for His own purposes. Any effort to reform society will fail unless initiated and empowered by God.

The question is asked, Can — or should — there be a Christian America? Surely there can be a Christian America, because "with God all things are possible" (Matt. 19:26). However, neither the Christian community nor the general American populace can ever bring it about by human effort. There is not the slightest chance that sinful human societies can purify or perfect themselves. However, as people yield to Christ, they become tools that God can use to bring about righteousness in their nation. It is every Christian's responsibility to "go and make disciples of all nations, baptizing them in the name of the Father and of the Son and of the Holy Spirit, and teaching them to obey everything I have commanded you" (Matt. 28:19-20). God is sending us out to transform both society and individuals. Christians are to disciple nations and to baptize individuals; both groups and individuals are to be taught obedience to God.

Should there be a Christian America? Is there anything that should *not* be Christian? It is widely acknowledged that America's foundation rests in part upon Christian principles, and Christian values and overtones can still be identified in our culture. But a movement away from biblical norms is obvious, especially in the attitude of our government, the media, and other public institutions. The Christian message is still proclaimed, but it is more openly attacked than ever before. Christians and pagans square off against each other more fearlessly now. But Christians must not stop laboring to bring all things under the dominion of Christ simply because of growing opposition.

The proposition to restore Christian America suggests reinstituting conditions that existed two hundred years ago. How can we find enthusiasm for returning to something that Christians know was faulty? Our efforts must aim at something better. While restoring the colonial American commitment to Christianity might be an improvement over the present situation, it is an insufficient goal.

The failures of England and France to restore certain historical arrangements in their lands warns us how not to go about our American efforts. Indeed, what is needed is not restoration but *restructuring*. We cannot bring about a Christian America by changing the form of government or turning the clock back two hundred years. Instead, we must focus on the government's authority and purpose for being, the rules for its conduct, and the place and limits of its control. Government should acknowledge the place and power of God and seek to promote righteousness.

Whether the United States is a nation, an empire, or a generic state, at least it is a cohesive body of people that is organized, powerful, wealthy, and has a world view. It manifests a personality — evident in the way Americans live, deal with their problems, conduct their businesses, and organize their affairs — and its owes a responsibility to its citizens, to people of other nations, and to God. Its failure to submit to God's authority is the chief threat to its continued existence.

To assess whether an individual is a Christian, we must consider a number of factors, such as his beliefs, conduct, self-control, relationships, motivation, and service. Likewise, in analyzing whether a nation is Christian, similar factors must be evaluated; these would include its government, judicial system, laws and legal procedures, customs, social ethics, institutions, concern for truth and righteousness, treatment of people, and vision. We cannot address all of these areas here, but let us examine one aspect — America's government — by asking four questions.

1. *Has our government ever been Christian?* Considering its early history and many of its early documents and pronouncements, the answer is a qualified yes.

2. *Is our American government currently Christian?* Considering its present foundational concepts, laws, activities, and scandals, the answer is a qualified no.

3. *Will our American government ever be Christian?* Considering the dominance of non-Christian elements in our pluralistic society, the answer is a probable no, or a hopeful maybe.

4. *Ought our American government to be Christian?* This is by far the most important question. If this were put up to a public vote, the response would very likely be negative. But considering the biblical perspective regarding nations, the answer is definitely yes.

Why should the United States have a Christian government? The first reason is that such is the demand of eternal truth. "Therefore, you kings, be wise; be warned, you rulers of the earth. Serve the Lord with fear and rejoice with trembling. Kiss the Son, lest he be angry and you be destroyed in your way, for his wrath can flare up in a moment. Blessed are all who take refuge in him" (Ps. 2:10-12).

Second, the government ought to be Christian because this is what God expects. A sizable portion of the Scriptures is addressed to nations or to corporate society. The Bible's premise is that God is the one and only sovereign ruler of the universe. He gives the orders, makes the rules, owns the world and everything in it. He rules over nations and grants authority to earthly governments. He expects to be heard and demands to be obeyed; He bestows His blessings on His followers and brings His judgments on all who rebel. He sentences sinners to death and hell; yet His mercy abounds, and eternal safety is provided for those who submit to the King who has all the authority and power. This truth applies to every phase of human activity.

Third, the government ought to be Christian because a nation or an individual that denies or ignores the sovereignty of Christ is under divine condemnation — ultimate death. This is the status of our American government and society.

America's only hope lies in surrendering to the reigning King, Jesus the Christ, and in accepting His gracious invitation to come into His kingdom.

What actions are necessary for America to become Christian?

1. We must acknowledge and accept God's authority over our nation. Individuals become Christians by yielding to the person of Jesus Christ, submitting to His rule, and serving Him in the world. A nation becomes Christian when its people and institutions do these same things. Because human beings are depraved, sin will not be totally eliminated, but it is counterbalanced by the work of Christ. Righteousness will grow and flourish in such a society.

2. In a Christian America, biblical truth will be interwoven throughout the structure of the culture. This will be expressed in the laws and practice of the governing authorities and of the governed. Divine and civil laws will be harmonious. Biblical norms will influence every segment of life, resulting in a fresh understanding and experience of freedom. "The truth shall make you free" (John 8:32).

3. In a Christian America, citizens will search after righteousness, which is revealed in the person of Jesus Christ. His advice will be taken seriously: "Seek the Lord while he may be found, call on him while he is near. Let the wicked forsake his way and the evil man his thoughts. Let him turn to the Lord and he will have mercy on him, and to our God, for he will freely pardon" (Isa. 55:6, 7).

4. In a Christian America, the government, schools, home, media, and even the marketplace will promote eternal biblical values instead of temporal, earthly, and material ones doomed to extinction with time.

5. In a Christian America, growing numbers of people will turn to God, confess their sins, and receive regeneration from the Holy Spirit.

All evil will not be eliminated in a Christian America, for Christians themselves are not made perfect in this world. Non-Christian elements will be tolerated until the time of judgment, even as God tolerates the sinfulness of each of us. Nevertheless, the government will punish acts of lawlessness before the final day of God's judgment.

The United States can become a Christian nation only by the work of God's Spirit in response to the humble prayer, fervent desire, and heartfelt repentance of those who are already believers in Christ. "If my people, who are called by my name, will humble themselves and pray and seek my face and turn from their wicked ways, then will I hear from heaven and will forgive their sin and will heal their land" (2 Chron. 7:14).

Part Four
National Confessionalism

Advocates of the national confession position contend that all contemporary nations should officially declare allegiance to Jesus Christ in their public documents and devise political structures and policies that honor God and promote His justice. Proponents of this view argue that God expects nations to adopt the same practice of covenanting as Old Testament Israel did. These covenants affirmed the Jews' loyalty to God and pledged their intention to obey His statutes. A more recent example is provided by many towns in Puritan New England that covenanted to follow Christ during the seventeenth century. Scotland made the same pledge through its National Covenant of 1638 and its Solemn League and Covenant sworn with England and Ireland in 1643. In the United States the leading supporters of the national confession position have been Reformed Presbyterians whose roots lie in Scottish Presbyterianism.

In 1864 Reformed Presbyterians joined other concerned Christians to establish the National Reform Association, an organization that has sought to combat the secular drift of American politics and to amend the Preamble to the Constitution of the United States. Supporters of the NRA have argued that the Constitution is a secular covenant because it does not explicitly acknowledge the authority of Jesus Christ as the sovereign Lord over this nation. The NRA's proposed amendment aims to have the United States government officially recognize Christ's kingship over this country. In 1874 and 1896 members of the House Judiciary Committee discussed this proposed amendment, but they rejected it both times.

During the late nineteenth century the NRA had wide support, and its members campaigned for many social reforms. By the early 1870s its honorary vice presidents included one United States senator, two governors, three federal judges, three state school superintendents, twenty-five college and university presidents, and eleven Methodist and Episcopal bishops. In the first two decades of the twentieth century the NRA spon-

173

sored three international congresses, which drew thousands of delegates from around the world. Since 1867 the organization has published a periodical, *The Christian Statesman*, to advocate its views. The membership (chiefly Reformed Presbyterians) and impact of the NRA are substantially less today than they were during its first fifty years of existence. Nonetheless, the effort of NRA members to have the United States officially declare its allegiance and commitment to Jesus Christ represents a longstanding concern among Calvinists that nations covenant to be the Lord's.

William Edgar, a Reformed Presbyterian minister and teacher in the Philadelphia area, presents the national confession position in his essay. The most significant political fact of the present age, he argues, is that Jesus Christ by virtue of His incarnation, death, resurrection, and ascension has been given "all authority in heaven and on earth" (Matt. 28:18). Jesus, Edgar maintains, commanded His disciples to teach the kings of the nations that they must submit to His sovereign authority.

Edgar traces the historical impact of Christianity in Western society from apostolic days to the present. The faithful witness of the early Christians led to the conversion of the Roman Empire. As a result of this "stupendous change," Constantine and his successors professed faith in Christ and sought to make their administrations Christian. During the thousand years between Charlemagne and the French Revolution (approximately 800 to 1800), the peoples of Western civilization continued to recognize Christ as Lord over all kings, nations, and churches, and the Bible strongly influenced the development of Western law. About 1750, however, a dramatic change occurred as the nations of Christendom began to rebel against God and rulers ceased to recognize Christ's lordship. Repudiating the longstanding belief that governments derived their authority from God, Enlightenment philosophers argued instead that a nation's people, through drafting a constitution, granted legitimacy to its government.

Unlike the nations of Western Europe, the United States, Edgar contends, has never acknowledged officially the sovereign authority of Jesus Christ. From the Declaration of Independence and Constitution onward, Americans refused to "honor God as God," establishing instead a government that "recognized the people alone as the source of its authority" (p. 182). America's Founding Fathers were not militant secularists, but the Constitution they devised, especially as compared to colonial charters and the European heritage, displays indifference toward God and attributes final authority to the people.

Edgar argues that as a result of increasing secularization during the past hundred years American public life has departed further and further from biblical ideals and practices. To reverse this trend, the most important political reform Christians can pursue is to convince our government to confess faith in Jesus Christ as Lord and to apply His law to society. The American people should amend the Preamble to the Constitution to acknowledge the authority and power of Almighty God and Jesus Christ and to establish an officially Christian government. Christians are obligated to do this because (1) Christ instructs the church to witness to kings; (2) Christ calls nations, not just individuals, families, and churches, to be part of His kingdom; and (3) Christ commands governments to rule justly, which is possible only if they base justice explicitly upon biblical norms. Only such an amendment will provide a secure basis for bringing American law into conformity with biblical principles. Nations in the past have been Christian; America can become Christian in the future.

13

The National Confessional Position
*William Edgar**

In Rudyard Kipling's novel *Captain's Courageous* a spoiled brat falls overboard into the Atlantic Ocean. A fishing boat rescues him, but instead of being grateful he is mouthy and insulting. Exasperated, the boat's captain finally decks him, remarking to his son that the flowing of blood has a powerful effect of clearing the head.

Growing numbers of American Christians are becoming concerned about the biblical role of civil government. Why? Because God has been clearing our heads, removing our smug satisfaction with America. He is giving our society over to all kinds of gross evils. As His judging hand rests upon our country, people grow afraid. Our pride shaken, we are ready to look again at the Bible and at the experience of believers in other times and places to learn God's will for our government and our nation's laws.

This chapter begins by showing how Jesus Christ after His ascension subdued emperors and kings in the Roman Empire and in later European governments, but how the nations, when they replaced their kings with themselves, also rebelled against God Most High. The middle part of the chapter examines the spiritual character of the American nation and its government. The final section suggests what Christians, kings of this land, along with all Americans, should be doing.

Kings Subdued, Nations in Rebellion

In biblical times political sovereignty usually belonged to kings. The emperor or king claimed to be a god and demanded to be obeyed as such. The kings of ancient Israel, however, knew that they were not gods on earth, and they did not expect their subjects to worship them. The good Hebrew kings, and even some of the wicked ones, understood that

---

*William Edgar was born in New York City; raised near Philadelphia; and schooled at Swarthmore College, the Reformed Presbyterian Seminary, and the University of Pennsylvania. He worked for four years as a missionary-teacher in Cyprus, and he is now pastor of a Reformed Presbyterian Church in Broomall, Pa.

the Lord was the true King of Israel: genuine sovereignty belonged only to Him (Pss. 10:16; 29:10; 44:4; 89:18; 149:2).

Not only did God anoint Jewish kings, He also gave the law in Israel. The kings did not make law; they enforced God's law. Kings were expected to "learn to fear the Lord" their God "by keeping all the words of this law and these statues" (Deut. 17:18-20).[1] Kings ruled in Israel by the grace of God.

The ancient heathen kings of the nations around Israel, who pretended to be divine and who made their own law, were in rebellion against the King of all the earth. Israel knew that their God was King of every nation. "For God is the king of all the earth; sing praises with a psalm! God reigns over the nations," they sang (Ps. 47:7-8). Even though the nations did not know or obey God, He overlooked their ignorance for a time (Acts 17:30).

When Jesus was born, conflict between Him and the usurping kings of the world was inevitable. Jesus came to King Herod's attention as the newborn King of the Jews whose star the wise men had seen (Matt. 2:1-2). Herod tried to kill the child. Over thirty years later the Roman governor Pilate ordered the execution of Jesus after Jewish leaders had falsely portrayed Him as a rebel against Caesar. Roman soldiers crucified Jesus. Written above His cross was the accusation "The King of the Jews!"

But death could not hold God's Anointed One. Jesus rose to life again and "presented himself alive after his passion by many proofs" (Acts 1:3). He left His disciples with this claim: "All authority in heaven and on earth has been given to me"; and these instructions: "Go therefore and make disciples of all nations, baptizing them in the name of the Father and of the Son and of the Holy Spirit, teaching them to observe all that I have commanded you"; and this promise: "And lo, I am with you always, to the close of the age" (Matt. 28:18-20). Then Jesus ascended to heaven, taking His seat of rule at the right hand of God.

Totally transformed by His resurrection and empowered by the Holy Spirit, Jesus' disciples began to preach. They defiantly called Jesus the *Christ*, meaning that He is the anointed and chosen King of Israel and of all nations. They insisted so often and so strongly that Jesus is the Christ that in Antioch the Gentiles misunderstood and began calling Jesus' followers Christians, thinking that Jesus' other name must be Christ. In

---

1. Scripture quotations in this chapter are from the Revised Standard Version, 1952, 1971.

Thessalonica Paul and his companions were accused of "saying that there is another king, Jesus" (Acts 17:7). The New Testament actually begins with the claim that Jesus Christ is the Son of David, that is, the rightful heir to the throne of Israel (Matt. 1:1). It ends with Jesus' testimony that He is the "root and the offspring of David, the bright morning star" (Rev. 22:16).

Because Jesus has come, the time when God overlooks the ignorance of kings and nations is past! God now "commands all men everywhere to repent, because he has fixed a day on which he will judge the world in righteousness" (Acts 17:30-31). As an indication of His coming final judgment, Jesus' exercise of authority sometimes includes interim judgments. When Herod allowed the people of Tyre and Sidon to cry, "The voice of a god and not of man!" the Lord sent His angel to take his life (Acts 12:22-23). The lesson is clear: God will no longer tolerate kings who blasphemously claim divinity. Jesus is now the ruler of all things, and He will not allow earthly kings to steal His glory. "All authority in heaven and on earth has been given to me" (Matt. 28:18). That is the most important political fact of our time.

Jesus told His disciples clearly that through their witness He intended to tell the kings of the earth that they must submit to His sovereign authority. Their testimony would be borne in a setting of conflict and violence: the usurping kings of the earth would resist Christ (Mark. 13:9; Acts 9:15). Paul quite openly tried to convert King Agrippa, and from jail in Rome he wrote the Philippians with joy that believers in Caesar's household sent them greetings (Acts 26:28-29; Phil. 4:22).

Why did Jesus tell His followers that they would witness to kings? He intended the kings of the earth to be converted and to bow before Him. Converted kings have to give up claims to their own divinity and, like every Christian, publicly confess Jesus. Then, like all Christians, they must obey God in their callings here on earth. For kings, that means ruling according to the law of God, not according to what merely seems good to them.

Because Jesus alone is the divine-human King, the early Christians would not worship Caesar. The Bishop of Smyrna, Polycarp, dragged to the stadium as an old man, refused to offer incense to Caesar or to swear by the genius of Caesar. He refused to revile Christ, saying, "Eighty and six years have I served him, and he never did me wrong; and how can I now blaspheme my King that has saved me. . . . I am a Christian."[2]

---

2. Eusebius, *Ecclesiastical History* (Grand Rapids: Baker, 1955), p. 146.

The final outcome of the Christian's unyielding witness to the unique lordship of Christ was the conversion of the Roman Empire. What a stupendous change that was! The Emperor Constantine confessed Jesus as the Messiah, the King of kings.

For at least a generation after Constantine, it was unclear whether Christianity would supplant paganism as the official religion of the empire. But after Julian's failed attempt to restore paganism, it became clear that the power of the Roman government would firmly support the church and would discourage paganism.[3] According to Theodoret of Cyprus, writing in 450, Julian cried as he died, "Galilean, you have conquered."[4] While it is doubtful that Julian said those words, they express the truth. Jesus had conquered. The kings of Rome had been subdued. They no longer claimed to rule by reason of their own divinity. They acknowledged that they ruled by the grace of God just as the kings of ancient Israel had so ruled. Real sovereignty belongs to God alone and to His Christ.

Emperor Constantine began a process whereby Roman laws started to reflect the Bible's law. For example, laws transforming the first day of the week, the Lord's Day, into a day of rest were enacted. Under Christian influence laws protecting slaves, peasants, children, and women were passed, and branding criminals on the face was forbidden because "man is made in God's image."[5] After the Roman Empire adopted Christianity as its official religion, it split into two parts, East and West. In the East the empire continued for many centuries. It survived barbarian invasions and Muslim attackers, but fell to the Crusaders in 1204 and finally to the Ottoman Turks in 1453.

In the West the empire disintegrated under repeated invasions of barbarian tribes. In the years that followed, a new civilization gradually emerged. On Christmas Day, A.D. 800, Pope Leo III surprised the Frankish king Charlemagne by crowning him Emperor of the Romans. The act began a tradition in the West in which kings received their crowns in coronation ceremonies conducted by the church. In sincerity or in hypocrisy, kings had to recognize the authority of Jesus the Christ. The old divine kingship was dead! The West had become Christendom, and both church and state acknowledged Christ as the source of their authority and law.

3. Kenneth Latourette, *A History of the Expansion of Christianity* (Grand Rapids: Zondervan, 1970), 1:158-60, 181.
4. Henry Chadwick, *The Early Church* (Baltimore: Penguin Books, 1967), p. 159.
5. Ibid., p. 128.

Within Christendom church and state competed for power. The pope claimed political authority, while kings tried to appoint bishops. At its best, the medieval church sought to exert political influence, not merely for power's sake, but more basically to develop a Christian state. Two fundamental points about civil government were established during the early Middle Ages: first, kings ruled by the grace of God, and, second, particular laws should apply the law of God to society.

Through all of the warfare, new discoveries, and spiritual ups and downs of the millennium from Charlemagne to the French Revolution, the peoples of the West unmistakably continued to think of their civilization as Christendom. They recognized the lordship of Jesus Christ over kings, nations, and churches. From the Christian Roman Empire and from the Middle Ages came a tradition of law in the West that owed a great deal to the Bible, both in its general conception of law and in particular instances of law. Family law, for example, reflected the Bible's teaching about marriage and divorce, and Christian ideals led to rules of war. Even theories of natural law that owed an important debt both to Greek philosophy and to the Bible viewed law in its deepest sense as God-given. Governments did not "make" law, they only codified and applied the law of God.

While persecution of Jews and dissenting Christians and battles between kings and popes were prevalent during these ten centuries, we must not lose sight of the forest for the trees. The West remained Christendom. Church and state, heretic and believer, argued from the Bible and often looked to God for strength. Just as an individual who confesses faith in Christ continues to sin after his conversion, so the Christian West sinned grievously. In ancient Israel, also, even the best kings — David, Solomon, Hezekiah, Josiah — failed to live up to all parts of God's law. But the Bible set the standard by which the kings of Israel and of Christendom could be judged! Jesus subdued the kings of the West, and they knew that they were not gods. They ruled only by the grace of God and would have to answer to Him.

Since about 1750, however, Christendom has rebelled against God Most High. While missionaries from the West have carried the gospel to the whole world, the West has collectively turned its back on God. In 1804 Napoleon Bonaparte crowned himself emperor, reversing the symbolism of Charlemagne's coronation a thousand years earlier. Jesus reigns, but in the modern West there is no fear of God.

Historians identify two revolutions that have transformed the West during the last two hundred years — the Industrial Revolution and the

Democratic Revolution. Although neither is as fundamental as the revolt against God, both contributed to that revolt.

The wealth and power conferred on Europe by means of the Industrial Revolution produced unbounded pride. "How can we explain our great success compared to the rest of the world?" Europeans asked. They concluded simply that the white race was biologically superior and that progress was a law of nature. The West forgot God and did not heed the warning that God had addressed to Israel: When the Lord makes you rich, "then take heed lest you forget the Lord, who brought you out of the land of Egypt" (Deut. 6:12).

The Democratic Revolution, meanwhile, changed the way people thought about themselves, their governments, and their laws. Enlightenment intellectuals taught that any government that claimed its authority came from tradition or from conquest or from God had no moral right to rule. Only the people, through a constitution drawn up according to Reason, could grant a government legitimacy.

In ancient times, kings claiming to be gods ruled by their own genius. Today whole nations claim autonomous authority to direct their own affairs. The dogma of self-determination is the foundational postulate of modern political thinking: the people have a right to rule themselves and to make their own laws, and every nation should be independent of every other nation. Almost every government on earth today claims to draw its authority from the people and from them alone. Even the socialist countries call themselves democracies.

When modern countries write constitutions or particular laws, people believe that they are merely giving law to themselves. In the constitutional republics such as Great Britain and the United States, popular sovereignty is limited by protections given individuals who dissent from the majority will. Nevertheless, even in these countries the most widespread understanding of law and, indeed, of ethics is that it emanates from society as a whole. The memory of a higher law, the memory of the law of God, continues to recede from popular consciousness. The people have forgotten God, and the nations have taken His place.

In the West we inherit many centuries of Christian thought and practice relating to civil government. We find it difficult to appropriate much of that experience, however, because democracy has replaced monarchy as the norm for governments. A more basic change, though, has taken place: the governments of modern nations do not admit to ruling by the grace of God, as Israel's and Christendom's kings did. Even Christians generally confine Jesus Christ and His law to private, family, and church circles.

As a result, public life in the West is being thoroughly de-Christianized, while ethical and legal standards are becoming more and more openly pagan.

Because of the apostasy of the West, the most basic issue today with regard to civil government is whether nations and governments should be self-consciously and explicitly Christian, as they once were. If the answer is no, and over a thousand years of Christendom was simply a colossal mistake on the part of Christians, then Western Christians should continue adjusting to the modern world, oppose certain moral evils as just one more special interest group, and maybe try to carve out a secure niche for themselves somewhere. If, however, the Lord calls nations and governments to acknowledge His rule and obey His law, then Christians must tell nations and governments what the Lord demands: open and explicit obedience to Him. The church itself must assert the principle of Christian government and the goal of a Christian nation.

The basic political fact of our times remains this: Jesus the Messiah has all authority in heaven and on earth. He will not allow His glory to go to another. The tragedies of the twentieth century warn that God will not be patient forever. And like Isaiah who saw Assyria coming, we are not unaware of the threats of nuclear warfare, financial collapse, and worldwide plague. The gospel that is such wonderful perfume to us is a loathsome stench to a rebellious world, because Jesus Christ is a rock that will make those who reject Him stumble and fall (2 Cor. 2:14-16; 1 Pet. 2:6-8).

Christ Known, but Not Honored

After the European explorers discovered the Americas, the Christian gospel spread to new territories. Offspring of the West, the United States is also the New World. Is it Christian? No!

From its beginning as a new nation in 1776—and that is the proper time to date the beginning of our country as Abraham Lincoln declaimed in his Gettysburg Address—the United States of America has refused to acknowledge the sovereignty of Jesus Christ. Christendom, the Old World, is apostate. America, the New World, is still pagan.

At the time of the Revolution of 1776 and the writing of the Constitution of 1787, the leaders of the nation chose not to honor God as God. Holding the truth in unrighteousness, they established a government that recognized the people alone as the source of its authority.

Their foolish failure to give glory to God has contributed to the glorification of man and the disappearance of God from our public life. "Life, liberty, and the pursuit of happiness" has replaced life, liberty, and the pursuit of godliness. As a collective whole, the American people serve and worship the creature rather than the Creator. Since Americans

> did not see fit to acknowledge God, God gave them up to a base mind and to improper conduct. They were filled with all manner of wickedness, evil, covetousness, malice. . . . Though they know God's decree that those who do such things deserve to die, they not only do them but approve those who practice them (Rom. 1:28-29, 32).

Pagan roots did not produce their noxious fruit all at once. Because of the godly beginnings of the colonies and the private faith of many individual believers, the United States throughout its history has experienced much good. In the minds of many believers, in fact, their country is — or was until very recently — a Christian nation.

In the 1780s there was not yet any clearly-defined category of a secular state. According to popular consciousness, America was a Christian nation because it was neither Jewish nor Muslim. Unlike the French Jacobins, who openly sought to replace the Christian God with the goddess Reason, the American Revolutionary leaders did not try to de-Christianize the country. They did not disturb state constitutions that recognized God or established churches. Traditional practices, such as appointing chaplains to official bodies or proclaiming days of prayer, continued.

Many of the basic principles of the 1787 Constitution reflect the influence of Christian tradition. The doctrine of express powers limiting the authority of the national government, for instance, implies the existence of another authority beyond the government's. All Christians can name that other authority, who is God speaking through His Son in the Scriptures, but the Constitution does not name Him. Current democratic theory considers that final authority to be the collective people. The doctrines of separation of powers and of checks and balances indicate a distrust of human nature. Christians know that such distrust is warranted because all men are sinners.[6]

6. Some of the more incidental aspects of the Constitution also assume a Christian society. The Christian Sabbath, for example, lies behind the provision that the president has "ten days (Sundays excepted)" to veto a bill from Congress. The Constitution's Framers concluded their work by signing it "in the Year of our Lord one thousand seven hundred and Eighty-seven."

In a phrase that reminds one of the later French Jacobin scheme to renumber the years beginning with the overthrow of the Bourbon Monarchy, however, they continued, "and of the Independence of the United States of America the Twelfth."

The effort to make the Founding Fathers appear as militant secularists, like their French contemporaries, is a distortion of history. When today's secular elites intone the First Amendment and rant about the wall of separation between church and state, so as to bludgeon Christians into public silence, they attribute a modern mentality to the architects of the Constitution, which they did not have. In fact, most of the Founding Fathers were *indifferent* to Jesus Christ (itself a terrible sin).

The Constitutional Convention never voted on Benjamin Franklin's motion to begin each day's deliberations with prayer. In total contradiction of the Bible, the Constitution permitted the man-stealing slave trade to continue until 1808. When asked why the Constitution did not mention God, Alexander Hamilton reportedly replied that the Framers had forgotten to.[7]

In 1797 the president signed and Congress ratified a treaty with Muslim Tripoli, which in its English translation stated:

> As the government of the United States is not in any sense founded on the Christian Religion, — as it has in itself no character of enmity against the laws, religion or tranquility of Mussulman . . . it is declared by the parties that no pretext arising from religious opinions shall ever produce an interruption of the harmony existing between the two countries.[8]

This treaty clause does not by itself prove that the Founding Fathers had adopted a clearly defined secularist philosophy of government. It does show, though, that the first leaders of our country were ready to exploit the Constitution's silence regarding Christianity to smooth the way to peace with a Muslim state.

The silence of the American Constitution regarding God is especially striking because the Founding Fathers wrote it against the background of Christian Europe and Christian colonial charters. As explained in the previous section, the kings and their governments in Western Christendom professed explicit faith in Jesus Christ. The coronation ceremonies emphasized that kings ruled by the grace of God. Through the centuries, moreover, the law of Christ had a deep and profound influence on the laws and life of Christendom. Consequently, the American colonies inherited a tremendous Christian body of law and custom.

---

7. Mark A. Noll, *The Search for Christian America* (Westchester, Ill.: Crossway, 1983), p. 107.

8. Ibid., p. 131.

The colonial charters issued by the kings of England acknowledged the reign of Jesus Christ, as did the documents written by the first colonists. The charter of Virginia named the spread of the Christian religion to the Indians as one of the reasons for its founding. In the Mayflower Compact the Pilgrims covenanted themselves together into a body politic "for the glory of God, and advancement of the Christian religion." The charter for the Massachusetts Bay Colony, the Fundamental Orders of Connecticut written in the New World in 1639, and William Penn's 1682 First Frame of Government for Pennsylvania all contained similar statements.

The colonial charters, like the kings in Christendom, openly professed commitment to the Bible and to the Christian religion. The Constitution's silence concerning God, Jesus Christ, the Bible, and the church is in striking contrast to the previous traditions of Christendom and to the colonial charters. Unlike the new Canadian constitution adopted in 1982, which begins modestly, "Whereas Canada is founded upon principles that recognize the Supremacy of God and the rule of law . . . ," the Preamble to the United States Constitution begins with a haughty boast of human power:

> We the People of the United States, in Order to form a more perfect Union, establish Justice, insure domestic tranquility, provide for the common defence, promote the general Welfare, and secure the Blessings of Liberty to ourselves and our Posterity, do ordain and establish this Constitution for the United States of America.[9]

Who gives the people the right to set up a government, pass laws, and enforce them? God does. But the American Constitution mentions no final authority except the People.

By their indifference toward God, the Framers of the Constitution unavoidably accepted the Enlightenment doctrine of popular sovereignty. And today lawyers, teachers, politicians, and voters understand the Constitution as deriving its power from the people alone.

How could the Founders of the American Republic so easily ignore God in their work? One explanation often mentioned is the existence in different colonies of competing churches. No church communion was ready to accept the establishment of some other denomination, and memories of Europe's religious wars made American Christians wary of asserting their claims too strongly. Pennsylvania, however, had already

---

9. See *Reformed Perspective* 1, 2 (February 1982): 28, where the contrast between the new Canadian and the American Constitutions is discussed.

shown that it was possible both to avoid an established church and practice toleration of all Christian denominations and still found the government on an open declaration of Christian principle. In adopting a Constitution that did not explicitly mention Christianity, the Framers had
more in mind than simply a desire to avoid religious strife.

The intellectual climate of the West in general had by 1776 begun to
turn against Christianity. The English Enlightenment, which simply
reasoned without God, was followed by the French and German En-
lightenments, which reasoned positively against God. Some of the
Founding Fathers, most notably Thomas Jefferson, were deists; few
could be called earnest Christians. There was, in fact, by the time of the
Revolution, a bifurcation in the colonies between the educated non-
clerical elite, which was readily absorbing Enlightenment thought from
Europe, and the mass of people who were listening to and believing orthodox preaching.

The Founding Fathers were literate men. They knew the Bible and
read the ancient classical writers, such as Cicero, Livy, Plutarch, and
Aristotle, and the many different Enlightenment philosophers. Drawing
on their reading and practical experience of governing, they framed the
Constitution. They did not try to reason from the Bible or from the great
Christian theologians like Augustine, Aquinas, or Calvin — all of whom
dealt significantly with civil government — for inspiration and direction.
Theirs was no clearly intended Christian theory of government like
William Penn's or the Puritan's. They went with the flow of developing
Western thought; and by the late eighteenth century that thought was
becoming decidedly secular in character, even if the concept had not yet
been clearly formulated or given a name. Even Presbyterian clergyman
John Witherspoon, who participated in the Constitutional Convention,
did not think in any distinctively Christian way about politics.[10]

While the nation's leaders shared in the general drift of Western thought
in the eighteenth century, among ordinary Americans the Great Awakening had lost some of its force and influence by the time of the Revolution.
By 1790 a lessening of spiritual intensity in the colonies was evident.

In God's mercy a second spiritual awakening revived American Christianity and spread across Europe after 1800. The French Revolution
shocked countless Europeans and Americans, many of whom blamed its
excesses on Enlightenment ideas of reason, human rights, equality, and
democracy. Deism ceased to be fashionable, and many of Western society's leaders returned to Christianity.

10. See Noll, *The Search for Christian America*, pp. 86-95.

In the new United States, Enlightenment understandings of equality and a belief in reason and liberty were institutionalized in political life, but there was an accommodation with Christianity.[11] It was accepted as the guarantor of moral behavior and hence of public order while its claims to truth were ignored in the public arena. The clergy, many of whom had at first supported the Revolution and had subsequently become alarmed by the increase in moral degeneracy and godlessness that they perceived during the war, adapted to the new American society. They accepted the new doctrine of the separation of church and state, but they reminded leaders and people alike of the importance of religion in maintaining public morals and public order.[12]

Throughout the nineteenth century in the United States there was an unstable synthesis of intense private religion and a public order that officially recognized no god except the people. Christians actively promoted a number of reform movements, but they did not challenge the Constitution's silence regarding Christ. Instead, they joined in the general American adulation of the Founding Fathers and their work. Public life was left to the realm of nature, while grace was reserved for private life.[13]

This arrangement of private religion and public irreligion produced religious peace for the most part, while American society slowly became secularized. In the years before the Civil War, education began to be removed from the private to the public sphere. By the end of the nineteenth century public schools with a lowest-common-denominator Protestant ethos had replaced church education and family instruction. After the Civil War institutions of higher education began to follow the German model, and clergymen ceased to be university presidents. By the end of the century judicial thinking began to think of the law not as God-given but as created by men.[14] Nature was slowly devouring grace. In other words, the parts of life governed by autonomous human reason expanded, and the areas devoted to Jesus Christ contracted. Worse yet,

11. D. H. Meyer, "The Uniqueness of the American Enlightenment," *American Quarterly* 28, 2 (1976): 165-86.

12. Emory Elliott, "The Dove and the Serpent: The Clergy in the American Revolution," *American Quarterly* 31, 2 (1979): 187-203.

13. The great medieval theologian Thomas Aquinas reconciled Aristotle's teaching with the Bible by arguing that unaided human reason could truly discover certain truths of nature, but that men needed God's revelation to learn the truths of grace. He divided knowledge therefore into two realms: that of *nature*, where human reason could work unaided, and that of *grace*, where men needed the Bible to assist their reason.

14. See John W. Whitehead, *The Second American Revolution* (Westchester, Ill.: Crossway, 1982).

those parts of life left outside the law of Jesus Christ tended to become hostile to Him.

The United States, which did not want to honor God as God in its public and corporate life, in the twentieth century has become increasingly confused about who God is. Sects and cults multiply, while a vague secular humanism functions as a new state religion. Religious confusion has produced moral confusion. Not only can millions of Americans no longer tell right from wrong, they cannot even think in moral terms. Psychology has replaced ethics, for example, as the basis for human relationships, and senators rely on opinion polls to tell them how to vote on moral issues. In today's popular mind the United States is a secular country where religion is tolerated but must keep its place. The public schools maintain a rigid silence about religion and ethics but, in fact, undermine Christian faith. The state constitutions, which once acknowledged God's authority, have been rewritten in line with the federal Constitution. The Supreme Court leads the federal courts and the Congress in revising our laws to eliminate remaining traces of biblical influence.

Nature is rapidly consuming Grace, but American Christians refuse to criticize the Constitution.[15] Instead, along with other Americans, Christians continue to praise the Constitution as the foundation of our country's peace and prosperity.

The United States in the last thirty years has been swept with a religious and moral revolution. Now a reaction is taking place. Will the reaction merely restore an earlier balance between Christianity and secularism, with a little bit of "values" teaching in the public schools to slow the moral rot? If so, the reform will not be lasting. Instead, Christians need to rethink radically the relationship between government and Jesus Christ and reform America as a Christian nation covenanted to be the Lord's. Nothing else will continue the traditions of Christendom. Nothing else will honor the Son as He should be honored. Jesus Christ will not long allow His glory to be stolen by anyone, not even by the collective people. The basic political fact of our times remains this: Jesus the Messiah has all authority in heaven and on earth.

National Confession: A Covenanted People

The American people have agreed to govern themselves by a secular covenant, a basic written law — the Constitution. In it the people have

---

15. See Francis Schaeffer, *Escape From Reason* (Downers Grove, Ill.: Inter-Varsity Press, 1968) for a discussion of the historical process by which an autonomous realm of Nature in human affairs "eats up" a restricted realm of Grace.

given elected representatives and appointed judges certain defined powers and have prohibited them from doing certain things. The people are king, and through their representatives they can change laws and even amend the Constitution. The Constitution is secular because it is not enacted in the name of any god but only by the authority of the people.

To become a Christian nation the American kings, the people, should covenant together to be the Lord's. The American nation, that is, should confess its faith in Jesus Christ, recognize His rule, and submit to His law. The Preamble to the Constitution should be amended to read:

> We the people of the United States, humbly acknowledging Almighty God as the source of all authority and power in civil government, the Lord Jesus Christ as the Governor among the nations, and His revealed will as of supreme authority, in order to constitute a Christian government . . . do ordain and establish this Constitution for the United States of America.

The National Reform Association, founded in 1864, actually proposed such an amendment once. It attracted the support of such noted people as Charles and A. A. Hodge of Princeton Seminary, Associate Supreme Court Justice William Strong, a U.S. senator, and some state governors. The House of Representatives debated the proposal in 1874 and again in 1896, rejecting it both times.[16]

One can imagine the authors of the Constitution beginning their work with such a statement of national Christian faith. They did not. It is almost inconceivable that the present pluralistic populace would accept such a proposal. It would be looked upon as an effort to impose the Ayatollah's government on the United States. So why demand it?

Christ Commissioned His Church to Preach to Kings

Once, when there were kings who ruled, Christians preached to them. The conversion of one of them, Constantine, led to the adoption of Christianity as the religion of the West and the gradual reshaping of its laws under the Bible's influence. Earlier conversions of Roman governors and officials certainly made them better officials, but only the public profession of faith by the emperor began to change the laws by which the governors ruled.

The American president, Congress, and judges are in the subordinate position that governors and local officials of the Roman Empire used to

16. See Gary Scott Smith, *The Seeds of Secularization. Calvinism, Culture, and Pluralism in America, 1870-1915* (Grand Rapids: Eerdmans, 1985), pp. 53-73.

occupy. The American people and their Constitution are in the position of emperor. Simply telling elected officials to obey Christ is, therefore, not sufficient to produce a radical redirection of America, for it fails to recognize that American officials are subordinates. It is to the highest political authority that we must preach; it is the people who must be converted.[17]

When the American church, or a good part of it, demands that the people amend their Constitution to recognize the law and authority of Jesus Christ, it will be preaching to kings again, "Serve the Lord with fear, with trembling kiss his feet" (Ps. 2:11). Without preaching national submission to Jesus our evangelism can never be more than proclaiming a private Jesus, and our claim that He has all authority lacks public meaning.

Why can we not just accept the present religious pluralism of American life as an unchangeable fact and adjust to it? Christianity is a missionary religion that claims universal validity and universal authority; therefore, its adherents cannot accept religious pluralism as a satisfactory state of affairs. Whenever Christians do not preach Christ's demand that all people in all their capacities obey Him, they fail to declare the unique claim of the gospel: all authority in heaven and on earth has been given to Christ, and therefore in Christ alone is there salvation. Explicit or implicit acceptance of religious pluralism unavoidably undercuts the church's evangelism.

Sometimes Christians think that if they produce a model community then others in society will see it and embrace the gospel. That did not happen with ancient Israel, however, and it will not happen in the gospel age. Instead, Christians must urge people to accept Christ and become part of His kingdom.

In the Turkish Ottoman Empire the Sultan enforced a kind of religious pluralism. Everyone had to accept it. Orthodox Christians, Armenian Christians, and other religious groups were organized into their own distinctive communities or *millets*. Each *millet* had its own schools and enforced its own laws on its members. All paid taxes to the Sultan. Because religious conversions disrupted society, evangelizing was forbidden. In the popular mind "changing your religion" became one of the greatest sins. In Cyprus — part of the Ottoman Empire until 1878 — I knew Christians during my four years there in the early 1970s who shrank from encouraging their Muslim neighbors to commit such "sin."

---

17. I write as a naive democrat, of course. The people do not all exercise equal political power in America. Various educated and wealthy elites and certain well-organized pressure groups possess influence far in excess of their numbers. Nevertheless, there is some real truth in official democratic theory that the people rule as sovereign in America.

In the Netherlands today society is organized along religiously pluralist lines. This kind of political and social organization will inevitably, if it has not already, end aggressive Christian evangelism. When Christianity does not claim universal validity and authority, the church loses its power to call outsiders to repentance and faith.

In the United States, despite the recent earnest preaching of pluralism, people have tended to think of the country as a unitary society, a "melting pot" in which all immigrants become Americans. Many Christians have naively considered the country Christian and have not thought that attempting to evangelize their neighbors would disrupt the social fabric. But if we finally and clearly accept the idea of the legitimate existence and maintenance of different "faith communities," then proselytizing will become an offense against social peace. If the church accepts the doctrine of religious pluralism, it will, without meaning to do so, give up its claim to call all men to repentance.

But if the church broadens its message to address the American people as the kings of this land, calling them in their capacity as rulers to repent and trust in Christ, then its evangelism will take on a fresh clarity and urgency. We seek a Christian amendment to the Constitution in order to preach to the American kings that they must repent and confess Jesus the Christ as Lord and Savior.

Christ Is Calling the Nations Into His Kingdom

American Christians, like Christians in the West generally, are deeply demoralized. Over the last two hundred years the church has endured so many defeats that believers no longer think that it is Jesus' plan to call whole nations to be Christian. The most that American believers hope for is to convert individuals, establish Christian families, influence a few minor institutions on the fringes of society, and slow down society's moral degeneration. American Christians have been so affected by defeatist theologies and by history textbooks that make the Puritans seem like ogres and the Carthaginians like good neighbors that they unthinkingly reject the possibility or desirability of a Christian nation. The truth is, however, that Christ is calling the nations to be His. Nations in the past have professed the Christian faith, and nations in the future will do the same.

Isaiah prophesied:

> It shall come to pass in the latter days that the mountain of the house of the Lord shall be established as the highest of the mountains . . . and all the nations shall flow to it, and many peoples

shall come, and say: "Come, let us go up to the mountain of the Lord . . . that he may teach us his ways and that we may walk in his paths" (Isa. 2:2-3; see also Zech. 2:10-11).

The "latter days" are the gospel age. The conversion of the nations began on the day of Pentecost when the Jews and proselytes from all over the Roman Empire and beyond heard the Good News in their own languages. No longer did one have to leave his own nation to become part of the kingdom of God! The kingdom of God, once limited to Abraham's family and then to the single nation of Israel, could embrace all nations.

Over the last two thousand years entire nations have professed Christian faith: Armenia, Ethiopia, the Roman Empire, and those nations which called themselves Christendom. Like Israel, these nations are now largely apostate, but that does not negate the reality of their earlier profession.[18]

But how can a *nation* be Christian? Is not the church the new nation of God? Of course it is. To the church Peter wrote, "But you are a . . . holy nation" (1 Pet. 2:9). The church is also a household, a bride, a priesthood, a building, and a body. But the church is not literally a household, a bride, a priesthood, a body, or a building; nor is it a nation.

The church, as the household of God, for example, does not replace ordinary human families, even though it inherits the promises made to Abraham and his family. Families still exist, and like Abraham's family, they can be part of the kingdom of God, but they can never be identical with God's kingdom on earth as Abraham's family once was. God wants families to be in the kingdom. In some families only individuals belong to Christ—often a child or a wife. In other cases whole families are distinctively committed to Christ—usually because the head of the family has declared with Joshua, "But as for me and my house, we will serve the Lord" (Josh. 24:15). Some family members may be rebellious, but the conscious identity, the ideal of family life, and the manner of living together are Christian and are drawn from the Scriptures.

The church is also like a nation, but it does not replace nations, even though it inherits the promises made to Israel. Since the coming of Christ nations still exist, and like Israel they can be part of the kingdom of God, but they can never be identical with the kingdom of God on earth as Israel once was. God wants the nations to come to Christ. Jesus told His followers to disciple the nations. In some nations individuals

---

18. See Romans 11 on how Christ will cast out unfaithful Gentile branches that have been grafted into His kingdom.

and families belong to Christ, gathered usually into the church. In some cases whole nations have professed Christian faith.[19]

Throughout history, a king's profession of Christian faith often led to the adoption of Christianity by his kingdom as a whole. Christian kings often supported the church's evangelism, listened to Christian counselors, and issued laws influenced by the Bible.

As democracies replaced monarchies and Christendom gave way to apostasy, the devil seems to have won a great victory. Modern nations are very conscious of their identity, and that identity does not include belonging to Jesus Christ. But God has a way of turning Satan's triumphs into his greatest defeats. Perhaps the adoption of a national Christian profession in a democratic rather than a monarchical context will lead to a more thorough national obedience than has yet occurred. Kings sometimes made nations Christian from the top down; but a democratic nation that became explicitly Christian would do so from the bottom up, providing the basis for radically biblical reforms. That may seem impossible. With men it is. But it is no more impossible than the conversion of the Roman Empire or the outbreak of the Reformation or the salvation of a rich man.

Christ Tells Government to Rule Justly

Everyone demands justice from a government, but what is the standard of justice? When Christians speak of justice, they mean justice according to the law of Christ. There is no other eternal, absolute standard of justice. The call for a Christian amendment to our Constitution explicitly affirms Christ's claim that His law should be obeyed.

What does the Bible teach about civil government? God has given civil government a three-fold task: to regulate and organize the life of the whole territory or tribe for the common good, to restrain open expressions of wickedness, and to foster the work of the church.

Even if there were no sin in the world, promoting the common good would be the first task of civil rulers. For the common good, civil governments create and enforce rules of the highway. Likewise, governments usually coin money to facilitate business transactions. Jesus indicated that the use of a government's money implied acceptance of its authority and the consequent duty of paying taxes (Mark 12:14-17).

19. See David M. Kemmerer, "Of Mass Baptisms, National Churches, and the Great Commission," *Christian History* 7, 2 (1988): 16-18, for a discussion of the conversion of Kievan Rus c. 988.

Sin's intrusion into the world makes restraining evil a second necessary work of civil government. After the Flood God announced His intention of partially punishing and restraining evil by human means. God's Word warns: "But if you do wrong, be afraid, for he [the civil authority] does not bear the sword in vain; he is the servant of God to execute his wrath on the wrongdoer" (Rom. 13:4).

Christ's ascension to God's right hand as King of kings and Lord of lords gives civil government its third task—fostering the work of the church. Christ is now head over all things, including governments, for the sake of the church, which is His body (Eph. 1:22). Many of the most important decisions of the Councils of Nicaea and Chalcedon and the Westminster Standards were written by church officers meeting at the call of and under the protection of civil rulers.

In God's providence civil governments usually fulfill, at least partially, His intentions. They organize the life of society so that all people benefit from certain rules and regulations. They arrest and punish murderers and thieves. They maintain a certain level of peace so that the gospel can be preached. This occurs because "the king's heart is a stream of water in the hand of the Lord; he turns it wherever he will" (Prov. 21:1). God instructs us to pray "for kings and all who are in high positions" (1 Tim. 2:2).

Even though civil governments cannot help fulfilling in part God's purposes for them, they often do evil as well as good. They attempt to hinder the church by persecuting it. They reward evil rather than good and, at their worst, make war on their own people. Exceeding their authority, states suffocate human freedom by trying to regulate every aspect of life. Because of such sin, God periodically judges civil governments, destroying one even while He makes another prosper. God punishes rulers for breaking His law.[20] Such sin springs from the refusal of rulers to hear God's voice and bow in repentance and faith before God's anointed King, Jesus.

The Bible clearly teaches Christians to obey even pagan governments (Rom. 13:1-2; 1 Pet. 2:13-14). In monarchical contexts these instructions imply a certain political quietism on the part of most believers; their political responsibilities are only to obey the law except where it requires them to sin, to respect authority, and to pay their taxes conscientiously. The biblical command of obedience still holds under democratic governments, but, as citizens, Christians are now rulers as well as subjects. All

---

20. See Daniel 5, for example, for God's judgment of Belshazzar and the Kingdom of Babylon.

the biblical commands to rulers to do justice apply to them as citizens; political activism, rather than quietism, is demanded.

However, the Christian citizen has a major problem when he tries to become politically active in a modern democracy. In a democracy authority flows in theory from the bottom up rather than from the top down. Laws are not given *to* the people, rather they come *from* the people. Citizens of democracies tend to think, therefore, that the people can do no wrong in any absolute sense, that a nation cannot be unjust to itself.

Only by rejecting the doctrine of popular sovereignty can Christians in democratic countries have a solid foundation for assuring justice. Jesus, not the people, is sovereign. The words addressed to kings in Psalm 2 apply in a democracy to the people or to the nation as a whole. God commands rulers to accept the law of His Son, the one to whom He has given the nations (Ps. 2:8, 10-12).

Rejecting the theory of popular sovereignty does not mean repudiating the system of constitutional representative government. It means, instead, that in political discussion American Christians will reason from the Scriptures, not because that is their particular bias as another pressure group, but because the Bible is the only finally valid basis for law. There is no other standard of justice in the universe than God's law. In addressing rulers the Lord portrays Himself as judge of the judges. He does not merely demand justice: "How long will you judge unjustly and show partiality to the wicked?" He also spells out what justice means: "Give justice to the weak and the fatherless; maintain the right of the afflicted and the destitute. Rescue the weak and the needy" (Ps. 82:2-4). Public opinion, even Christian public opinion, is not the proper basis for law; only the Bible is.

Which laws in the Bible should be applied to modern industrial democracies? That is an important question. Yet it is not germane to the American situation as long as Christians accept the dogma of popular sovereignty and the nation refuses to acknowledge Jesus as King. And the barrier in people's minds to recognizing Jesus as King over America is not primarily concern about which biblical laws would be enforced, but, rather, that sinful and unregenerate man will not confess that Jesus is Lord. Those who assert Jesus' sovereignty over nations can begin to change the nature of political debate in our country by continually asking, What does the Bible say?

Which biblical laws should apply? America's law should be based on the Ten Commandments. Spoken aloud by God Himself at Mount Sinai, engraved on tablets of stone, and stated in universal language, they hold a special place in the Old Covenant. Much of the rest of the Old Covenant law shows how God applied the Ten Commandments to a whole nation, Israel, and it concretely explains the implications of the Ten Commandments for a nation's law code.

What will be the place of non-Christians in a Christian nation? Jesus' parable of the wheat and tares teaches clearly that believers and unbelievers will always be mixed together in this life (Matt. 13). The mixing occurs in all human contexts — families, churches, nations. For the sake of the wheat, the owner of the field tells his workers not to destroy the tares. In a Christian nation unbelievers will not be "uprooted." There will be no forced conversions; the attempt to do so would harm everyone. The presence of "tares," and of continuing sin in believers, means that a Christian nation, like any Christian family or church or individual, will be imperfect. Sin will remain; all utopianism is excluded.

In summation, the United States of America should amend its Constitution to recognize the sovereignty and law of Jesus Christ. The theory of popular sovereignty must be rejected. The amendment is necessary because Christ warns kings to submit to Him, because He claims the nations for Himself, and because such an amendment will enable us to begin basing our laws on the only sure foundation of law, the revelation of God.

Even though such an amendment is politically impossible at this time, the church should still demand it for three reasons: (1) to preach God's Word to the kings of this land and make it clear that the gospel is not just a private matter; (2) God promises the nations to His Son (nations have been Christian in the past and will be Christian in the future); and (3) to provide Christians a clear platform from which to demand reforms of the law in a biblical direction.

*   *   *   *   *

Appendix: Social Covenanting

The Puritan settlers of New England organized many of their towns on the basis of town covenants.[21] Unlike colonial charters, which were issued from the top down (from the king), the New England town cove-

---

21. During those same years in the British Isles the Scots signed a National Covenant in 1638 to further the Reformation in that country, and in 1643 they formed a Solemn League and Covenant with England and Ireland. All of those covenants were written in the name of God in Christ and were subscribed to in obedience to Him.

nants were drawn up by local leaders and endorsed by the townsmen. They provided the legal framework for that region's famous town meetings.

Much of the materials in the town covenants were based upon biblical teachings, while reverence for the God whom they worshiped in common motivated the settlers to live peaceful and orderly lives. The covenants helped to create social order in a new environment with a minimal use of force. Writing covenants enabled Americans to cooperate and establish civil authority under God among themselves.

Like the town covenants, the American Constitution also created authority peacefully, deriving it from the consent of the people, bottom up, rather than from the concession of a king or the "natural" authority of a patriarchal tribal leader. However, the American Constitution differed from the town covenants in a crucial respect: it made no clear reference to God as the source of its authority or to God as the goal of human life. In short, the Constitution is a secularized town covenant.

The writing of town covenants clearly owes much to the example of covenants found in the Bible. There we find the great covenants that God made with mankind (Noahic, Abrahamic, Mosaic, Davidic, New) and instances of Israel renewing the Mosaic covenant in great national ceremonies (the entire Book of Deuteronomy; Josh. 8:30-35; 24; 2 Chron. 15:12-13; 34:29-32). We also find numerous examples of covenants made between individuals and social groups, which we will call social covenants.

The Mosaic covenant established two regulations concerning social covenants. First, God did not allow Israel to make a covenant with any Canaanite nation (Exod. 23:32; 34:12; Deut. 7:2). Second, all oath-taking had to be done in the Lord's name (Deut. 10:20), and anything sworn in the Lord's name had to be fulfilled (Exod. 20:7).

Israelites swore oaths in support either of individually made vows or of covenants that bound two or more people together. In the oath they called on God to witness their words and to punish nonfulfillment of the private vow or the social covenant. Covenants had to be consistent with God's law.

Social covenants could be of several kinds. Two individuals could make a covenant together. David and Jonathan, for example, covenanted to be friends (see 1 Sam. 18:3-4; 20:8, 12-17; 23:15-18; 2 Sam. 3:12-13; 5:1-3; 23:1-5).

A somewhat different sort of covenant united not two individuals but a leader and his followers. David and Israel covenanted together to make him king (2 Sam. 5:1-3). Years later, Jehoiada and the temple guards covenanted together to make Joash king (2 Kings 11:4). After the return from exile, Nehemiah and the people covenanted together to obey the law, even signing their names on the covenant document.

Social covenanting was a part of Israel's life from the time the Jews entered Canaan until the days of their return from Babylon. The practice of covenanting, in fact, predated the Old Covenant: Jacob and Laban made a covenant together (Gen. 31:43-54). The social covenants united individuals, or a leader and his followers, or Israel and a foreign nation. The Mosaic law itself recognized the practice of social covenanting by regulating it.

The New Covenant brought by Jesus Christ has today fulfilled the Mosaic covenant as a second administration of the Abrahamic covenant. The Mosaic covenant, also called the Old Covenant, was the first dispensation of grace according to the promises made to Abraham; the New Covenant is the second and final dispensation of grace. The Old Covenant included only Israel; the New Covenant includes all nations and exhibits grace and salvation, not by the types and ordinances of the Old Covenant, but directly and fully in Jesus Christ.

What is the place of social covenanting under the New Covenant? In particular, can natural social groups such as families and nations covenant together for purposes consistent with the New Covenant the way Israelites could under the Old Covenant? Yes. As we have noted, whole nations in past centuries have identified themselves as Christian. Scotland, in fact, signed a covenant to be the Lord's and to further the Reformation, and early New England's towns covenanted to serve the Lord.

Isaiah prophesied that one day the Egyptians and the Assyrians would worship God (Isa. 19:19-25). Jesus phrased the Great Commission in a way that sounds odd to us: "Go therefore and disciple all the nations, baptizing them . . . teaching them . . ." (Matt. 20:19). On the day of Pentecost Peter addressed "all the house of Israel" (Acts 2:36); he and Paul clearly thought that the whole Israelite nation should acknowledge its Messiah (see Rom. 9-11). The Bible ends by picturing the New Jerusalem with a river flanked by the tree of life with its twelve kinds of fruit, "and the leaves of the tree were for the healing of the nations" (Rev. 22:2).

In the New England town covenants and in the Scottish National Covenant civic groups were covenanting to fulfill purposes consistent with the New Covenant. They unmistakably thought of themselves, not simply as Christian individuals, families, or churches, but as Christian towns and a Christian nation.

Tragically, the American Constitution is a secular covenant. The Founding Fathers divided life into a public sphere where Christ and His law were not recognized and a private sphere where they could be. Two hundred years later the public sphere has expanded, and the private sphere has shrunk — public life has turned in an anti-Christian direction as God's law is blatantly broken.

Repentance is always possible, however. America can return to its colonial roots and turn away in horror from the awful sin now tolerated in this land. Elected leaders in cooperation with church leaders can renounce murder (abortion), theft, (from future generations through budget deficits and environmental ruination), and adultery (encouraged by easy divorce and remarriage laws and legal pornography). They can end the secular public education that ignores God and, thereby, teaches children that He is irrelevant to life. In addition to a national turning from these and other sins, America can amend the Constitution to recognize the law and authority of the Lord Jesus. Such an amendment would transform the Constitution from a secular covenant into a Christian social covenant, laying the groundwork for the progressive refashioning of American life along biblical lines.

"Blessed is the nation whose God is the Lord, the people whom he has chosen as his heritage" (Ps. 33:12). "Righteousness exalts a nation, but sin is a reproach to any people" (Prov. 14:34).

14

The Theonomic Response to National Confessionalism

Gary DeMar *

What criteria should be used to determine whether America can be described as a "Christian nation"? Do we go to the character of the people or to the documents they draft? Some belief system, some prevailing ideology makes up the warp and woof of every civilization. An analysis of any nation at any point in time will tell us what gives meaning to the people and their institutions. A nation's religious foundation can be determined by looking at its economic system, judicial pronouncements, educational goals, and taxing policy. Look at a nation's art and music, and there you will find its religion. Read its books and newspapers. Watch its television programs. The outgrowth of civilization will be present on every page and in every program. These are all determiners of a nation's religious commitment.

God evaluates a nation's allegiance to Him based on behavior, not slogans. God considers ethics and not merely profession. Behavior is a more accurate barometer of a nation's religious commitment than profession. "What people *do* frequently speaks louder and is more revealing than anything they *say*, or *claim to believe*."[1] It is not unusual, therefore, to see the emphasis that the Bible places on behavior as evidence that a profession is true (e.g., James 1:22).

In Jeremiah's day the people believed that having the temple was evidence enough of faithfulness to God. Their prior commitment to the Lord was thought to ensure present and future security.

*Gary DeMar received the B.A. from Western Michigan University in 1973 and the M.Div. from Reformed Presbyterian Seminary in Jackson, MS in 1979. Following pastoral service and teaching at Mt. Vernon Christian Academy in Atlanta, he became president of American Vision in Atlanta in 1986. Among his numerous publications are *God and Government: A Biblical and Historical Study* (1982), *God and Government: Issues in Biblical Perspective* (1984), *God and Government: The Restoration of the Republic* (1986), *Ruler of the Nations: Biblical Blueprints for Government* (1987), and *Reduction of Christianity* (1988).

1. Timothy P. Weber, *Living in the Shadow of the Second Coming: American Premillennialism: 1875-1982*, rev. ed. (Grand Rapids: Zondervan, 1983), p. 7.

Thus says the Lord of hosts, the God of Israel, "Amend your ways and your deeds, and I will let you dwell in this place. Do not trust in deceptive words, saying, 'This is the Temple of the Lord, the temple of the Lord, the temple of the Lord.' For if you truly amend your ways and your deeds, if you truly practice justice between a man and his neighbor, if you do not oppress the alien, the orphan, or the widow, and do not shed innocent blood in this place, nor walk after other gods to your own ruin, then I will let you dwell in this place, in the land that I gave to your fathers forever and ever" (Jer. 7:3-7, NASB).

The temple was a symbol of God's presence with the nation and of the nation's former allegiance. It was not enough. God wanted the people to keep His covenant demands as well as maintain the temple.

We make a mistake if we believe that religious pronouncements make us a Christian nation or that an absence of them makes us a non-Christian nation.[2] For example, President Reagan declared 1983 to be The Year of the Bible after the Senate and House of Representatives authorized and requested him to do so. This Joint Resolution stated the following:

The Bible, the Word of God, has made a unique contribution in shaping the United States as a distinctive and blessed nation. . . . deeply held religious convictions springing from the Holy Scriptures led to the early settlement of our Nation. . . . Biblical teachings inspired concepts of civil government that are contained in our Declaration of Independence and the Constitution of the United States. . . . the history of our nation clearly illustrates the value of voluntarily applying the teachings of the Scriptures in the lives of individuals, families, and societies.[3]

The slaughter of unborn innocents continued even as the ink dried on the proclamation. Can a nation assuage its guilt with words minus deeds? Does a document, declaration, or proclamation make a nation

---

2. The same reasoning process is sometimes used with the Book of Esther: "There can be no doubt that the historicity and canonicity of Esther has been the most debated of all the Old Testament books. Even some Jewish scholars questioned its inclusion in the Old Testament because of the absence of God's name." Edward G. Dobson, "Esther," in *Liberty Bible Commentary*, executive editor, Jerry Falwell (Lynchburg, Va.: The Old-Time Gospel Hour, 1982), p. 909.

3. Public Law 97-280, 96 Stat. 1211, approved October 4, 1982.

Christian?[4] Presidents from George Washington to Ronald Reagan
have been sworn into office with their hands on an open Bible.[5] Have
their actions reflected an understanding of the Bible's demands? Do the
people vote in terms of their biblical allegiance? Do our laws reflect biblical absolutes? Horace Greeley's adage speaks to the issue: "The name of
God on a plow beam would not make the plow run any better." Perhaps
we need both the name of God and the plow beam — both the official pronouncements and the moral character to back them up, both the Lord-

4. Many official pronouncements and declarations speak of our nation's religious and
Christian commitment. The Ten Commandments hang over the head of the Chief Justice
of the Supreme Court. In the House and Senate chambers appear the words, "In God We
Trust." In the Rotunda is the figure of the crucified Christ. On the walls of the Capitol
dome, these words appear: "The New Testament according to the Lord and Savior Jesus
Christ." On the Great Seal of the United States is inscribed the phrase *Annuit Coeptis*, "God
has smiled on our undertaking." Under the Seal is the phrase from Lincoln's Gettysburg
address: "This nation under God." President Eliot of Harvard chose Micah 6:8 for the
walls of the nation's library: "He hath showed thee, O man, what is good; and what doth
God require of thee, but to do justly, and to love mercy, and to walk humbly with thy
God." Engraved on the metal cap on the top of the Washington Monument are the words:
"Praise be to God." Lining the walls of the monument's stairwell are numerous Bible
verses: "Search the Scriptures," "Holiness to the Lord," and "Train up a child in the way he
should go, and when he is old he will not depart from it." The crier who opens each session
of the Supreme Court closes with the words, "God save the United States and the Honor-
able Court." At the opposite end of the Lincoln Memorial, words and phrases of Lincoln's
Second Inaugural Address allude to "God," the "Bible," "providence," "the Almighty," and
"divine attributes." The plaque in the Dirksen Office Building has the words "IN GOD
WE TRUST" in bronze relief.
Our national anthem, "The Star-Spangled Banner," contains these lines:

> Blest with victory and peace,
>   may the heav'n rescued land
> Praise the power that hath made
>   and preserved us a nation.
> Then conquer we must,
>   when our cause it is just
> And this be our motto
> "In God is our trust."

Our coins have the phrase "In God We Trust" stamped on them. This practice was sanc-
tioned by an official governmental pronouncement made by Congress in 1956. The president is authorized to proclaim at least two National Days of Prayer each year. Public Law
82-324 requires the president to proclaim a National Day of Prayer on a day other than a
Sunday. Under Public Law 77-379 the president proclaims the fourth Thursday of
November each year as a National Day of Thanksgiving. The words "under God" were inserted into the Pledge of Allegiance by Congress in 1954.
5. Washington's Bible was opened to two pictures illustrating Gen. 49:13-15 on the left
page and the text of Gen. 49:13-50:8 on the right. (From a letter of Robert C. Gooch,
Chief, General Reference and Bibliography Division, Library of Congress, April 6, 1945).
President Reagan took the oath of office on the King James Bible used by his mother,
Nellie Reagan, opened to 2 Chron. 7:14 (*New York Times*, January 12, 1981).

ship of Jesus Christ mentioned in the Constitution and the will of the people to serve Him.

But fundamental questions remain. Did our constitutional Framers intend to disestablish Christianity as the national religion and thereby make the people independent sovereigns? Can we assume that our constitutional Framers believed, rightly or wrongly, that Christianity resided in the character of the people, and therefore the citizen's expression of self-government under God would be enough to hold the nation together? Did they believe that because the state constitutions were explicitly Christian that they did not need to repeat this affirmation in the federal Constitution? Were the states so fearful of a national establishment of religion that the Framers did not want to include any reference to religion? This is R. J. Rushdoony's conclusion:

> When reference is made to the Christian nature of the United States, the objection immediately raised is the *absence* of reference to Christianity in the Constitution. The Constitution would never have been ratified had such a reference been made, and to safeguard themselves, the people sought and gained the further protection of the First Amendment. . . . All the constituent states had in some form or other either a Christian establishment or settlement, or specifically Christian legislation. Religious tests for citizenship, blasphemy laws, singular or plural establishment, and other religious settlements were the rule, jealously guarded and prized, first against British interference, then against Federal usurpation. To preserve the integrity and freedom of the specific forms of Christian statehood of the constituent states, the Constitution forbade any jurisdiction to the Federal Union in this area.[6]

6. Rousas J. Rushdoony, *This Independent Republic: Studies in the Nature and Meaning of American History* (Nutley, N.J.: Craig Press, 1964), pp. vii-viii. Thomas Jefferson broke from the tradition established by Washington and Adams of issuing proclamations of national prayer, because he believed that the national government is prohibited "by the Constitution from intermeddling with religious institutions, their doctrines, discipline, or exercises. This results not only from the provision that no law shall be made respecting the [*sic*] establishment or free exercise of religion, but from that also which reserves to the States the powers not delegated to the United States. Certainly, no power to prescribe any religious exercise, or to assume authority in religious discipline, has been delegated to the General Government. *It must then rest with the States, as far as it can be in any human authority.*" Jefferson's letter as reprinted in Robert L. Cord, *Separation of Church and State: Historical Fact and Current Fiction* (New York: Lambeth Press, 1982), p. 40, my emphasis.

While Jefferson was wrong in his application of the Constitution, he did understand that the states retained their religious freedoms. Madison, the architect of the First Amendment, reestablished the tradition of issuing proclamations for national prayer. It is interesting to note that the American public is more familiar with Jefferson's infamous "separation between church and state" phrase than Madison's more constitutional nonestablishment clause. Jefferson was not present at the Constitution's drafting, and he had no hand in the construction of the First Amendment.

The questions raised above are difficult to answer. It is impossible to read the minds of the Framers. Reading too much into what they did or did not do is risky. Is it possible that they saw the Constitution as nothing more than a mechanical device to bind the states together, so the many states could operate optimally as one nation? While we might prefer that the Preamble affirmed Jesus' sovereignty over the nation, the Framers might have inadvertently rather than deliberately failed to include it. A display of our nation's Christian heritage is evident on nearly every page of our nation's history. As federal judge Frank McGarr recently declared in a case involving the placement of a creche in Chicago's city hall:

> The truth is that America's origins are Christian with the result that our fondest traditions are Christian, and that our founding fathers intended and achieved full religious freedom for all within the context of a Christian nation in the First Amendment as it was adopted, rather than as we have rewritten it.[7]

But not everyone agrees with Judge McGarr. "The view that the United States began as an explicitly Christian nation, only to have that status snatched away by activist judges, is a misreading of history — and of the Constitution."[8]

It seems that history is in the eye of the beholder. This is why a detailed consideration of the facts is in order. Of course, we know that all historians bring certain presuppositions with them in the evaluation of the facts. But the task of digging up the facts is still ours, in spite of what slant our detractors might put on them.

Much of William Edgar's argument is commendable. I agree with nearly all of his propositions. He is correct in his insistence that the character of the American people and their government cannot be separated. But Edgar goes further. He contends that since the Constitution does not mention the Lord Jesus Christ in a *direct* way, and the states — embodied in "We the People" — ratified the Constitution without this written acknowledgment, then the nation at the time of the Constitution's drafting rejected Jesus Christ as the sovereign ruler of the nations by substituting "We the people" as the reigning deity.

Edgar correctly observes that today our nation refuses to confess Jesus Christ as Lord, and our laws increasingly have no basis in God's law. But does the absence of a *direct* reference to Jesus Christ in our Constitution

7. Cited in Morten Borden, "Faith of Our Fathers," *Reason*, June 1987, p. 35.
8. Ibid.

mean that our Founders willfully steered the nation toward secularism and that people today have willfully abandoned the lordship of Jesus Christ? Will an amendment to the Constitution as advocated by Edgar and the National Reform Association make any difference?

The transformation of a nation comes from the bottom up. As Christians, we should be more concerned about the commitment of the people to Christ than about their commitment to the propositions of a Constitution. An amendment to the Constitution will mean something when it grows from the will of the people, since "the character of the American people and their government . . . cannot be separated." Legislating Christianity from the top down will not make us a Christian nation. The people of Israel repeatedly covenanted before God, and yet they still followed "other gods" (Judg. 2:12). Their official constitution never changed, but their personal commitment did. As a nation, we need *both*.[9]

The Constitution and a Christian World View

Edgar shows that Christianity formed the backdrop for the Constitution's framing:

1. Colonial charters explicitly professed faith in Christianity.[10]

2. The leaders of the American Revolution, unlike the French Jacobins, did not work to eliminate Christian influences from the nation.[11]

3. These leaders made no attempt to change state constitutions that recognized God or to abolish established churches on the state level.[12]

9. The following words are inscribed on the Department of Justice Building in Washington, D.C.: "Justice in the life and conduct of the state is possible only as first it resides in the hearts and souls of the citizens."

10. The New England Confederation, put into effect on May 19, 1643, established a union of like-minded civil bodies: "Whereas we all came into these parts of America with one and the same end and aim, namely, to advance the Kingdom of our Lord Jesus Christ and to enjoy the liberties of the Gospel in purity with peace; and whereas in our settling (by a wise providence of God) we are further dispersed upon the sea coasts and rivers than was at first intended . . ."

11. The French "proclaimed the goddess of Reason in Notre-Dame Cathedral in Paris and in other churches in France. . . . In Paris, the goddess was personified by an actress, Demoiselle Candeille, carried shoulder-high into the cathedral by men dressed in Roman costumes." Francis Schaeffer, *How Should We Then Live?* (Old Tappan, N.J.: Fleming H. Revell, 1976), p. 122. Such a spectacle sent a message to the entire nation.

12. *The Connecticut Constitution* (until 1818): "The People of this State . . . by the Providence of God . . . hath the sole and exclusive right of governing themselves as a free, sovereign, and independent State . . . and forasmuch as the free fruition of such liberties and privileges as humanity, civility, and Christianity call for us, is due to every man in his place and proportion . . . hath ever been and will be the tranquility and stability of Churches and Commonwealth; and the denial thereof, the disturbances, if not the ruin of both."

The Delaware Constitution (1831): Recognized "the duty of all men frequently to assemble together for the public worship of the Author of the Universe." The following oath of office

4. They continued to appoint chaplains to official bodies and to proclaim days of prayer.[13]

5. The Constitutional Framers "concluded their work by signing it 'in the Year of our Lord one thousand seven hundred and Eighty-seven' " (p. 183).[14]

was in force until 1792: "I . . . do profess faith in God the Father, and in Jesus Christ His only Son, and in the Holy Ghost, one God, blessed for evermore; I do acknowledge the holy scriptures of the Old and New Testaments to be given by divine inspiration."

The Maryland Constitution (until 1851): "That, as it is the duty of every man to worship God in such a manner as he thinks most acceptable to him; all persons professing the Christian religion, are equally entitled to protection in their religious liberty. . . . The Legislature may, in their discretion, lay a general and equal tax, for the support of the Christian religion." The constitution of 1864 required "a declaration of a belief in the Christian religion" for all state officials.

The North Carolina Constitution (1876): "That no person who shall deny the being of God, or the truth of the Protestant religion, or the divine authority of the Old or New Testaments, or who shall hold religious principles incompatible with the freedom and safety of the State, shall be capable of holding any office or place of trust or profit in the civil department within this State."

For a list of state constitutions and their reference to the sovereignty of God, see Charles E. Rice, *The Supreme Court and Public Prayer: The Need for Restraint* (New York: Fordham University Press, 1964), app. B.

13. In the Capitol Building a room was set aside by the Eighty-third Congress to be used exclusively for the private prayer and meditation of members of Congress. In this specially designated room there is a stained-glass window showing George Washington kneeling in prayer. Behind Washington a prayer is etched: "Preserve me, O God, for in Thee do I put my trust" (Ps. 16:1). The two lower corners of the window each show the Holy Scriptures and an open book and a candle, signifying the light from God's law: "Thy Word is a lamp unto my feet and a light unto my path" (Ps. 119:105).

14. "DONE in convention by the unanimous consent of the States present, the seventeenth of September, in the year of our Lord one thousand seven hundred and eighty seven and of the independence of the United States of America the twelfth." The French Revolution divorced itself from a *Christian* history, while the United States Constitution perpetuated an already established Christian order. "The French Revolution, which felt the need of a new Year One and a new calendar, was a revolution against history" (Pieter Geyl, *Uses and Abuses of History* [New Haven: Yale University Press, 1955, p. 22]). Edgar, however, sees something of the "French Jacobin scheme to renumber the years" by writing that their efforts for independence were accomplished on "the Twelfth" year from the writing of the Declaration of Independence (p. 183n). This is reading sinister motives into the minds of these men. They simply dated their efforts from the time of their independence from Great Britain in 1776. But even 1776 follows the progression of the Christian calendar: one thousand, seven hundred and seventy-six years *from the birth of Jesus Christ.*

An earlier proclamation announcing a day devoted to "Fasting, Humiliation and Prayer" (1782) mentions "the Goodness of the Supreme Being . . . His absolute Government of the World . . . our multiplied Transgressions of the holy Laws of God, and his past acts of Kindness and Goodness," and describes God as "the Ruler of the Universe." It ends with these words: "[T]hat he would incline the hearts of all men to peace and fill them with Universal Charity, and benevolence and that the religion of our divine Redeemer with all its benign influences may cover the earth as the Waters cover the sea." The conclusion is similar to that of the United States Constitution: "Done by the United States in Congress Assembled this nineteenth day of March in the Year of our Lord one thousand Seven hundred and eighty two and in the Sixth Year of our Independence." Cited in J. Bruce Kremer, *John Hanson of Mulberry Grove* (New York: Albert and Charles Boni, Inc., 1938), pp. 161-63. This proclamation is filled with solid Christian doctrine. The dating in no way reflects the motives of the "French Jacobin scheme."

This in itself is significant. If it was the Framers' purpose to exclude Jesus Christ, then why mention Him at all? Why not just the date — September 17, 1787?

6. The Constitution assumes "the existence of the Christian Sabbath: The President has 'ten days (Sundays excepted)' to veto a bill from Congress."[15]

Despite emphasizing these Christian influences, Edgar goes on to maintain that our Founders evidently did not think that they needed God's guidance, rejecting, for example, Benjamin Franklin's appeal for prayer.[16] On the surface, this seems like a logical explanation. But James Madison, "the Father of the Constitution," gives a different interpretation. After the motion was seconded, "[Alexander] Hamilton and several others expressed their apprehensions that however proper such a resolution might have been at the beginning of the convention," it might now "lead the public to believe that the embarrassments and dissensions within the Convention, had suggested this measure."[17] On September 24, 1789, the same day that it approved the First Amendment, Congress called on President Washington to proclaim a national day of prayer and thanksgiving. The First Congress resolved

---

15. Article I, Section 7.

16. Franklin's appeal reads in part: "In the beginning of the contest with Britain, when we were sensible of danger, we had daily prayers in this room for Divine protection [an indicator in itself of our nation's reliance upon Christian principles]. Our prayers, Sir, were heard — and they were graciously answered. All of us who were engaged in the struggle must have observed frequent instances of a superintending Providence in our favor. . . . And have we now forgotten that powerful Friend? Or do we imagine we no longer need its assistance? I have lived, Sir, a long time, and the longer I live the more convincing proofs I see of this truth, that God governs in the affairs of men. And if a sparrow can not fall to the ground without His notice, is it probable that an empire can rise without His aid?

"We have also been assured, Sir, in the sacred writings, that 'except the Lord build the house, they labor in vain that build it' [Ps. 127:1]. I firmly believe this and I also believe that, without His concurring aid, we shall succeed in this political building no better than the builders of Babel. . . ." Benjamin Franklin, "Motion for Prayers in the Convention" in *The Works of Benjamin Franklin*, fed. ed., ed. John Bigelow (New York and London: The Knickerbocker Press, 1904), 2:337-38.

17. "Debates in the Federal Convention of 1787 as Reported by James Madison" in *Documents Illustrative of the Formation of the Union of the American States* (Washington, D.C.: Government Printing Office, 1927), p. 297. There is some evidence, however, that Franklin's suggestion was taken up at a later date: "Mr. Randolph proposed that in order to give favorable aspect to the measure [proposed by Franklin], a sermon be preached at the request of the Convention on the 4th of July, and thence every morning. This was agreed to." Warren P. Mass, "Will the Convention Have a Prayer?" *The New American*, July 6, 1987, p. 59.

that a joint committee of both Houses be directed to wait upon the President of the United States to request that he would recommend to the people of the United States a day of public thanksgiving and prayer, to be observed by acknowledging, with grateful hearts, the many signal favors of Almighty God, *especially by affording them an opportunity peaceably to establish a Constitution of government for their safety and happiness.*[18]

A Christian preamble to the Constitution would have been beneficial, but it alone would not have stopped our nation's drift into secularism. State constitutions that were explicitly Christian did little to reinforce the Christian character of the people. At worst, the Constitution is filled with compromise. The defects have come to light over the two centuries since its drafting. The problem, however, is not with the Constitution, but with a nation that has refused to rest in the undeserved grace of the Lord Jesus Christ and with Christians who have abandoned the law of God as the standard of righteousness in family, church, and state. The church's duty is to convince hearts and minds of the merits of the gospel and the goodness of the law. From this new people will flow a nation that will be Christian.

Again, I concur with Edgar when he writes:

> To become a Christian nation the American kings, the people, should covenant together to be the Lord's. The American nation, that is, should confess its faith in Jesus Christ, recognize His rule, and submit to His law (p. 189).

But this will not be accomplished by amending the Constitution to acknowledge "Jesus Christ as the Governor among the nations." Legislating that Jesus Christ is the sovereign Lord will do little to change the direction of the nation if the people first do not change their beliefs and actions. Such an amendment, if needed at all, will only follow on the heels of a great revival and reformation. Edgar himself hints at this when he states that "such an amendment is politically impossible at this time" (p. 196).

A call to the whole nation to amend the Constitution and obey Christ will not be popular with most Americans. If pressed with any vigor and

18. *The Annals of Congress, The Debates and Proceedings in the Congress of The United States*, vol. I, *Compiled from Authentic Materials by Joseph Gales, Senior* (Washington, D.C.: Gales and Seaton, 1834), pp. 949-50, emphasis added.

publicity, it will provoke a strong negative reaction. Only a revival among the American people will produce a revision of the Constitution. Transformation must begin in the least of things before we will see it in the greater things.

> In that day there will be inscribed on the bells of the horses, "HOLY TO THE LORD." And the cooking pots in the Lord's house will be like the bowls before the altar." And every cooking pot in Jerusalem and in Judah will be holy to the Lord of Hosts; and all who sacrifice will come and take of them and boil in them. And there will no longer be a Canaanite in the house of the Lord of hosts in that day (Zech. 14:20, 21, NASB).

We the People

One last point needs to be made. Edgar states that "the Constitution is secular, because it is not enacted in the name of any god but only by the *authority of the people*" (p. 189, emphasis added). His assumption is that the people as a collective whole now have become new sovereigns. This does not accurately represent our constitutional system. The phrase "We the People" in the Preamble to the Constitution "shows the Federal Union to be a government of States, and not of all America, as a consolidated body. . . . The qualifying adjective 'united' is annexed to the word states, and not to the word 'people.'"[19] James Madison, the primary architect of the Constitution, replied to Patrick Henry's question of how the "people" can institute a national government over the sovereignty of the states: "Who are the parties to the government? The people; but then not the people as composing *one great body*; but the people as composing *thirteen sovereignties.*"[20]

So then, the *states* created the national government. The national government is the creature of the *states* and not of the people generally.

> The Constitution of the United States is a grant by grantors to a grantee. The grantors are the "several States," not as a consolidated people, but as separate and independent sovereignties — "the people" as organized into "several" distinct sovereign communities. Thus the Supreme Court of the United States declares that: "The States form a confederated government; yet the several states re-

19. Abel P. Upshur, *The Federal Government: Its True Nature and Character; Being a Review of Judge [Joseph] Story's Commentaries of the Constitution of the United States* (New York: Van Evrie, Horton and Co., 1868), p. 122n.
20. Ibid., emphasis added.

tain their individual sovereignties, and with respect to their municipal regulations, are to each other sovereign." (2 Peters, 590; 12 Wheaton, 334.) Again: "The powers retained by the States proceed not from *the people of America* but from the people of the *several States*, and remain after the adoption of the Constitution what they were before." (4 Wheaton, 193, 17, 54; 203, 9.) Thus all authority proves that the Government of the Union is one of the States *united*, not of the *People consolidated*.[21]

Now, what significance does this carry for our present discussion? First, the states only granted *enumerated* powers to the national government. Those powers not listed "are reserved to the States respectively, or to the people."[22] The Constitution did nothing to disestablish Christianity from the several states. At the time of the Constitution's drafting, a number of states had established churches.[23] The First Amendment only prohibited "Congress" from making any law "respecting an[24] establishment of religion, or prohibiting the free exercise thereof."[25] The eminent constitutional scholar Joseph Story wrote that

21. Ibid.
22. Amendment X.
23. When the Constitutional Convention assembled in Philadelphia in the summer of 1787, Georgia, South Carolina, Connecticut, Massachusetts, and New Hampshire still retained their religious establishments.
24. "Had the framers prohibited '*the* establishment of religion,' which would have emphasized the generic word 'religion,' there might have been some reason for thinking they wanted to prohibit all official preferences of religion over irreligion. But by choosing 'an establishment' over 'the establishment,' they were showing that they wanted to prohibit only those official activities that tended to promote interests of one or another particular sect.
"Thus, through the choice of 'an' over 'the,' conferees indicated their intent. The First Congress did not expect the Bill of Rights to be inconsistent with the Northwest Ordinance of 1787, which the Congress reenacted in 1789. One key clause in the Ordinance explained why Congress chose to set aside some of the federal lands in the territory for schools: 'Religion, morality, and knowledge,' the clause reads, 'being necessary to good government and the happiness of mankind, schools and the means of learning shall forever be encouraged.' This clause clearly implies that schools, which were to be built on federal lands with federal assistance, were expected to promote religion as well as morality. In fact, most schools at this time were church-run sectarian schools." Michael J. Malbin, *Religion and Politics: The Intentions of the Authors of the First Amendment* (Washington D.C.: American Enterprise Institute for Public Policy Research, 1978), pp. 14-15.
25. Our Founders had good intentions in wanting further assurances that the newly created national government would not interfere in the religious affairs of the states. The First Amendment was the result. I believe the inclusion of the First Amendment was a mistake. If the Constitution is a document of *enumerated* powers, then any power listed is power granted. An active role was given to Congress to search for and eliminate anything that hinted at being a religious establishment. This power was transferred to the Supreme Court. Now the Court considers cases dealing with religious establishment. Without the First Amendment, this power would never have been granted.

the real object of the First Amendment was not to countenance, much less to advance, Mahometanism, or Judaism, or infidelity, by prostrating Christianity; *but to exclude all rivalry among Christian sects, and to prevent any national ecclesiastical establishment which should give to a hierarchy the exclusive patronage of the national government. It thus cut off the means of religious persecution (the vice and pest of former ages), and of the subversion of the rights of conscience in matters of religion* which had been trampled upon almost from the days of the Apostles to the present age. . . .[26]

Second, the purpose of the constitutional Framers was to establish a national system of governance to bind the several states in a single nation without destroying state sovereignty. The document serves a limited purpose. Its purpose is stated succinctly and clearly in the Preamble:

WE THE PEOPLE of the United States, in Order to form a more perfect Union, establish Justice, insure domestic Tranquility, provide for the common defence, promote the general Welfare, and secure the Blessings of Liberty to ourselves and our Posterity, do ordain and establish this Constitution for the United States.

The Constitution was designed to accomplish what the several states could not do alone. The design was to create a "union" of the diverse state sovereignties. Nothing was destroyed in its creation. The single states became "the United States."

So, then, the states created a national political entity that in no way disestablished their Christian character. In fact, with the passage of the First Amendment the states believed they were insuring their religious heritage. Their state constitutions already acknowledged the sovereignty and providence of God over all their affairs. It has been only through a blind court and an ignorant public that the true meaning of our nation's Christian history has been obscured.[27]

Given this limited function, we should not make too much of the Constitution, for either good or evil. It has only been since the abandonment of state sovereignty rights that the Constitution has taken on a life of its own, touching every facet of society, something it was never designed to do. Those who deny Christ want us to consider the Constitution as *the*

26. Joseph Story, *Commentaries on the Constitution of the United States*, 2d ed., vol. 2 (Boston: Charles C. Little and James Brown, 1851), sec. 1872, p. 591. Emphasis added.

27. See *Jaffree v. Board of School Commissioners of Mobile County*, 554 F. Supp. 1104 (S.D. Ala. 1983) by Judge Brevard W. Hand in Russell Kirk, ed., *The Assault on Religion: Commentaries on the Decline of Religious Liberty* (Lanham, MD.: The Center for Judicial Studies/ University Press of America, Inc., 1986), pp. 72-115.

most important document; nothing else matters. We fall into their trap when we reason that the Constitution is our nation's sole document of values. While the Constitution is important, it is neither sacred nor inspired. Its history, the religious beliefs of the American people, and the political principles that shaped the development of the Constitution and other political documents are all important in understanding the nature and ideological basis of American government.

Conclusion

George Washington stated that "it is the duty of all nations to acknowledge the providence of Almighty God, to obey His will, to be grateful for His benefits, and humbly to implore His protection and favor."[28] He went on in his Thanksgiving Proclamation of October 3, 1789, to write that as a nation "we may then unite in most humbly offering our prayers and supplications to the great Lord and Ruler of Nations, and beseech Him to pardon our national and other transgressions."[29]

Substantial evidence supports the claim that our Founders did not reject all things Christian. Yes, the Constitution should have acknowledged the authority of the Lord Jesus Christ more explicitly. But countless numbers of documents show that Christianity *permeated* the nation. In 1892, the United States Supreme Court determined, in the case of *The Church of the Holy Trinity vs. The United States*, that America was a Christian nation from its earliest days. The court opinion, delivered by Justice Josiah Brewer, was an exhaustive study of the historical and legal evidence for America's Christian heritage. After examining hundreds of court cases, state constitutions, and other historical documents, the court came to the following conclusion:

> Our laws and our institutions must necessarily be based upon and embody the teachings of the Redeemer of mankind. It is impossible that it should be otherwise; and in this sense and to this extent our civilization and our institutions are emphatically Christian. . . . This is a religious people. This is historically true. From the discovery of this continent to the present hour, there is a single voice making this affirmation. . . . We find everywhere a clear recognition of the same truth. . . . These, and many other matters which might be noticed, add a volume of unofficial declarations to the mass of organic utterances that this is a Christian nation.[30]

28. James D. Richardson, *A Compilation of the Messages and Papers of the Presidents, 1789-1897*, vol. I (Washington, D.C.: Bureau of National Literature and Art, 1901).
29. Ibid.
30. Decision of the Supreme Court of the United States in the case of *The Church of the Holy Trinity v. The United States* (143 United States 457 [1892]).

15

The Principled Pluralist Response to National Confessionalism

Gary Scott Smith

Proponents of principled pluralism agree with many aspects of the national confession position. Among other things, those positions concur on the following principles and practical implications. God is sovereign over the universe and over individual nations. As Lord of all life Jesus Christ commands Christians to serve Him through their cultural activities. Christ's followers should resolutely resist efforts to secularize American society and to confine Christian faith to the private areas of life. We should respond obediently to biblical norms for all areas of our lives, and we should develop strong congregations and parachurch organizations to proclaim the gospel, nurture believers, help those in need, and promote biblical morality. Christians should protest the privileged status of secular humanism in our nation's schools and seek to retard its penetration into many other aspects of American culture. The Bible instructs us both to present the gospel to individuals (evangelism) and to structure institutions according to its norms (social reform). Thus, believers should actively labor to develop governmental structures and public policies based upon biblical principles. Finally, God expects governments to rule justly and to provide equal opportunities and the same rights for all their citizens.

Despite these fundamental agreements, however, advocates of principled pluralism disagree sharply with the fundamental goal of the national confession position: to amend the Preamble to the United States Constitution so that it would officially acknowledge the authority of Jesus Christ over our nation. Scriptural, historical, and practical arguments indicate that this proposed amendment is undesirable, causes division among theists, and diverts attention from other more important tasks.

The greatest problem with the proposal made by the National Reform Association (NRA) is that it lacks biblical support. Based on his understanding of the Scriptures, Edgar argues that contemporary nations such as the United States should profess faith in Christ in their public documents, give official preference to Christianity, and directly support the work of the church. His analysis of biblical teaching shows that God is sovereign over all of life, including the state, and that He expects nations to practice justice and righteousness. Edgar fails, however, to substantiate his contention that Jesus' claim to have all authority in heaven and on earth (Matt. 28:18) means that nations must openly recognize Christ's dominion in their constitutions and seek vigorously to become explicitly Christian in their political life. Clearly, Christ does reign over heaven and earth (Eph. 1; Col. 1-3). Where, however, does the Bible teach that Christ intends to dominate nations or desires to be explicitly recognized as their source of political and legal authority? Christ's authority and kingdom in this age, as described in the New Testament, are primarily spiritual, not physical or territorial. The reign of Christ on earth is expressed outwardly through the church, not through any nation(s) (Acts 1:6-8). The New Testament does not even hint that the kingdom of God is political or that it can be identified with a particular nation.

Moreover, Edgar's evidence does not justify his claim that Christ instructed His disciples to demand of kings that they submit their countries to His sovereign authority. Mark 13:9, which Edgar cites in this connection, simply declares that the disciples will be flogged in the synagogues and will stand before governors and kings for Christ's sake, as a testimony to Him. What we do know about the disciples' treatment by the Roman Empire would not lead us to assume that they entreated kings to make their empires "self-consciously and explicitly Christian" (p. 182). Edgar's claim that they did so is at best an inference.

Neither general principles nor specific New Testament laws teach that Christ expects nations to be formally committed to Him. The New Testament does not even imply that God will work in special ways through individual nations, as He did through Old Testament Israel. Instead, the gospels and the epistles emphasize that God's primary agent in the world is the church, which consists of individuals drawn from many nations. The limited New Testament statements about political life suggest that nations will not be distinctively Christian and that they will contain mixed populations of believers and unbelievers (see Matt. 13:24-30). As King of kings Christ is ultimately sovereign over all governments and rulers. But how does He express, or expect Christians to acknowledge and reflect, His ultimate sovereignty? Is it by seeking to make the governments of nations in which they live explicitly Christian? Or is it by encouraging governments to obey their biblical mandate to preserve order, govern justly, and protect the weak?

Our understanding of government and political life should be derived from the Bible's general principles and directives, which are valid for all ages. Because God is Lord of the universe, all persons, relationships, institutions, and nations are subject to Him and accountable to His creational and inscripturated Word. While the Bible does not systematically discuss social theory, government, or public policy, it does teach that all of life is under God's judgment and is in need of renewal.

Through His act of creation God provided for the development of basic structures to direct and shape life. These structures—marriage, family, state, church, work—establish the responsibilities, rights, and freedoms of persons as they function in various social relationships. Human beings, however, rebelled against God's creational laws and developed distorted social institutions and relationships. The Scriptures reveal God's plan for reordering social relationships and institutions. Despite sin's intrusion in the world, God's creational ordinances remain in force. The social order is neither autonomous nor created artificially by sovereign people. Societies are responsible to a holy and omnipotent God and His transcendent norms.

God established the state to preserve order and to regulate social interactions. Because of the Fall the state must also restrain evil. Its primary task is to promote justice and righteousness (see Pss. 2; 58:1; 72:1-2, 12, 14; 82:1-4; Isa. 16:5; 31:1-2; Jer. 23:5; Rom. 13:1-4; 1 Pet. 2:14). The Old Testament writers frequently chastised Israel and other nations for failing to follow the biblical norms for political life—practicing justice, acting righteously, and dealing equitably with all citizens. The Bible does not command governments forthrightly to express commitment to Christianity or to develop a covenantal relationship with Christ. It does, however, instruct the state to protect the functioning of the various societal institutions of family, marriage, school, workplace, and church and to treat the diverse faith communities fairly and equitably.[1]

In short, what New Testament principles or passages teach that nations must profess Christ as Lord and explicitly act as Christian governments? In the context of the entire New Testament the parable of the wheat and the tares (Matt. 13:24-30), as James Skillen writes, "seems to suggest that Christians must not try to establish an earthly state or political community that would be for Christians only" or that would in any

---

1. See Rockne McCarthy et al., *Society, State and Schools: A Case for Structural and Confessional Pluralism* (Grand Rapids: Eerdmans, 1981), p. 37.

way discriminate against non-Christians.[2] The way a nation treats its minorities, strangers, dispossessed, and poor is a much better test of its obedience to Christ than what its official documents profess. A nation that does not explicitly acknowledge God's authority may administer justice more evenhandedly than a declaredly Christian state. Many modern democratic nations promote public justice better than did European nations during the centuries of Western Christendom.

In addition to the lack of scriptural support for the national confession position, its evaluation and use of history seems highly questionable. "Christian" states have often forced Christianity on their citizens and have fostered many injustices. Edgar applauds the Roman Empire's adoption of Christianity as its official religion. Because of this change, emperor worship ceased, many laws became based upon biblical norms, and states supposedly sought to follow Christian principles in their administrations. Nevertheless, the Constantinian establishment of Christianity produced many problems. Despite their government's official profession of faith in Christ, many Roman emperors did not rule justly. Moreover, by making peace with the Christian church, rulers were often able to dominate the church and use it for their own purposes. As a result, neither the Eastern nor Western branch of the church did much, prior to the year 1000, to develop a distinctively Christian society.[3]

Worst of all, the empire's official commitment to Christianity made the church a coercive body, demanding monopoly. The power of the imperial state was used to enforce Christian orthodoxy. Refusal to join the church came to be seen as an act of disloyalty to the emperor. Christian mobs destroyed Jewish synagogues, and "heretics" were exiled or persecuted. Such cruel devices as the rack, whipping posts, and red hot plates were used to punish dissenters, and a large number of secret police, who masqueraded as civilians, detected heresy, exacted recantations, and enforced uniformity. Censorship was widely practiced.[4] By controlling belief the Christian state violated individuals' liberty of conscience.

The medieval state officially endorsed Christianity, but its application of the gospel was often superficial, inconsistent, and even destructive. The church conformed much more to worldly standards and values than

    2. James Skillen, "Public Justice and True Tolerance" in *America, Christian or Secular? Readings in American Christian History and Civil Religion*, ed. Jerry S. Herbert (Portland, Oreg.: Multnomah Press, 1984), pp. 284-85.
    3. See Kenneth Scott Latourette, *A History of Christianity* (New York: Harper and Row, 1953), p. 262.
    4. See Paul Johnson, *A History of Christianity* (New York: Athenaeum, 1976), pp. 76, 116.

it transformed them, especially as compared to its first three hundred years of existence. By the middle of the tenth century "Christianity in Western Europe was at a lower ebb than it was ever to be again."[5]

Between 800 and 1800, when Western Europe recognized Christ's lordship over its kings, nations, and churches, grave problems persisted. Popes and kings fought to control nations. The church organized crusades. Jews were harassed, oppressed, and even slaughtered. Christians persecuted other Christians, and religious wars were common. Few rulers actually followed Christian principles in governing their subjects. Throughout Western Europe in the late Middle Ages Christian ideals were officially accepted but cynically and practically disregarded. During these years most people's allegiance to Christ was "uncomprehending and superficial."[6]

In the years after 1800 officially Christian nations with state churches displayed less spirituality, vitality, and missionary impulse than countries with no explicit Christian commitment and disestablished churches. In America, for example, revivals, reform societies, and mission agencies flourished, and many individuals displayed deep Christian conviction and piety.[7] In Western Europe the practice of Christian faith was much more nominal despite, or ironically because of, the close relationship between church and state. In many ways, then, the end of Western Christendom and the disestablishment of the church have brought great benefits.

Finally, there are serious practical problems with the NRA's position. In 1874 and 1896 the House of Representatives rejected the association's proposed amendment. During those years the NRA had much wider support and better-known advocates than it does today. Despite this broad support, the NRA was unable to achieve its goal. Even though Christianity had significantly penetrated the culture, values, and ethos of mid-nineteenth-century America, NRA proponents could not convince large numbers of Christians that its proposal was biblical or the House of Representatives that it was just and prudent.

The objections that Christians living in the nineteenth century offered to the NRA's proposal still seem valid today. They asserted that American society could be (and to a significant degree was) based upon biblical values without official constitutional recognition of the authority of Jesus Christ over the nation. They contended that most Americans agreed

5. Latourette, *History of Christianity*, p. 330.
6. Ibid., pp. 555, 675.
7. See Winthrop Hudson, *The Great Tradition of the American Churches* (New York: Harper and Row, 1953), p. 262.

with William Seward that there was a "higher law" than the Constitution. Christian opponents of the NRA reasoned that reforming institutions, remedying social problems, and evangelizing the unsaved were much more important than pressing for a Constitutional amendment. Such an amendment would not make Americans more devout Christians. It would, however, logically require the state to punish citizens who disobeyed any of the Bible's fundamental requirements.[8]

The NRA position, today as a century ago, poses serious problems for a pluralistic culture composed of many different groups who hold conflicting ideologies and values. This amendment would force Jews, Unitarians, secularists, and proponents of Eastern religions to submit to the civil authority of one whom they do not consider divine: Jesus.

In the late nineteenth century the NRA's proposal tended to drive a wedge between its Reformed Protestant supporters and other theists, all of whom acknowledged God's sovereignty over nations and events and agreed that the second table of the Ten Commandments should be the foundation for political life and legislation. Efforts to pass such an amendment, now as then, divide theists and, therefore, inhibit their working together on the basis of other mutually held principles to shape governmental policies and practices.

The underlying problem with the NRA approach is that it is neither scripturally valid nor politically realistic to think that Americans can transform their society into a consistently Christian nation with laws that conform completely to God's commandments. The Bible teaches Christians living in the New Testament era not to expect to spread the gospel by the aid of the civil government. American society has become increasingly diverse and heterogeneous since the late nineteenth century, rendering the NRA's proposal undesirable and even offensive to greater numbers of Americans. This proposal highlights a political issue that seems even to many Christians to violate the separation of church and state. Supporting it could hinder our efforts to correct serious social injustices here and abroad.

In summary, the NRA's proposed Constitutional amendment involves substantial scriptural, historical, and practical problems. Christians should neither attempt to make the Bible the direct foundation for civil law nor allow militant secularists to eliminate all explicit Christian influence from public life. Instead, we should participate in public discourse

---

8. See Gary Scott Smith, *The Seeds of Secularization. Calvinism, Culture and Pluralism in America, 1870-1915* (Grand Rapids: Christian University Press, 1985), chap. 4.

about policy issues and political choices that confront our nation. As we do, we should remember that God's common grace provides a basis "for discussing and shaping public policy without explicit appeal to the Bible."[9] Christians should join with other concerned persons to support policies that promote justice in society. While we should work to base our nation's political life on biblical principles, we should make sure that non-Christians receive every opportunity and benefit in the political arena that Christians receive.

America's Founding Fathers intentionally did not mention God in the Constitution, because they were cognizant of the many problems that had resulted when governments had explicitly professed commitment to Christianity. They believed, however, that Americans would be deeply religious and that biblical norms and values would strongly influence American life. Certainly that has been the case. Recognizing God in the Constitution would probably not have made America any more Christian than it has been; given the history of Western Europe during the past two hundred years, it could have made our nation less Christian.

No group of Christian believers, not those living in the Byzantine Empire, Western Christendom, or Puritan New England, has been able to create a genuinely Christian culture. This is so, George Marsden argues, because most cultural ideals that persons esteem most highly and are committed to "reflect directly the values that predominate in fallen human nature"—sinful pride (expressed in tribalism, racism, nationalism, and class consciousness), materialism, and love of power.[10] Christian values improve civilizations and on occasions have transformed aspects of a culture. Nonetheless, Christians continue to sin, and the gospel is always amalgamated with the various anti-Christian forces underlying all societies. No large society has ever had a vast majority of strongly committed Christians. Moreover, the presence of a large number of such Christians or of Christians generally in a society has not necessarily meant that biblical values have become dominant there. While we can expect Christians to act as salt and light in the world, we cannot expect any country to become thoroughly or consistently Christian in its government and public life.[11]

Despite our nation's many social problems and extensive secularization, the Christian faith continues to be practiced more vigorously here

9. Mark A. Noll, Nathan O. Hatch, and George M. Marsden, *The Search for a Christian America* (Westchester, Ill.: Crossway, 1983), p. 136.
10. Ibid., p. 44
11. Ibid., pp. 43-46.

and to influence more aspects of public life than in contemporary Europe with its official Christian heritage. While opposing hedonism and relativistic secular philosophies, we should labor diligently to base American public policies on biblical principles. Efforts to amend the Constitution to acknowledge officially Jesus Christ's authority will not be helpful in this task.

16

The Christian America Response to National Confessionalism*

John Eidsmoe**

Is the United States of America a Christian nation? The answer to that question depends in part upon how one perceives America and its spiritual condition today and in the past. But a deeper question is involved: What is a Christian nation? Of what does a Christian nation consist? Does it rest upon the regenerate status of the nation's people? Or upon their moral character? Or upon the Christian values held by the people and embodied in their governmental system? Or upon an official statement of Christian dedication?

William Edgar, in his excellent presentation of the national confession position, argues persuasively that America is not a Christian nation because its founding documents contain no explicit confession of Christianity. He urges that the Preamble to the Constitution be amended to acknowledge "the Lord Jesus Christ as the Governor among the nations . . . in order to constitute a Christian government . . ." (p. 189).

I will argue neither for nor against the adoption of such a confession. Rather, my point is that the presence or absence of such a confession in the basic documents of our nation is largely irrelevant to the question of whether this is a Christian nation and sheds little light upon the spiritual state of America either now or at the time of its founding.

Obviously, a mere pretense of words in the Constitution does not make a nation Christian. The confession must be supported by the fervent convictions of the people. But how many of the people must support

*This paper was not presented at the consultation held at Geneva College in June of 1987. It was written especially for this volume.

**John Eidsmoe holds degrees from St. Olaf College (B.A.), the University of Iowa (J.D.), Lutheran Brethren Seminary (M.Div.), Dallas Theological Seminary (M.A.), and Oral Roberts University (D.Min.). He has taught at Oral Roberts University and Tulsa Seminary of Biblical Languages. Among his many published works are *God and Caesar: Christian Faith and Political Action* (1985) and *Christianity and the Constitution: Faith of Our Founding Fathers* (1987), which discusses in greater detail the ideas and men referred to in this response.

the national Christian confession for the nation to be considered Christian? One hundred percent? Ninety percent? Fifty-one percent? And how fervent must they be?

Such questions illustrate the difficulty of identifying a nation as Christian based upon a national Christian confession. Ultimately, nations cannot make a confession of salvation in Christ; only individuals can. And every nation is composed of wheat and tares, believers and unbelievers living alongside one another.

It is better to identify a nation as Christian based on values it holds that are consistent with the Word of God. Nations do have certain shared values, which, while perhaps not universal, are held by a general consensus of the population. If those values are rooted in Judeo-Christian tradition and consistent therewith, and if Christianity has been the primary source of those values, that is evidence that the nation may be Christian. If, in addition to that, a substantial portion of the population claims to be Christian (without considering whether they are personally regenerate), that may provide a further basis for calling the nation Christian.

Let us make a distinction, then, between individual salvation and national Christendom. Individuals are saved, not by holding certain values or behaving in a certain way, but by trusting in the Lord Jesus Christ and His finished work on the cross. Nations, however, are not saved in that sense. Whether a nation is Christian must be determined by asking (1) whether the basic underlying values of the nation are consistent with Christian values and are rooted in Christianity and (2) whether a substantial portion of the population considers itself Christian. A national confession of Christianity may be evidence of that, but not very strong evidence, nor the best evidence.

Rather, the best evidence may be found by examining the religious make-up of our nation at the time of its founding and by looking at the basic values underlying the Constitution and Declaration of Independence. As we do so, we will find that (1) the people and leaders of the United States in 1776-1787 were almost all professing Christians and (2) the basic principles of those documents are rooted in Christianity.

The Christian Beliefs of the Founding Fathers

In claiming that most of the Founding Fathers held Christian beliefs, I am not saying they were or were not personally regenerate or "born again." I argue instead, based upon extensive reading of the Founders' own writings, that the vast majority of them were professing Christians.

The vast majority either belonged to or supported Christian churches, and their spoken and written statements expressed Christian doctrine. First, few if any of the fifty-five delegates to the convention identified with deism. Dr. M. E. Bradford catalogs only three as deists (Benjamin Franklin, Hugh Williamson, and James Wilson.) I question even these. Of the rest, there were twenty-eight Episcopalians, eight Presbyterians, seven Congregationalists, two Lutherans, two Reformed, two Methodists, and two Roman Catholics (one delegate's religious preference cannot be determined).[1] Church membership was not a mere formality among the Founding Fathers. Most were faithful in church attendance, and of these many held church offices.[2]

Second, a study of what authorities the Founding Fathers read, cited, and respected in the years between 1760 and 1805 reveals that by far the most widely quoted source at the time was the Bible. The Bible accounted for approximately 34 percent of all their quotations and citations, with the Book of Deuteronomy being quoted most frequently. The other most frequently quoted and cited sources were various Christian authors.[3]

Third, the Founders were educated in a Christian world view. Education in colonial America took place largely in the home, supplemented

---

1. M. E. Bradford, *A Worthy Company: Brief Lives of the Framers of the United States Constitution* (Marlborough, N.H.: Plymouth Rock Foundation, 1982), pp. iv-v. It is not clear whether this list is based in various cases upon actual membership or simply expressed religious preference. In my book *Christianity and the Constitution* I explain why I question whether Franklin, Williamson, and Wilson were deists.

2. See the diaries of George Washington and John Adams. Washington was a church vestryman, and Roger Sherman was a deacon and held many other church offices. The strong church involvement of the Founding Fathers might seem surprising in light of Edgar's assertion that only 10 percent of Americans were church members in 1790. While others place the figure as high as 15 or 20 percent, it is agreed—and Edgar acknowledges— that, unlike today, church membership was far lower than church attendance. But there are reasons for this. For one thing, Americans reacted against the English state church to which everybody belonged regardless of spiritual condition, and they made church membership a position of authority and responsibility and imposed strict requirements for membership. Also, the population was very mobile at that time, and many moved too frequently to join a church, although they attended church and were personally devout. The point is that there are explanations for the relatively low church membership other than a lack of spirituality or Christian conviction.

3. Donald S. Lutz and Charles S. Hyneman, "The Relative Influence of European Writers on Late Eighteenth Century American Political Thought," *American Political Science Review*, 78 (1984): 189-97. Baron Montesquieu, an orthodox Catholic, was in first place with 8.3 percent of all quotations; Sir William Blackstone, an orthodox Anglican, was just behind him in third place was John Locke, a Christian, but not entirely orthodox, with 2.9 percent. Lutz and Lyneman reviewed an estimated 15,000 items and closely read 2,200 books, pamphlets, newspaper articles, and monographs with explicitly political content printed between 1760 and 1805.

by church schools. The two basic texts were the Bible and *The New England Primer,* which itself was Bible-based.[4] From about 1690 to 1800 this primer was the principal book used to teach beginning reading in American schools. At both school and home the Westminster catechisms were drilled into children. That the Founding Fathers received a Christian education, were involved with Christian churches, and read and quoted Christian sources indicates that Christianity was the major formative influence upon their lives and ideas.

Today many of the Founding Fathers are unfairly labeled deists. Deism—best described as the belief in an "absentee God," a god who created the universe and established physical and moral laws by which the universe is to be governed but who does not actively intervene in human affairs[5]—was popular in Europe in the 1700s. It was less popular in England and still less popular in America,[6] as the preceding evidence of church membership and Christian influence demonstrates. Even those Founding Fathers who were less than orthodox in their religious faith—most notably Benjamin Franklin and Thomas Jefferson—could not, strictly speaking, be called deists, for both repeatedly affirmed that God actively participates in human affairs.[7] Moreover, Franklin and Jefferson stood apart from the rest of the Founding Fathers. Both were, to some degree, children of the Enlightenment. Most of the Founders

4. Samuel Chester Parker, *The History of Modern Elementary Education* (Chicago: Ginn and Company, 1912), pp. 74, 76-77. The primer contained the Lord's Prayer, the Ten Commandments, many Bible verses, and the Westminster Shorter Catechism.

5. See "Deism," *Encyclopedia of Philosophy,* ed. Paul Edwards (New York: Macmillan, 1967), 2:326-36.

6. See Herbert M. Morais, *Deism in Eighteenth Century America* (New York: Russell and Russell, 1960 [1943]), pp. 15, 120-58; Henry F. May, *The Enlightenment in America* (New York: Oxford University Press, 1976), pp. 231-32.

7. Franklin had been a deist early in his life, but he moved away from deism as he grew older. At the Constitutional Convention it was Franklin, at age 81, who moved for daily prayers, declaring, "I have lived, Sir, a long time; and the longer I live, the more convincing proofs I see of this truth, that GOD GOVERNS IN THE AFFAIRS OF MEN"—an explicit rejection of deism, the fundamental premise of which is that God does *not* govern in the affairs of men. Benjamin Franklin, quoted by James Madison in *Notes on Debates in the Federal Convention of 1787* (Athens: Ohio University Press, 1966, 1985), p. 209. And Jefferson declared in his Second Inaugural Address, "I shall need . . . the favor of that Being in whose hands we are, who led our forefathers, as Israel of old, from their native land, and planted them in a country flowing with all the necessaries and comforts of life; who has covered our infancy with His providence, and our riper years with His wisdom and power; and to whose goodness I ask you to join with me in supplications. . . ." Thomas Jefferson, "Second Inaugural Address," 1805; quoted by M. Richard Maxfield, K. Delynn Cook, and W. Cleon Skousen, *The Real Thomas Jefferson,* 2d ed. (Washington, D.C.: National Center for Constitutional Studies, 1981, 1983), pp. 403-4.

were much more influenced by the Reformation. Many of them, including George Washington, Alexander Hamilton, John Jay, Patrick Henry, Samuel Adams, and John Witherspoon, clearly expressed commitment to Christian faith.[8]

Consider, for example, John Witherspoon. Edgar argues incorrectly (citing Marsden, Hatch, and Noll) that Witherspoon "did not think in any distinctively Christian way about politics."[9] While Witherspoon did not participate in the Constitutional Convention, he was a delegate to the New Jersey ratifying convention and a signer of the Declaration of Independence. His influence was nonetheless felt in that nine of the fifty-five Convention delegates were graduates of the College of New Jersey, of which Witherspoon was president. His writings and sermons clearly reveal that he based his political views squarely upon his Calvinistic theology. In particular, his concept of separation of powers and checks and balances was based upon his Calvinist view of the depravity of human nature. This conviction implied that political power must not be trusted to any one individual but must be separated among various branches, with each checking and balancing the others.[10]

8. Washington referred to Jesus Christ as "the Divine Author of our Blessed Religion." Shortly before Alexander Hamilton died, he laid plans for the establishment of an organization called the Christian Constitutional Society, which was to promote the two institutions essential for our free republic — the Christian religion and the rule of law under the Constitution. John Jay, co-author of the *Federalist Papers*, first chief justice of the U.S. Supreme Court, and a founder and national president of the American Bible Society, frequently wrote and spoke about his religious faith. Patrick Henry wrote in a letter to his daughter that "amongst other strange things said of me, I hear it is said by the deists that I am one of the number; and indeed, that some people think I am no Christian. This thought gives me much more pain than the appellation of Tory; because I think religion of infinitely higher importance than politics. . . ." And the man sometimes called "the Father of the American Revolution," Samuel Adams, was motivated largely by Christian conviction. His biographer John C. Miller says of him, "In his eyes, the chief purpose of the American Revolution was to separate New England from the 'decadent' mother country in order that Puritanism might again flourish as it had in the early seventeenth century." George Washington, "Circular Letter to Governors," June 8, 1783; quoted by Paul F. Boller, Jr., in *George Washington and Religion* (Dallas: Southern Methodist University Press, 1963), p. 71. Alexander Hamilton, "Letter to James Bayard," April 1802; cited by Broadus Mitchell, *Alexander Hamilton: The National Adventure 1788-1804* (New York: Macmillan, 1962), pp. 513-14. See Norman Cousins, *In God We Trust: The Religious Beliefs and Ideas of the American Founding Fathers* (New York: Harper and Brothers, 1958), pp. 364-65. Patrick Henry, "Letter to Daughter Betsy," August 20, 1796; quoted by Wiliam Wirt, *Sketches of the Life and Character of Patrick Henry*, rev. ed. (New York: M'Elrath and Sons, 1835), pp. 402-3. John C. Miller, *Sam Adams: Pioneer in Propaganda* (Stanford: Stanford University Press, 1936, 1960), p. 85.

9. Edgar, citing George Marsden, Nathan Hatch, and Mark A. Noll, *The Search for Christian America* (Westchester, Ill.: Crossway, 1983), pp. 86-95.

10. For a fuller exposition of the views of Witherspoon, see Eidsmoe, *Christianity and the Constitution* (Grand Rapids: Baker, 1987), pp. 81-92, 101-2.

Edgar's reference to the 1797 Treaty of Tripoli shows how one must grasp at straws in order to debunk America's Christian heritage. The treaty with Muslim Tripoli is said to contain the language, "As the government of the United Stated is not in any sense founded on the Christian religion . . ." (see p. 184). However, there is good reason to doubt that this language ever appeared in the original version of the treaty. The treaty itself is shrouded in mystery, but the language that appears in English as Article 11 probably was not part of the original Arabic. Rather, it is a handwritten note (inserted between what are numbered Articles 10 and 12 in English) from the Dey of Algiers to the Pasha of Tripoli, assuring him that it is all right to sign the treaty because the United States was not founded on Christianity. This apparently was translated into English along with the treaty itself. It is significant that when the treaty was renegotiated under President Jefferson in 1806, the above-quoted language was omitted.[11]

Why, then, did the Founding Fathers not include an explicit acknowledgment of Christianity in the Constitution? The real reason the Constitution contains no express acknowledgment of Christianity lies in the nature of federalism and our system of limited delegated powers.

As Edgar demonstrates, most of the state constitutions and colonial charters contained explicit recognition of Christianity. As late as 1776 established churches existed in at least eight of the thirteen former colonies and established religions in at least four of the other five.[12] But these established religions differed greatly. It was therefore generally agreed to give the newly created federal government no jurisdiction over religion, but rather to leave that matter to the states. Believing that the federal government they created had no powers other than those delegated to it by the people through the Constitution, the Founders thought they had effectively limited federal power over religion. They clarified that point in the Bill of Rights. For this reason the neutral word *respecting* was used in the First Amendment: "Congress shall make no law respecting an establishment of religion, or prohibiting the free exercise thereof. . . ." This meant two things: (1) no official federal religion; (2) no interference with established state religions.

Another clue to the meaning of the First Amendment is the little word *an* before "establishment." If the word had been *the* it might be inter-

---

11. For a fuller exposition of the controversy surrounding the Treaty of Tripoli, see John Eidsmoe, *Christianity and the Constitution*, app. 1, pp. 513-15. See also, Gary DeMar, "A Response to Dr. William J. Edgar and National Confession" (Atlanta: American Vision, 1987).

12. See Justice Hugo Black, Engel v. Vitale, 370 U.S. 421, 427-28 (1962).

preted to mean no federal involvement with religion, period. But prohibition of "an establishment" meant simply that no one denomination was to be given official recognition above and beyond the others.[13]

In the true sense of the word, religious liberty is perfectly compatible with Christianity. Old Testament Israel was a theocracy, in that God was the ruler of the nation. However, the civil authority (the state) and the religious authority (the priesthood) were distinct offices with distinct personages and distinct functions. The kings always came out of the tribe of Judah, and the priests always came out of the tribe of Levi. Nevertheless, both received their authority from God, and both were subject to the law of God (Deut. 17:14-21).

In the same way, church and state have separate spheres of authority in America; yet we are "One Nation Under God." And while the offices of civil servant and minister of the gospel are separate and distinct, occasionally the same person can fill both offices.[14]

Edgar states that the Framers of the Constitution replaced the sovereignty of God with the sovereignty of the people by beginning the Constitution with "We the people. . . ." I respectfully disagree. The notion of popular sovereignty properly understood, is compatible with Christianity. Repeatedly we read in Scripture that the people chose their rulers (see Judg. 8:22; 9:6; 2 Kings 14:21). This does not mean Old Testament Israel practiced perfect democracy, but it does mean that its government ultimately depended upon the consent of the governed.

On the other hand, the Founders firmly rejected the French notion that "the voice of the people is the voice of God." John Adams declared that *vos populari est non vox dei*; the voice of the people is "sometimes the

---

13. Joseph Story, the Supreme Court justice and Harvard law professor whose *Commentaries on the Constitution* (1833) were the definitive work on the Constitution in the nineteenth century, cannot be accused of pro-Christian bias, since he was himself a Unitarian. But he wrote, "Probably at the time of the adoption of the Constitution, and of the amendment to it now under consideration, the general, if not the universal sentiment was, that Christianity ought to receive encouragement from the state, so far as was not incompatible with the private rights of conscience and the freedom of religious worship. An attempt to level all religions, and to make it a matter of state policy to hold all in utter indifference, would have created universal disapprobation, if not universal indignation." Justice Joseph Story, *Commentaries on the Constitution of the United States*, vol. 2 (Boston: Little, Brown and Co., 1905 [1833]), sec. 1874, p. 593; quoted by Robert L. Cord, *Separation of Church and State: Historical Fact and Current Fiction* (New York: Lambeth Press, 1982), p. 13.

14. When the First Amendment was introduced in Congress in 1789, the Speaker of the House was the Rev. Frederick Conrad Augustus Muhlenberg, an ordained Lutheran clergyman—and he was an enthusiastic supporter of the First Amendment!

voice of Mahomet, of Caesar, of Catiline, the Pope, and the Devil."[15] For this reason, the Founders distrusted pure democracy and, instead, favored a confederate republic in which no one, not even the majority of the people, has absolute power. They devised a system in which the majority has basic control, subject to certain checks, but in which the minority has certain basic rights that even the majority must respect.

Edgar cites Christ's words in Matthew 28:18: "All authority in heaven and on earth has been given to me." He contends that the time Christ assumed this authority was at His ascension. However, Christ spoke those words before His ascension, and the aorist passive indicative does not suggest a continuous action. I believe, rather, that Christ has always had such authority, starting before creation in eternity past, and that He has delegated a small portion of His authority to civil rulers (Dan. 2:21; Ps. 82; Rom. 13:1-7). In other words, Christ's authority, and the authority of civil rulers, is the same in the Old Testament, in the New Testament, and in the church age.

Whether America's founding documents are Christian depends not so much upon whether they bear Christ's name as upon whether the basic principles they contain are compatible with the principles of Christ's Word, the Bible. I believe they are. The concepts of human equality and God-given human rights have their roots in the Judeo-Christian view of man.[16]

The concept of government by consent of the governed, as we have seen, has its roots in Scripture and in the Judeo-Christian view of respect for human dignity. Likewise the concept of limited, delegated powers — that our government has only such power as we, the people, have delegated to it through our Constitution, and no more — is a Judeo-Christian view epitomized in Christ's words in Luke 20:22-25. Commenting on those words, Lord Acton said, "When Christ said 'Render unto Caesar the things that are Caesar's and unto God the things that are God's,' He gave to the state a legitimacy it had never before enjoyed, and set bounds to it that had never yet been acknowledged."[17]

15. John Adams, quoted by Gilbert Chinard, *Honest John Adams* (Boston: Little, Brown and Co., 1933, 1961), p. 248. Adams declared further, "If the majority is 51 and the minority 49, . . . is it certainly the voice of God? If tomorrow one should change to 50 vs. 50, where is the voice of God? If two and the minority should become the majority, is the voice of God changed?" This is typical of the Founding Fathers' sentiments.

16. Even Jefferson stated such concepts in theological terms: "We hold these truths to be self-evident, that all men are created [not evolved] equal, that they are endowed by their Creator [not their government] with certain unalienable rights. . . ."

17. Lord Acton, quoted by Gertrude Himmelfarb, *Lord Acton* (London, 1955), p. 45; in E. L. Hebden Taylor, *The Christian Philosophy of Law, Politics, and the State* (Nutley, N.J.: Craig Press, 1966), pp. 445-46.

A further Judeo-Christian concept is respect for the law of God. In Deuteronomy 17:14-20 God commanded each king of Israel, at the beginning of his reign, to write out a copy of the biblical law and to keep it with him and read it "all the days of his life." When Jefferson wrote in the Declaration of the "Laws of Nature and of Nature's God," he used language borrowed from Sir William Blackstone and others.[18] Blackstone's view of the law of nature is totally consistent with the law of God written upon men's hearts, as Paul describes it in Romans 2:14-15. There need be no sharp dichotomy between the law of nature and the law of Scripture, as both are the law of God.

The Founders held to these Judeo-Christian ideals: human equality, God-given human rights, religious liberty, and government under the law of God. There remained two basic questions.

First, how can one implement these ideals in a society of sinful, fallen men? The Founders recognized that a theory of government must be based upon a realistic view of human nature — and they knew that man is a sinner. They therefore devised a government that prohibited any individual or group from obtaining too much power. First, they limited the governed to certain delegated powers. Second, they divided the powers vertically among local, state, and federal levels. Third, they separated the powers of government horizontally among the legislative, executive, and judicial branches. Fourth, they employed checks and balances so that each branch would check the other. Fifth, they reserved certain individual rights that even a majority may not violate.

The second question was: How can civic virtue, or national morality, be preserved? The Founders knew that a free society cannot survive without civic virtue. Unless men are willing, to some extent, to exercise self-discipline and sacrifice their own desires and interests for the good of the nation, that type of discipline must be imposed from above by a dictator. But the Founders also knew that, human nature being what it is, man is incapable of producing that kind of self-discipline and civic virtue on his own.

18. Sir William Blackstone, *Commentaries on the Laws of England*, quoted by Verna Hall, *Christian History of the Constitution of the United States of America* (San Francisco, Foundation for the American Christian Education, 1962, 1979), pp. 140-46. As Madison put it in *Federalist No. 51*, "But what is government itself but the greatest of all reflections on human nature? If men were angels, no government would be necessary. If angels were to govern men, neither external nor internal controls on government would be necessary. In framing a government which is to be administered by men over men, the great difficulty lies in this: You must first enable the government to control the governed; and in the next place, oblige it to control itself."

So what is the source of civic virtue? The answer according to the Founding Fathers was: religion in general, Christianity in particular. Washington wrote that "Religion and Morality are the essential pillars of civil society."[19] And John Adams declared, "Our constitution was made only for a moral and religious people. It is wholly inadequate for the government of any other."[20]

Can free, limited constitutional government survive in the United States today? I believe it can, because the principles of our Declaration of Independence and Constitution are timeless — but only to the extent that twentieth-century Americans hold to the faith of our Founding Fathers, the Judeo-Christian principles found in the Word of God.

19. See Washington, quoted by Ashabel Green, *The Life of Ashabel Green, By Himself* (1849), p. 615; quoted by Boller, *George Washington and Religion*, p. 82.
20. John Adams, 1789; quoted in *War on Religious Freedom* (Virginia Beach: Freedom Council, 1984), p. 1.

Part Five

Major Responses

displayed the righteousness of God, which will be evident (at least) in all affairs of life in the ultimate form of the kingdom after Christ returns (the eternal state). But I completely disagree with any notion that the civil laws served *the same* soteriological *function* as the ceremonial laws, or that they "foreshadowed" the work of the Messiah in *the same way* that the sacrificial laws did so. To think that they did is exegetically groundless and theologically misleading. The civil laws of Old Testament Israel did not, as was characteristic of the ceremonial laws, expound the way of gaining redemption or symbolize the setting of God's people redemptively apart from the world.[6]

A similar rejoinder is called for when, later in his response, Schrotenboer insists that redemption (salvation) is "as wide as societal life, even as wide as the new creation where righteousness will be the order of the day" (p. 58). Even as I have done above, he alludes to the new creation that is to come (e.g., 2 Pet. 3:13). I have no objection to using the word *redemption* to encompass everything pertaining to the restoration of the fallen creation (cf. Rom. 8:23; Eph. 1:14; 4:30; Col. 1:13-20), thus including the righteous behavior and attitudes that are expected of God's redeemed people and that will characterize the new creation. However, it would be a grave theological mistake to overlook the fact that the word redemption is here being used *broadly* to cover both *the means* of redemption (Christ's sacrificial, substitutionary death) and *the effects* of that redemption (the holy conduct of His people). To intermingle or confuse those two different senses of *redemption* is a grave theological mistake, one bound to mislead God's people away from the purity of the gospel; we are not saved *by* our righteous behavior, but rather saved *unto* righteous behavior (e.g., Eph. 2:8-10; Rom. 3:28; 8:4). I fear that Schrotenboer and many others in our day teeter precariously on the edge of that misleading error when they speak ambiguously of "the laws that define the righteousness of God" as being "*redemptive*" in nature. To eschew theological equivocation, theonomists concur with the Reformed heritage in discriminating between laws that display the *way* of redemption (ceremonial) and laws that define the righteousness of God (moral, civil) to be emulated as an *effect* of redemption.[7]

6. See my essay's discussion of the New Covenant surpassing the Old Covenant in realization. Cf. *By This Standard*, pp. 135-38, 162-66, 281-82.

7. An analogous confusion is detected when Schrotenboer argues that all of the Old Testament legislation was "redemptively oriented," since some regulations (e.g., Lev. 19:35-37) are "related" to God's deliverance of Israel and others are "grounded on" the call to be holy because God is holy (e.g., throughout Leviticus). What we need to ask, of

6. Twice in the early portion of his response, Schrotenboer cites New Testament texts (1 Cor. 9:21; Gal. 4:1-7) in order to mitigate the normativity of the Old Testament law as such. In both cases he fails to utilize sound historico-grammatical and contextual exegesis to understand the meaning of the passages.[8] He treats them as applying *categorically* to the Mosaic law in its entirety—thus creating a self-contradiction in Paul's own teaching (e.g., Rom. 7:12; 13:8-10). In fact the passages pertain specifically to the law in its ceremonial functions or aspects. (We must not forget that Paul and others used the simple word "law" [*nomos*] with a variety of different senses.)

course, is what specific kind of "relation" or "grounding" these examples represent. Upon reflection it seems Schrotenboer has confused the *nature* of these commandments (which is moral in itself) with the *motive* declared for keeping them (which is often a matter of redemptive gratitude or divine emulation). The motive-clauses in the law do not transform God's moral demands into ceremonial regulations.

8. For instance, the "adaptation" of which Paul speaks in 1 Cor. 9:21 is certainly not the one suggested by Schrotenboer, namely, a cultural or pragmatic flexibility about God's *moral* laws. It is certainly not our prerogative to make just any changes in that law that seem good to us in "working for the coming of Christ's kingdom" (to use Schrotenboer's words). In 1 Cor. 9, Paul's adaptability was concerned specifically with the *ceremonial* laws that culturally separated the Jews from the Gentiles (e.g., the prohibition on eating pork). He said that he would observe such strictures among the Jews, but live as someone without such strictures among the Gentiles. Notice, for instance, how "becoming as a Jew" is placed in parallel to "becoming as under the law" in v. 20. Paul does this even though *only some* of the regulations of "the law" imposed a difference between Jewish and Gentile lifestyles (e.g., Deut. 14:21); in most cases the law's stipulations bound Jew and Greek alike (cf. Rom. 1:32; 2:14-15; 3:19). Alteration in Paul's conduct was permissible because he was not morally bound by the ceremonial code in the first place, thus leaving him free to follow or ignore its provisions for symbolizing Jewish separation, according to the governing principle that he should become all things to all men in order to gain some for Christ. It would be absurd to think that Paul intended to teach that he was allowed to break God's moral law (by stealing, raping, blaspheming, etc.) among the Gentiles, but was obligated to refrain from doing so among the Jews, in order that both groups might be drawn to Christianity! Cf. *By This Standard*, pp. 187-98, 308.

Schrotenboer also refers to Gal. 4:1-7, indicating that Old Testament Israel was under "the law" as a schoolmaster, or tutor, which has in some sense passed away now that Christ has come. Again, however, detailed exegesis reveals that Paul's specific denotation was the ceremonial character of the law. The language (semantics) of Paul, the illustrations used in literary context, the historical setting, and the very way Paul described the law as a "tutor unto Christ" all point to the fact that he was not speaking of the moral law, but rather the ceremonial law. He spoke of those "rudiments" (Gal. 4:3, 9) which Col. 2:16-17 says were a foreshadow of things to come, the body of which is Christ. He spoke in the historical context of a contest with the Judaizers who insisted upon circumcision for salvation (Gal. 2:3-4), and he used the illustration of the ceremonial calendar (Gal. 4:10). It was the ceremonial law that was a tutor for those in their spiritual minority that pointed to Christ and taught justification by faith (Gal. 3:24); the moral law itself contained no such gospel, but only the demand that convicts sinners and brings them under judgment. Unfortunately, Schrotenboer does not interact with this understanding of the passage as it is mentioned in my essay or other published materials. Cf. *By This Standard*, pp. 189, 309-10.

7. Schrotenboer considers it a drawback that, when Israel received the Mosaic law, the nation did not *distinguish* the life "zones" we call ecclesiastical, civil, and industrial. He later speaks of the Mosaic regulations being "geared to the primitive state of Israel's societal structure." I remarked earlier in 2 that Schrotenboer offers no objective means of determining what these alleged life-zones are. Nor has he offered any reason to think that ancient Israel's perspective on this matter might not have been closer to reality (or to the divine intention) than his own outlook. But more significantly, we must simply deny Schrotenboer's claim that Israel did not "distinguish" religious cult (ecclesiastical affairs) from state (political affairs). Such a misconception, though popular, is simply not true to historical fact and divine revelation.[9] The functions and the qualifications for office were recognizably different for priests and civil leaders in Old Testament Israel. Regardless of the form of civil government Israel had at any particular time in her national history, and regardless of how "primitive" her "societal structure" may seem to Schrotenboer, there was still a difference between those laws which God revealed for political rulers to obey and those which were revealed for the priests to follow.

8. But, says Schrotenboer, the moral, civil, and ceremonial laws were not "strictly delineated" in the Old Testament. He later explicitly questions the distinction. Still later he criticizes it for being "misleading." I believe that his failure to recognize the distinction is a serious literary, ethical, and theological mistake—a mistake compounded by a muddled understanding of it,[10] as well as by a fatal misperception of the theonomic conception.[11]

9. See my book, *Theonomy in Christian Ethics* (Phillipsburg, N.J.: Presbyterian and Reformed, 1977), chap. 20; cf. *By This Standard*, pp. 286-90.

10. It is evident that Schrotenboer confuses *different types* of discontinuity that hold between our day and Old Testament legislative literature. He runs together the "cultural forms" of Old Testament laws with the "shadows" contained in the law, which look ahead to the work of Christ (midway through his section 3). Likewise, later in the same section, he merges the "redemptively" oriented aspects of the Mosaic law-system with the "culturally conditioned" aspect of it. Treating these two as belonging to the same category of discontinuity inevitably leads to garbled conclusions. As I explained in my essay, some discontinuities with the Old Testament, even as with the New, are merely a matter of *cultural* lifestyle (affected simply by the natural course of time and circumstances of place), while others are necessitated by *redemptive-historical* changes (affected by the supernatural intervention of God to accomplish redemption, fulfill prophecy and promise, and give substance to foreshadows of salvation). These are logically distinct matters, answering to different factors and leading to different kinds of treatment. But he does not interact with the analysis of this in the essay at all.

11. Toward the beginning of the conclusion of his response, Schrotenboer opines that we might find a port of entry to "a haven of agreement" with pluralists if theonomists would only treat "the civil provisions" of the Mosaic law in the same way that my essay

The first thing that Schrotenboer misses is that these categories of law did not *need* to be written out in *delineated* literary subsections in order for them to be, nevertheless, clearly *distinguishable* by the Israelites. So his objection about the moral/civil/ceremonial breakdown invents a difficulty where one hardly existed. [12] Second, with the coming of New Covenant revelation (which helps us understand even better the meaning and purpose of Old Covenant commands), the cogency and necessity of something like the moral/civil/ceremonial distinction becomes *all the more* apparent. It accounts for Paul's insistence on submission to case-law ("civil") provisions of the Old Testament (e.g., 1 Tim. 5:18) and his refusal to see other ("ceremonial") laws as obligatory (e.g., Gal. 2:3; 5:2, 6). Third, if Schrotenboer wishes to call into question the legitimacy of the traditional Reformed categorization of the Old Testament law (cf. Westminster Confession of Faith XIX), he really should have dealt in some detailed fashion with that part of my essay (or other publications) which offers biblical evidence of its theological propriety. He offers no rebuttal. [13]

treated the validity of the specific case laws; namely, in terms of their "broader, underlying principle" or "general equity" (although Schrotenboer *himself*, earlier in the first paragraph of his section 2, actually *contrasted* "culturally conditioned" regulations with the "civil laws" of the Pentateuch). This, however, is precisely the way that theonomists *do* interpret the civil case-laws of the Old Testament — and always have! (One can find this in my original treatise, *Theonomy in Christian Ethics*, in subsequent journal articles, and most recently in *By This Standard*). Thus when Schrotenboer concludes by recommending the Westminster Confession's statement (XIX, 4) that Israel's judicial laws no longer oblige anyone beyond their general equity, he has come to a position with which theonomists entirely concur (*Theonomy in Christian Ethics*, pp. 539-41; cf. *Journal of Christian Reconstruction* 5, 2 [Winter 1978-79]), *passim*. Having misunderstood from the outset what the theonomic position actually is, his opposition to that view is weakened considerably.

12. A category distinction is unmistakable in God's declaration, "I desire faithful love, not sacrifice" (Hos. 6:6). That statement would have made no sense whatsoever if Israel could not tell the difference between the laws demanding sacrifice (which we call "ceremonial") and the laws demanding faithful love (which we call "moral" and "civil"). Are we to believe that the ancient Israelites lacked the mental acumen to catch the contrast between laws that bound Jews and Gentiles *alike* (e.g, the death penalty for murder, Lev. 24:21-22) and those which bound Jews but *not* Gentiles (e.g., the prohibition of eating animals that died of themselves, Deut. 14:21)? Whether they used the verbal labels of "civil" and "ceremonial" (as we do) is beside the point. The category difference was hardly beyond an Israelite's mental discernment. Moreover, surely even the ancient Israelites recognized the difference between commands pertaining to kings (e.g., Prov. 31:4-5) and to judges (e.g., Deut. 16:18-19) and to parents (e.g., Deut. 6:7-9) and to merchants (e.g., Lev. 19:36) and to farmers (e.g., Lev. 19:9-10) and to children (e.g., Exod. 20:12) and to priests (e.g., Lev. 1:5), and so on.

13. Instead of rebutting the rationale for the categorization, Schrotenboer merely repeats his questionable notion that Israel was an "undifferentiated society" (see *8* above) and then his equivocal remark that all of God's laws "are redemptively oriented" (see *5* above). He also, at two different places, makes strange (and undefended) comments about the dietary provisions of the Mosaic law.

First, he insists that the dietary laws were an indissoluble "blend" of moral and redemptive. But this is hardly believable since the Gentiles were never obligated to observe such

9. Schrotenboer says that Israel, breaking both parts of the love commandment, failed as a model to the nations. I agree. However, it was the nation that failed, not the divine revelation delivered to Israel. That revelation of God's law was Israel's great advantage (Rom. 3:1-2). Since theonomists promote the advantage of God's law (not the deplorable disobedience of Israel to it), the relevance of Schrotenboer's remark is not at all clear.

10. Exegetically speaking, Schrotenboer is quite mistaken to pit the "summary" and "comprehensive commands" of God's law against its "specific regulations." After all, it really makes no sense to say someone complies with the summary command of love (Lev. 19:18) when he violates the "specific regulation," for instance, of not tripping a blind person (v. 14 preceding). It is precisely the *specific regulations* that the "summary" commands *summarize*! What rationale does Schrotenboer offer for such shaky reasoning? He says the summary or comprehensive commands of

---

regulations, and "moral" laws are those by which God has "bound *all* [of Adam's] posterity, to personal, entire, exact and perpetual obedience . . . [as] a perfect rule of righteousness" (Westminster Confession of Faith, XIX, 1-2). I indicate in my essay and other publications that, based on Acts 10, the dietary provisions symbolically taught the separation of Jew from Gentile, and such provisions were not meant to be perpetually binding: "what God has cleansed do not treat as unclean" (v. 15). Because the New Covenant brings together Jews and Gentiles on an equal footing, there is no offense in eating pork or shrimp today. We have here a paradigm case of the theonomic approach: Old Testament regulations are set aside, but only when there is textual warrant from God's own Word.

The second odd thing about Schrotenboer's references to the dietary laws is that he first says that they "need no longer be observed" (end of section 3 in his response), but then later contends, based on Acts 15, that "the New Testament prescribes them for us Gentiles" (midway through his conclusion). This contradiction needs to be resolved by correcting his misinterpretation of Acts 15:20, 29 (where the only dietary regulation *as such* that is taken from the *Mosaic law* is the prohibition of eating blood, which includes meat killed by strangling instead of butchering). The Old Testament taught that blood was prohibited, not for any inherently moral reason, but because of its symbolism and place in the sacrificial ritual (cf. Lev. 17:10-11; Deut. 12:23, 27). When Christ's redemptive work put aside the law's sacrificial practices (e.g., Heb. 10:8-14), it likewise ended the corresponding dietary regulation. The reason this (otherwise nonbinding) stipulation was imposed on converted Gentiles in a particular local circumstance was not that it was a "moral" law, but simply to smooth social contact and table-fellowship between them and converted Jews, for whom eating blood was traditionally repulsive. That is, the obligatory first principle on which the Jerusalem Council acted was that of the Christian's need for loving sensitivity and church unity, *not* the dietary law itself. This being the case, Christians need to observe such a law (as with Paul, 1 Cor. 9:20-21), *only when* dictated by the moral mandate to avoid causing disharmony or a stumblingblock. That this was exactly the import of the Jerusalem Council's decree is quite obvious from a study of its other demand, that Gentile converts not eat meat sacrificed to idols. Paul declared this practice to be entirely *permissible* in itself (1 Cor. 8:4, 8; 10:25), *but* ruled it out only when in a particular situation it caused stumbling for a brother with a weak conscience (8:9, 13; 10:23-24).

the Old Testament have "abiding significance" (in contrast to the specific regulations) *because* for them "we have Jesus' word." But, of course, we just as much *have Jesus' word* for "every jot and tittle of the law" (Matt. 5:18), for "every word that proceeds from God's mouth" (Matt. 4:4), for even "the least of these commandments" (Matt. 5:19)! Schrotenboer's reasoning is self-refuting. Even when Jesus reminds us that we ought to attend to the weightier matters of the law, He immediately adds that the lesser matters "should not be left undone" (Matt. 23:23). Those minor, specific regulations of the law do not dispense with the summary command of love; they rather *define* it. As Jesus said, "*If* you love Me, you will keep My commandments" (John 14:15).

11. Although it was not part of my essay (or in any way essential to its argumentation), the use of *pleerosai* in Matthew 5:17 is broached by Schrotenboer. I believe that the debate over how to translate or interpret that Greek word is really irrelevant, *as long as* one is faithful to the literary context where it appears.[14] However, Schrotenboer's exegesis of the text is superficial and faulty — straining against and ignoring the context to make "fulfill" create *discontinuity* with the Old Testament and applying the word to Christ's *redemptive* acts.[15]

14. A detailed treatment of this word and the passage in which it appears may be pursued in *Theonomy in Christian Ethics*, chap. 2. For a detailed treatment of Rom. 10:4, also cited by Schrotenboer, a passage that calls Christ "the end" (*telos*) of the law, see Daniel P. Fuller, *Gospel and Law: Contrast or Continuum?* (Grand Rapids: Eerdmans, 1980).

15. Schrotenboer portrays "fulfill" in Matt. 5:17 as supporting the "discontinuity" (as opposed to identity-continuity) side of Christ's relation to the Old Testament law. But that is obviously and completely at odds with the local context! The point, which is made in many ways over again, is that we dare not pit Jesus against even the least commandment of the Old Testament (vv. 18-19); He, not the Jewish elders, gives the law its full authority and intention (vv. 20ff.). The thrust in this particular pericope is upon Jesus' *continuity* with the law, not discontinuity.

Schrotenboer does further violence to the exegetical context of Matt. 5:17 when he claims that "fulfill" is there applied to the "redemptive acts" of Christ's own ministry and mission — the actions ("happening") by which He fulfilled the "promise" made in the Old Testament, as well as "all that was yet preparatory and incomplete and in itself ineffective." However, there is not the slightest *linguistic evidence* for these things in the text of Matt. 5; they are completely read into the passage from outside. Not one word is spoken of prophecies, promises, or foreshadows of the Old Covenant. Not one word is spoken of the redemptive work of Christ leading to the cross and resurrection. We read rather about ethics. The passage begins with "hungering and thirsting" (indeed being "persecuted") "for righteousness sake" (vv. 3-12), then proceeds to an elaboration of the "good works" of Christ's disciples as light and salt (v. 16), the status of the law's "commands" (vv. 18-19), and the genuine demand they make of us (vv. 20ff.) — all climaxing in the call for moral "perfection" (v. 48) and then instructions about "doing your righteousness before men" (6:1; cf. 5:16). Schrotenboer is simply riding roughshod over the actual text of Matthew here, wrongly assuming that he may take the connotation of "fulfill" as it is found in other passages altogether and pour it back into its use at Matt. 5:17.

Finally, although Schrotenboer alleges that it does "serious injustice to Jesus' words" to interpret "fulfill" in the sense of confirming the law and giving it its full measure, he offers

12. Based on his preceding lines of discussion, Schrotenboer comes to the judgment that pluralists "obviously find a different kind of discontinuity" than do theonomists between God's work in Israel and His work in Christ. Pluralists see the discontinuity as being greater,[16] "because the civil regulations *as such* no longer apply" (p. 57). The problem here, though, is that he has not presented even one specific biblical text to support or insinuate that the civil regulations of the Old Testament law are abrogated under the New Covenant. Not one line of biblical exegesis or argumentation is offered for this conclusion — over against the multitude of scriptural proofs adduced in my essay. Not only is his claim naked of any textual warrant; none of his preceding considerations supply premises from which he could soundly deduce that the civil laws are abrogated. Those foregoing considerations are either factually mistaken, or the conclusion does not logically follow from them. In short, he has failed to supply any good reason for his assertion. Hearkening back to response *1* above, I would simply challenge Schrotenboer and other pluralists to prove that the civil legislation of the Old Testament no longer holds validity, and to prove it *by means of* "the Holy Spirit speaking in the Scripture." Without that, their polemics can have no persuasive power.

13. Schrotenboer finds it "a mystery" that my essay was relatively silent about the Holy Spirit. But the explanation is simple. I was not allotted sufficient space in my essay to talk about everything.[17] In light of

not the slightest line of reasoning to refute the detailed studies that substantiate that approach. This (alleged) "serious injustice" is not solely the province of *Theonomy in Christian Ethics*, after all; others "guilty" of it include John Murray, George Eldon Ladd, David Wenham, the latest edition of the Bauer-Arndt-Gingrich Greek lexicon, W. H. P. Hatch, G. Dalman, B. H. Branscomb, and so on. Schrotenboer owes us argumentation, not mere accusation.

16. By the way, Schrotenboer here offers an excellent illustration of the strange "theologian's talk" that so often frustrates analytical philosophers. He says that "the discontinuity is greater" *because* "the continuity is greater." This kind of paradoxical (if not illogical) talk is baffling — and must continue to be so until he clearly and cogently explains the particular *sense* of "discontinuity" he intends, as well as the particular *sense* of "continuity" he intends, the *logical relation* that holds between those two senses or notions, and the substantial *evidence* he has for asserting the greater continuity, the greater discontinuity, and the way the former warrants the latter. There may be rhetorical value in declaring greater *dis*continuity on the basis of greater *con*tinuity, but without some conceptual clarification it is dubious that it makes good sense.

17. If I did not elaborate on the work of the Holy Spirit, it is certainly not because I minimize it (any more than I slight the doctrine of the virgin birth by not discussing it in my essay). The work of the Holy Spirit as it bears upon the Christian and God's law is precisely the subject of chap. 7 in *Theonomy in Christian Ethics* and of chap. 8 in *By This Standard* (cf. also the index of each book for further references). It seems to me that all of us who are part of this consultation already take for granted what Schrotenboer writes about the Holy Spirit. It did not require distinctive mention by any of us.

the precarious tendency toward subjectivism and imaginative theologizing all around us in our day, however, I do regard it worth repeating that the Holy Spirit enlightens our understanding of the written Word, rather than taking the place of that objective standard or giving us supplemental revelations. That is, the Spirit testifies to Christ and His Word, rather than testifying of Himself (John 16:13-14). The Spirit leads *by* the Word, not outside of or against that Word. This brings Schrotenboer's discussion back to the Scripture and to the need for textual exegesis of it in order to make the points he wishes to make (cf. response *1* above).

14. That is precisely what is lacking with respect to those substantial claims in Schrotenboer's response which I find the most dangerous of all. For instance, he asserts at the end of section 2 of his response that "what carries over from the Old Testament civil legislation" for our day is *simply* the amorphous, abstract principle: "God wills that justice prevail" (entailing "release from oppression"). The danger, of course, is that anybody can pour whatever content he wishes into this generic notion of "justice" (or "oppression") — and conflicting schools of thought obviously interpret the ideal of justice in vastly different ways! One man's "justice" is another man's "oppression," unless we have the written, objective, and absolute standard of God's *detailed* moral revelation by which to judge.

By contrast, Schrotenboer sets aside the details of God's wisdom for civil affairs; as he later puts it, "God does not intend us" to "superimpose on our society" the positive civil laws of the Old Testament, which gave concrete expression to God's "abiding law of love and justice" (midway through his conclusion). He maintains, instead, that the formal principle of justice is to be *situationally* defined today: "the form in which justice is to be maintained . . . should fit the situation" (p. 57). Such a suggestion is shocking from an advocate of Reformed Christianity, since Calvinism characteristically *distrusts* fallen man's imagined moral judgments. Calvinism points men to God's special revelation to *correct* the details of their distorted ideas of right and wrong: one of Scripture's key benefits is that it offers "reproof, correction, and instruction in righteousness" (2 Tim. 3:16), and indeed "through the law comes the knowledge of sin" (Rom. 3:20; cf. 7:7; 1 John 3:4). By recommending a situationally defined idea of justice, he opens the door to moral relativism, which, in turn, opens the door to political tyranny with its attendant social *oppression* and physical *brutality.* For that reason his political outlook fails the most elementary test in Christian ethics: Does it show genuine "love for your neighbor as yourself" (Matt. 22:39-40)? Love would not work harm to one's neighbor (Rom. 13:10) by opening the door to political violence in the amorphous name of "justice." Rather, "hereby we know that we love God's children, when we love God and do His commandments . . . and His commandments [in contrast to every politician's own idea of justice] are not burdensome" (1 John 5:2-3).

Without any attempt to offer scriptural justification, Schrotenboer alleges that the role of civil government is "broader" than coercive power to enforce God's criminal law. He claims that the civil government also has a proper "educational" function. *Where* does "the Holy Spirit speaking in the Scripture" say such a thing? To grant educational authority to the state is to arm it with the most efficient weapon of despotism: control over the minds and outlook of its citizens, especially the young. Today we increasingly suffer the evil effects of having allowed the state to assume jurisdiction in schooling: antagonism to the independence of Christian schools, the enforced "secularism" of the public school mentality, declining scholarly achievement, and degenerating morals. In light of these things, Schrotenboer must be challenged to adduce some very strong biblical justification for his dangerous opinion that the state has an "educational" function. None has been yet given.

He should also bring forth a cogent analysis and exegetical justification for the hazardous thesis that the laws of Jubilee (Lev. 25) "meant in essence that land, which was the means of production, would periodically be redistributed." In the New Testament, he maintains, this "requires an equalization in ownership" (p. 60). He leaves no doubt about his appalling socialist intentions here: "land reform" and freedom to be "communally responsible"—which entails his objection to the alleged circumstance that a small number of families own most of the land of El Salvador! To read an advocate of the Reformed faith endorse socialism ("equalization in ownership" as the state's duty in the name of "public justice") in this brazen way is ominous. It ought to be clear by now (from both reasoned analysis and historical experience) that state-enforced socialism is about as morally repulsive and fallacious a social theory as one can find. It involves the oppressive intrusion of the state into the individual's right of private property and contract (cf. Exod. 20:15; Matt. 20:15) and the "beastly" presumption to control the marketplace (cf. Rev. 13:17). It unlovingly turns the state into a tyrannical thief that shows respect of persons (Exod. 23:3; Lev. 19:15, 18; cf. Exod. 30:15) and frames mischief by a law (Ps. 94:20). Nowhere does "the Holy Spirit speaking in the Scripture" delegate to the state the authority to redistribute wealth and equalize possessions. Schrotenboer's unproven supposition that the state has such competence and right necessitates a very negative verdict on pluralism. As is evident in this paragraph and the previous two, pluralism's ideal of "public justice" (disregarding the details of God's civil laws) is the Christian's slippery-slope to statism.

15. By way of summary, let me here add a concise bottom-line evaluation of confessional pluralism (see note 1). I believe that pluralism is *neither* faithful to Scripture *nor* even logically cogent. (1) Contrary to the biblical demand that all the kings and judges of the earth "serve Jehovah" specifically (Ps. 2:10-11), pluralism instead calls upon the rulers of the state to honor and protect all religious positions, regardless of their negative attitudes toward Jehovah. Furthermore, by subtracting the civil commandments from God's law without relevant and specific biblical warrant, pluralists come under the condemnation of the law itself (Deut. 4:2; 17:20) and under the censure of our Lord (Matt. 5:19). (2) But not only is pluralism morally wrong, it is logically impossible. When one religious philosophy *requires* the death penalty for murder and another *forbids* the death penalty for murder, the state cannot conceivably give "equal protection" to both viewpoints; whether it executes the murderer or not, the state will have violated one of the competing religious convictions, thus not honoring both equally. The "King of kings," Jesus Christ, requires certain things to be done by the kings of the earth, and about those requirements we may not (morally) and cannot (logically) be "pluralists." As Jesus declared, "He who is not for Me is against Me" (Matt. 12:30). As faithful disciples of the Lord, we must urge the state to base its actions and policies upon the *one* and *only* sound moral perspective, the one revealed by Christ — not some blend of "plural" religious views and attitudes.

16. Turning briefly to the national confession response to my essay, I wish to reassure Harrington that the use of the word "explicitly" in the first sentence of my essay was not at all meant to disparage "good and necessary consequences" that are deduced from what Scripture explicitly teaches (Westminster Confession of Faith, I, 6). It was, rather, meant as a challenge to those who claim the Bible for their authority without proving their theses or conclusions by means of sound hermeneutical principles applied to particular texts of Scripture. There are too many unjustified, vague, subjective, and virtually mystical claims for what "the message" of the Bible is in our day.

17. When Harrington expresses agreement with the direction theonomists take, but doubts some of the conclusions they have reached, I would only repeat what I have said in note 4 to my essay. I too find some of the interpretations and applications of the law that modern theonomists

propose to be highly questionable[18] (and sometimes rooted in a positively objectionable hermeneutic).[19] Nevertheless, the foundational program is a sound one, even if some attempts to build on it need correction or refinement.

18. Harrington proposes that it is the duty of the civil magistrate to apply and enforce the moral law of God under modern conditions. This is, contrary to his statement, precisely the theonomic solution. We would simply add that "the moral law" is not restricted to the Ten Commandments; they are rather "the summary" of the moral law (Westminster Larger Catechism, 98), the details of which illustrate what the Ten Commandments specifically mean.[20]

19. I am glad to repeat for Harrington (cf. note 9 to my essay) that postmillennial eschatology is not *logically* integral to the theonomic understanding of the civil magistrate.[21] Moreover, the literature that sometimes expresses the opposite view in rather irritating and divisive terms is as offensive to me as a postmillennialist as it is to Harrington as an amillennialist. Those who insist that postmillennialism is logically demanded by theonomy usually do not accurately grasp what logic or logical inference really is. They end up talking about a *psycho*logical connection between theonomy and postmillennialism, or they think that since the two positions are both biblical concepts (with which I agree) they must "logically" entail each other (which I dispute). Christ's humanity and Christ's deity are both taught in the Bible, but that does not at all mean that the concept of someone's being human logically entails that this person is divine! We logically distinguish Christ's deity from His humanity, and similarly we should logically distinguish the theses of ethics (about what ought to be the case) from those of eschatology (about what will actually be the case).

18. A notorious example is R. J. Rushdoony's view that believers ought to observe the dietary laws today, but they are not subject to discipline (even by the church) for failing to observe the law's Sabbath regulations (*Institutes of Biblical Law* [N.p.: Craig Press, 1973], pp. 131-33, 151-54, 297-302). But a whole host of secondary detailed disagreements in interpretation of application could be mentioned: e.g., David Chilton treats the head tax of Exod. 30:11-16 as the province of the civil government (*Productive Christians in an Age of Guilt Manipulators* [Tyler, Tex.: Institute for Christian Economics, 1981], p. 35).

19. An example is the fanciful stream-of-consciousness connections, allegorical flights, and even numerology proposed by James Jordan (e.g., *The Law of the Covenant* [Tyler, Tex.: Institute for Christian Economics, 1984], apps. F, G) or the artificial imposition of an imagined blanket outline (with imprecise, pre-established categories) on biblical materials suggested by Ray Sutton (*That You May Prosper* [Tyler, Tex.: Institute for Christian Economics, 1987] e.g., apps. 1-5).

20. Cf. Carl Bogue, "What Does the Decalogue Summarize?" *Covenanter Witness* 103, 5 (May 1987): 4-6.

21. Contrary to the misleading argumentation of some theonomists (e.g., Gary North, *Dominion and Common Grace: The Biblical Basis for Progress* [Tyler, Tex.: Institute for Christian Economics, 1987], chap. 5, esp. pp. 138ff.).

18

The Principled Pluralist
Major Response

Gordon J. Spykman

I will respond briefly to three issues that David M. Carson of the national confessional position raised in response to my essay.

First, he asked if there is not a contradiction involved in trying, in the name of Christ, to reclaim all spheres of life for the honor of God and, yet, at the same time treating all religions as equal before the law. To do what I suggest is simply to recognize that structural pluralism is normative, but that confessional diversity or religious heterogeneity is a historical reality. Acknowledging both of these is not a contradiction. Instead, it recognizes the dialectic that exists in history because of sin and the counteracting effect of God's grace; a conflict is occurring between the city of God and the city of the world, between the kingdom of light and the kingdom of darkness. But that is not a contradiction; that is the antithesis.

Second, Carson noted that my essay offers no definition of justice. I do provide a definition of sorts, although it is implicit. I argue that there is no universally accepted definition of justice. Each community defines justice in terms of its own religious convictions, in terms of its own world view. Justice for some means giving every man his due; justice for the capitalist means giving every man what he deserves; justice for the socialist means giving every man what he needs. Justice from a biblically Reformed position means enabling people to fulfill their offices as marriage partners, as parents, as elders in the church, as teachers in the school, and so forth. In biblical teaching, the universal office of every believer is differentiated into a spectrum of offices, which points once again toward a pluralistically structured society.

Third, Carson asks, what holds a society together? For the last sixteen hundred years the Judeo-Christian tradition has been considered the major source of social cohesion in Western civilization. Attacks upon that tradition have weakened its ability to serve as a foundation for social life. Francis Schaeffer argued that secularization began in the 1920s. I think it began much earlier. Perhaps the disintegration of Western society's Christian foundations first became widely apparent in the 1920s, but the roots go back in the eighteenth century. As Hitler's Germany experienced a crisis in the 1930s, we may be headed for a similar cultural crisis, but stemming from different sources.

What holds a society together? Until now our secularizing society has depended on the public school system to provide social coherence. Our public school system supposedly creates national unity out of the melting pot of ethnic and cultural groups. When you suggest alternatives to the system or question its value basis, you are questioning the fundamental source of cultural integration which provides security for many Americans. We should not, however, expect one sphere called education to bear the whole weight of society in holding it together. Other social institutions should share in this task.

Turning to T. M. Moore's response for the Christian America position, four times he asked, What do I mean by "word of God?" There is a word of God that precedes the written Word of God in the Scriptures. The law, the will of God, was not born on Mount Sinai with the giving of the Ten Commandments. It began at creation. God spoke all things into existence: "The heavens declare the glory of God and the skies proclaim the work of his hands" (Ps. 19:1, NIV). Revelation, Hebrews, and John's Gospel make this same point. Scripture teaches that what God brought into existence by the power of His word was a coherent creation that makes sense. God's original creative word still holds. Paul refers to this word when he declares in Romans 2 that even those who do not have the law that was promulgated on Mount Sinai are still aware inwardly of God's basic laws, which either accuse or excuse them. Thus we have some point of contact with those who are not Christians.

Because the grace of God still preserves some creational sense of right and wrong, we can appeal to that original and abiding revelation and say to non-Christians, "Do you not agree that it is wrong, for example, to engage in sexual promiscuity?" No one can disobey the word of God with impunity. The Word inscripturated reinforces, reiterates, and republishes the creational word in written redemptive form. Scripture does not negate God's creational word. That word is abiding; it holds for all creatures. Since Christ's death we know this word only through the Scriptures. That is why John Calvin described the Bible as a pair of glasses. For example, I could not discern one face from another in a crowd without my glasses. But with them, I can see clearly who people are. So also the light of God's Word dispels the darkness of sin; it gives sight to eyes blurred by sin. That is how the Scriptures work. The Scrip-

tures do not draw us away from creation; rather, they bring us back to
the creation in a meaningful way. Only by being grounded in God's creative work can we understand what redemption is all about; redemption
restores the fallen creation to what God meant it to be.

I now turn to Moore's concern about mediating structures. To relate
them to Islam, Marxism, and Christianity, as he does, is to confuse
structure and direction. Structural pluralism refers to the rightful existence of a plurality of institutions in society, such as homes, schools, and
churches. Religious pluralism refers to the spirit that pervades these societal structures: there are, for example, Christian homes, but also
homes directed by an Islamic spirituality or a Marxist ideology. To say
that I look to the state for reconciliation instead of to Christ is to misread
what I said. Both the church and state are to promote reconciliation in
society, but in different ways. Christians, however, have not sufficiently
called the state to be an agent of reconciliation and justice in society.

To help common Christians on the street and in the pew, we need organizations like the Association for Public Justice and other Christian
political movements. Supporting these groups with our time and money
is more important than ever before. Let us put our efforts where our
mouths are.

Representing theonomy, Carl Bogue accuses me of deducing confessional pluralism from structural pluralism. He alleges that I make one
follow logically from the other, that I make one equivalent to the other.
He misreads my paper. I do not see that kind of connection between
structural and confessional pluralism. Structural pluralism is a normative given of God's creation. Confessional pluralism, the diversity of
religious convictions, results from distortions in God's creation. The one
must be kept normative. The other must be accepted as a historical reality and addressed with a strategy derived from the gospel.

During the consultation one important question arose from the floor.
The questioner agreed that confessional pluralism is a historical reality.
But is it, he asked also a *de jure* reality, that is, is this a situation that God
wills? The answer is no. Religious diversity is an antinormative state of
affairs. Yet, as the parable of the wheat and the tares reveals (Matt. 13),
God does not intervene directly to change this religiously mixed situation until the judgment day. He exercises an eschatological forebear-
ance. The day of grace, with its call to repentance, faith, and obedience,
continues. To convert others we are not to use the civil sword of the
state, but the sword of the Spirit, which is the persuasive power of the
Word of God. During these end times, the task of civil government in

administrating public justice evenhandedly is, therefore, not to revert to the "Christendom" models of the past, with their favored religions and established churches, but to deal equitably with all faith communities within its jurisdiction. The blemishes of the past notwithstanding, a state based on Christian principles should be best equipped to assure (religious and confessional) liberty and justice for all.

19

The Christian America
Major Response
Harold O. J. Brown

My essay analyzes civil government primarily from a political and historical perspective, rather than strictly in terms of the implications of biblical a priori assumptions concerning society.

In his response for the national confessional position, D. Howard Elliott makes several pertinent observations about the disastrous course on which the United States is embarked. He does not, however, refute my contention that this course results from specific errors in navigation and that it can be changed if we as a society make certain adjustments which, in principle, lie within our power to make. That potential for change is due to the common grace that God imparts to all men and the biblical principle that at least certain of the judgments of God are known to unregenerated natural man (Rom. 1:31). It seems to me that God's Word has in the past been used by individuals and societies as a lamp guiding them to prudential conduct and civic justice, even when those individuals were not committed Christians and when those societies were not consciously and deliberately under the sovereignty of Christ. An example of this is post-Puritan (i.e., largely Unitarian) New England, where there was a good measure of biblically inspired civil justice despite considerable apostasy from orthodox christological doctrine.

If the United States should suffer sweeping disaster, it will not be simply because we did not make the right prudential decisions about political and economic matters based on biblical principles. It will happen because God in His wisdom has determined to let judgment fall upon us. Nevertheless, the fact that we sense elements of present judgment should not cause us to despair and embrace disaster as inevitable; it is surely possible that God means to warn us lest we remain heedless and His judgment become inexorable.

None of the other participants was particularly happy with my use of Switzerland as an example. The residual establishment of Christianity and relics of a Christian state do not seem to further the proclamation of the biblical gospel and true conversion. Indeed, this is the case. Personally, I am not satisfied with my four years of ministry in Klosters. There, to some extent, my biblical message was self-muzzled by my integration into a formally Christian, practically pagan, order; at the same time I was criticized for not fitting in, in consequence of the fact that I kept appealing to biblical standards and criticizing the substitution of pagan ones for them. Nevertheless, Switzerland, a society where two Christian confessions enjoy status as part of the establishment, is at least as generous to dissenting minorities as is the United States with our radical separation of church and state. Switzerland does not make things difficult for minority religions or atheists, but neither does it swallow the ACLU-type of argument that any official recognition of a people's Christian heritage and sentiments (or folklore) is an unacceptable affront to atheists and other non-Christians.

Fundamentally, I am in agreement with those who say that the troubles in American society today largely stem from our failure, initially, and, more recently, from our refusal to acknowledge the sovereignty of God theoretically, symbolically, or practically. Those who advocate theonomy or the national confession position propose a direct, frontal assault on this problem. If they could succeed in establishing the principle of the sovereignty of Christ in law, either in a full-fledged or a modified form, there would be good, prudential reasons for supporting them. However, inasmuch as they seem to me to risk creating *more* opposition than already exists, I have serious doubts as to whether either of these positions merits vigorous support.

The theonomist says that he is not concerned with success, but merely with obedience, and this is certainly a forthright position. The difficulty with it is that we are supposed to be discussing politics, which includes the art of the possible, not merely axioms or first principles.

Principled pluralism seems simply to accept the present situation as inevitable and rejoices in the fact that nonestablishment has permitted a vigorous flourishing of Christian institutions, more vigorous, indeed, here than elsewhere. The difficulty with this position also lies with the future. Principled pluralism seems to offer no defense against value pluralism; in the long run, that leads to the dictatorship of the 51 percent, which may well suppress the pluralism that we hope guarantees our continuing freedom and prosperity.

In the light of my critics' objections, it seems to me that I must acknowledge attempting to sell a watered-down version of Christian ethics to the general non-Christian public, banking on what I take to be the biblical fact that there is a measure of divine law and common sense left in natural man, and that, given a proper choice and good conditions, he may well choose biblical justice without himself being biblically converted. My critics propose vigorous evangelism, and I agree. Indeed, in the time that has passed between our conference and the publication of these remarks, I have been forcefully struck by the fact that we in the United States have a "two cultures" situation of the type described by scientist-novelist C. P. Snow in his book bearing that name. However, whereas Professor Snow envisaged scientists and humanists living in two different worlds, it is becoming evident that our two cultures are Christian and pagan. The Christian culture is composed, in part, of Bible-believing Christians, with some enthusiastic support from traditionalist Roman Catholics and a few others, but these constitute a minority of the population. Among the rest, however, quite a few sympathize more with Christian culture; though they do not fully understand it and would not be willing to go all the way to the Cross, they prefer it to paganism, the consequences of which in the last analysis are distasteful to natural man, too.

Of course, evangelism is our imperative; but we must do other things as well, just as the Christian farmer must plow, plant, weed, and harvest in addition to praying, reading the Bible, and witnessing to others. No one suggests that a converted farmer need not pay attention to sound principles of agriculture, and we should not suggest that the converted politician need pay no attention to sound governmental principles largely found in Scripture. I see the possibility of a measure of cooperation between natural law and biblical law. And it is possible to use the law written in the heart of man (Rom. 2:14-15) to appeal to non-Christians to model behavior along God-pleasing lines. This appeal can and must never substitute for evangelism, just as crop rotation must never substitute for personal conversion; it is possible to have the one without totally ignoring the other.

Why is it not a proper goal to restore former social conditions that were faulty if, in fact, they were better and more consistent with divine justice than present substitutes? When a man with a club-foot breaks his leg, the doctor does not say, "There's no use setting this leg, as it was not right before." The Christian physician is well aware that the only full healing of physical infirmities comes with the glorified resurrection body, but that does not prevent him from making efforts to repair what exists today.

Government will not accomplish everything. No legislation at all can produce love, for example, either of God or of neighbor. Legislation cannot prevent people from having racist attitudes, but it can prevent them from exhibiting them in the ugliest and most harmful ways. Legislation cannot prevent a small, peace-loving society from being subjugated by a more powerful, warlike neighbor. Even good civil defense procedures cannot prevent damage from natural disasters. By acknowledging its limitations, government may do a better job in those areas where it possesses competence.

Elliott wants the United States to acknowledge the sovereignty of God in a formal way. I agree, but many evangelicals do not. One hears the contention that "under God" in the Pledge of Allegiance, "In God We Trust" on coins, school prayers, and other such external forms, being superficial, have no value. I disagree. It seems to me that Romans 1 makes it plain that God expects a measure of formal respect and gratitude from natural man and holds him accountable if he refuses to pay it. The practice of prayer and Bible reading in many public schools prior to the 1961 and 1962 Supreme Court decisions hardly was a great salvation ministry, *but* their prohibition has been followed by the consequences predicted in Romans 1:28: "Just as they did not see fit to acknowledge God any longer, God gave them over to a depraved mind . . ." (NASB). The unnatural practices of homosexuality and abortion followed almost immediately upon those court decisions. The mere acknowledging and honoring of God as indicated in Romans 1:18ff. does not have direct salvific consequences, *but* refusal to honor Him has dreadful *educational* ones — resulting in a darkened mind and making it much more difficult for individuals to recognize biblical truths and, consequently, to attain salvation.

The words of 2 Chronicles 7:14, to which Elliott refers, certainly are addressed to believers, but surely in the original context the whole Jewish people was meant. "My people" have wicked ways; that applies both to those who consciously embrace the covenant and to those who are merely fellow-travelers on board the ship of state — Israel or the church. Even a formal and external national repentance would have beneficial effects on social conditions, and those beneficial effects would be recognized and would produce an evangelistic impact as well. If I understand Elliott correctly, he makes the point that 2 Chronicles 7:14 directly challenges believing Christians to repent. With this I agree. This is not *merely* a generalized appeal to the citizenry, like "Buy U.S. Savings Bonds!" Inasmuch as from a classical Reformed perspective we proclaim the external call to repentance to all, knowing that only the elect will sincerely respond, it seems that here too we must make the appeal to *all*, leaving it to the grace of God to see who responds.

As a principled pluralist, James W. Skillen accuses me of misunderstanding the work of Christ largely in terms of a kind of societal improvement. I have vigorously attacked liberation theologians for substituting social improvement (as they see it) for repentance and salvation. But it seems undeniable that the teachings of Christ, if heeded in the social order, do work improvement in social conditions and, in fact, would even make liberation theology less attractive. It is true that Emperor Constantine retained some of the sacerdotal functions of his pagan predecessors, and he intervened in a dramatic way at the Council of Nicea. He certainly thought himself in a sense analogous to David, and his admirers called him Isoapostolos (equal to the apostles). But they did not suggest Isochristos, which would have been recognized as blasphemy. His Arian sons and successors did rather want to see themselves as a bit lower than the Father, but above the generality of mankind. Arian theology permits this arrogance, because Christ the Redeemer Himself is seen as a created being; thus, another created being, the emperor, might conceivably pose as close to Him in dignity. For Constantine to abandon paganism and accept Christianity was a tremendous change, and it is not surprising that he did not make the transition smoothly. After 380 A.D., Theodosius I abandoned the old pagan title Pontifex Maximus (Highest Priest) — a title later to be assumed by the pope.

In contrast to my view that the Constitution itself does not contain religious values (as the Declaration of Independence does) and needs to be supplemented, Skillen argues that it does contain a nonsectarian theism. It certainly was *compatible* with such a theism and probably presupposed theism, but it does not explicitly contain it; and, so, it did not need to be amended, but interpreted, to get rid of one theistic principle after another. Jefferson's variety of nonsectarian deism was implicitly hostile to Christianity, although even Jefferson would probably be dismayed at the frankly atheistic stance of American government today. I believe that Skillen sees the Constitution as more favorable to monotheism than it really is and reads too much into our early national symbols. America's symbolism is not really theism at all, even of an Old Testament variety. The Seeing Eye is sometimes found in Christian art, but on the Great Seal of the United States it, like the pyramid, reflects the vague "Great Architect" deism of American Freemasonry rather than faith in the personal God of Christianity.

The criticisms of my fellow presenters bring home the fact to me that my position, in a sense, is neither fish nor fowl. Unwilling to espouse theonomy in the full sense or even to say as a nation we need a confessional acknowledgment of Christian doctrine, and yet also unwilling to concede that principled pluralism is adequate, I seem to be pleading for an America that is "just a little bit" biblical and Christian. It is, of course, dangerous to settle for half-way measures where salvation is concerned. However, we are not talking about "saving" society, but merely about "uplifting" it — and I think that we may legitimately draw on the implications of Paul's comment, "A little leaven leavens the whole lump" (1 Cor. 5:6, NASB). But this obviously involves borrowing some of the theonomist agenda and attempting to sell it to people who are not yet converted and, indeed, may never be. To do this is a far cry from ushering in the kingdom of God, though it will, I think, "produce a more perfect union" than that which the Preamble to the Constitution envisages. Principled pluralism is overly optimistic about what pluralism will mean in the era of the encroaching total state, and I would like to head off some of its potential consequences before they become realities.

Perhaps I am not far from the national confessional position. Indeed, because in politics as in life one must often aim higher than one can reach to attain anything worthwhile, I can endorse much of that effort as well as of theonomy — provided that we do not so provoke minority religions and nominal Christians into fearing such a threat to their survival and freedom that we ruin our chances of accomplishing anything positive at all.

20

The National Confessional
Major Response
William Edgar

What makes a nation Christian? asks theonomist
Gary DeMar. I answer: When a nation self-consciously identifies itself as
owing love and obedience to Jesus Christ, and when a dominant goal of
its public life is to order its common affairs by the law of Christ revealed
in the Bible, then it can fairly be called a Christian nation. Perfection is
not required.

The United States today is not a Christian nation. Was the United
States a Christian nation in 1789? Americans in 1789 thought of their
country as Christian, and the Bible had a great role in shaping law and
public affairs generally. The educated political elite, well read in Enlightenment thought, however, were no longer reasoning on clearly biblical
grounds. They were not notably pious men personally, and the two crucial
documents they produced — the Declaration of Independence and the
Constitution — are at best lukewarm in their recognition of the Christian
God. A comparison of the colonial charters and constitutions with the
Declaration of Independence shows how markedly different were the religious views of the political leaders of the seventeenth and eighteenth
centuries. In his response to my essay DeMar concludes that "the Constitution should have acknowledged the authority of the Lord Jesus Christ
more explicitly" (p. 212). "A Christian preamble to the Constitution would
have been beneficial . . ." (p. 208). On these things we are agreed.

But would a Constitutional amendment committing us as a nation to
obeying Jesus Christ in and of itself make us a Christian nation? Put the
question that way and the answer seems to be no. "Legislating Christianity from the top down will not make us a Christian nation," DeMar
writes (p. 205). But who is going to carry out such top-down legislation
in the United States? We are a democracy, and the procedures for amending the Constitution are well known. No Christian amendment could be
adopted without a prior massive religious transformation in which millions changed their personal commitments and collectively decided to

govern their public affairs by the law of Christ. A Christian amendment is not politically practical at this time, but advocating it does present a way to educate individualist American Christians, who practice a privatized religion, that Christ rules public as well as private affairs.

Should we, however, so readily dismiss the influence of top-down legislation? Law reflects the religious and moral beliefs of a people, but it also shapes them. For example, as long as gambling was illegal, many Americans concluded that it was also immoral, and they would not gamble. Now that gambling is widely legalized in various forms, people who before would never have gambled now think nothing of doing so. The history of the nation of Israel under the kings shows, in fact, how extraordinarily influential in a nation's life is the religious commitment of the king and his court. A secularizing educated elite in the United States have had tremendous and growing top-down influence in American life — through their control of education, the media, the courts, and the legislature. The prevalent view that the Constitution provides a mandate for secularizing public life has had a powerful influence upon American life. Would not a Constitution that was explicitly Christian have a similar influence, pointing us in the direction of biblical obedience in civil affairs?

Finally, we must remember that the Constitution of today is not the same document as the one adopted in 1789. Many amendments have been passed. Even if DeMar were correct about the Constitution's Christian character in 1789, he must admit that today it is almost universally understood as a strictly secular document. He attributes this understanding to a "blind court and an ignorant public" (p. 211), but it is the way people now understand the Constitution. No one could ever mistake the Mayflower Compact or William Penn's "Preface to his First Frame of Government for Pennsylvania" as secular documents. They were explicitly Christian. Historical arguments are not going to convince Americans, especially our opinion-forming elite, that the Constitution affirms America's status as a Christian nation; only a Christian amendment can do so.

While DeMar and I agree about the ideal of a Christian nation and even about a Constitutional statement to affirm a national Christian commitment, Gary Scott Smith (for the principled pluralist position) seems to disagree totally. He describes a proposed Christian amendment to the Constitution as divisive, useless, and generally undesirable. He argues that the ideal of an explicitly Christian nation is not biblical and that it misunderstands the Bible's teaching about civil government. And he claims that the history of attempted Christian culture building shows its futility. "No group of Christian believers, not those living in the Byzantine Empire, Western Christendom, or Puritan New England, has been able to create a genuinely Christian culture" (p. 219). We seem to disagree almost totally. And yet . . .

And yet, Smith thinks that "Christ's followers should resolutely resist efforts to secularize American society and to confine Christian faith to the private areas of life" (p. 213). Christians should not "allow militant secularists to eliminate all explicit Christian influence from public life" (p. 218). Why should we resist secularization and privatization? It must be because the public influence of religion has been good and right. Where did such influence come from in the first place? It came from Western Christendom! What was the theoretical basis for Christians transforming at least parts of their cultures? Most often this impulse arose from the conviction that Christ rules the nations and calls His disciples to teach them to obey all that He has commanded. The influence of the Bible on the laws of nations comes from earlier times when Christians exercised political power and used it to write laws that reflected the Bible's view of right and wrong. Smith evidently thinks that much that is worthy came from Western Christendom, and he does not want to lose any more of it. Neither do I. We both oppose any further secularization of American society.

Nevertheless, Smith thinks that the European Christians during the Middle Ages, those living in the Byzantine Empire, and New England Puritans went about Christianizing their cultures in the wrong way. The cultures they created were certainly not perfect. Yet the remnants of what they built are to be resolutely conserved! And would Smith apply what seem to be perfectionist standards to individual Christians as he seems to do to Christian nations? It should be noted that the weight of Christian thinking and experience through the centuries is on the side of trying to build a Christian culture within an explicitly Christian nation. Smith argues that "in many ways . . . the end of Western Christendom and the disestablishment of the church have brought great benefits" to the Western world (p. 217). Really? Is the Europe that finally ceases in earnest after 1885 to be Christendom really preferable to what went before? It is post-1885 Europe that first conquered most of the world in an orgy of imperialism and racism and then gave us communism, fascism, and two world wars. I wonder if Smith really believes that the end of Christendom was such a blessing; he opposes further secularization as I do. I wonder how deeply we really disagree.

Smith writes that the state's "primary task is to promote justice and righteousness" (p. 215). I agree. But justice and righteousness by what standard? The Bible certainly teaches that the knowledge of God and His law are revealed in the creation, but it leaves no doubt that His written Word is clearer, more complete, and necessary for sinners. "Then what advantage has the Jew? . . . Much in every way. To begin with, the Jews are entrusted with the oracles of God" (Rom. 3:1-2, RSV). Christians, equipped with God's Word and committed to opposing any further secularization of society, should appeal to the authority of Scripture to defend biblically based proposals and positions in the public arena. After all, the secularists can appeal to Freud, Darwin, and the latest social science research.

For Christians not to refer to the Bible when arguing public policy issues does not make sense, except that it is very difficult in the American context for Christians to do other than find secular arguments to support biblical positions. Why? Because we are working in a secular political context, defined in great measure by a Constitution understood as requiring public life to be secular. And as long as Christians do not challenge the premise that America should be a non-Christian nation governed only by the will of the people, they will be unable to do more than resist further secularization. If they use only feeble arguments drawn from nature, not Scripture, they will not build anything; they will only defend remnants of the past. But Smith does not want only to resist secularization; he wants to build a more just and righteous society. So do I. And we both, in fact, find the content of justice and righteousness in the Bible.

In the century since Congress rejected the National Reform Association's plea for a Christian amendment, American Christians have not been notably successful in promoting justice and righteousness in America. We must value not only some remnants of Christendom, but also Christendom's ideal of a nation obedient to Jesus Christ—the King of kings and Lord of lords who has all authority in heaven and on earth and has commissioned His followers to disciple the nations. Then, standing confidently on the Bible, we not only can resist further secularization, but actively continue the task at which our fathers in the faith worked—building a Christian culture that honors our Savior in word and in deed.

I have two brief observations about John Eidsmoe's interesting response from the Christian America perspective.

1. The significance of the 1797 Treaty of Tripoli is that it was adopted by President Adams and the United States Senate *according to its English translation.* They could not read Arabic! Whether the original treaty contained the words about the non-Christian nature of the United States government, and where those words came from, is interesting historical

trivia, but it is not important in determining the mentality of the Founding Fathers. The ratification of the English version of the treaty, however, reveals that the earliest leaders of the United States gave their assent to a document that denied the Christian character of the nation's government.

2. To find the "real reason" for the absence of something is difficult. Eidsmoe finds the "real reason" the Constitution makes no reference to Jesus Christ "in the nature of federalism and our system of limited delegated powers" (p. 226). Certainly, the principle of federalism can explain the absence of a national established church, but the principle of federalism clearly did not require that the Constitution in its Preamble make no reference to God, the Bible, or Jesus Christ. Something else was at work—a rather lukewarm and indifferent spirit toward Jesus Christ. That same indifference is evident in the Constitutional Convention's refusal to open its sessions with prayer, in its toleration of the abominable slave-trade, and a few years later in the government's disavowal of Christian commitment in its signing a treaty with Tripoli.

Appendix A

Questions and Answers

In order to explain each of the four positions further and, especially their implications for public policy, this appendix presents an edited summary of responses from the four major presenters— Bahnsen (for theonomy), Spykman (for principled pluralism), Brown, (for a Christian America), and Edgar (for a national confession)—to questions asked at the Consultation on the Biblical Role of Civil Government.

Questions Addressed to Greg L. Bahnsen

Q: If America were to become a theonomic nation, what functions would the federal government have and what would be implemented?

Bahnsen: Many major changes would occur. Our nation would stop murdering unborn children and promoting sexual promiscuity and perversion; the government would no longer give special protection or funding to these activities. The government would no longer promote such virtues as charity toward our neighbor; instead, the family and the church would be responsible for encouraging such interpersonal virtues. Moreover, the sanctions of the marketplace, not the government's strong arm, would be used to pressure companies or individuals to refrain from oppressing and exploiting others. Thus, one major part of what our government is doing now would cease.

On the other hand, in a theonomic society the civil government would promote virtues that it often works against today.[1] It would reinstitute laws protecting the observance of the Sabbath. It would allow families to educate their children as parents see fit. The government would stop interfering with church schools and in the marketplace as it presently does. Instead of discriminating in favor of the wealthy and special interest

---

1. Theonomists disagree among themselves on some of these particular proposals.

groups, it would promote equity between poor and rich. In short, civil government would be more limited and regulated by the Constitution.

Q: How do you define *pluralism?* Do you advocate pluralism in any areas of public life?

Bahnsen: I support the pluralism of the First Amendment—that the federal government is not to establish a religion. This means that our government must not establish one Christian denomination among others as the official state-supported religion of this land. However, our government should establish, or work in terms of, a *religious* preference. It should obey the laws of Jesus Christ. I reject the pluralist argument that any number of religious conceptions and world views should be balanced with one another to determine civil law. We should evangelize extensively and elect Christian legislators from various denominational backgrounds, who, guided by biblical teaching, will work to pass laws based on Jehovah's revelation.

Q: What should the relationship of the United States be to other countries that may want to observe God's laws?

Bahnsen: First, from the theonomic perspective, each nation's own sovereignty must be honored. God appoints the governors of every land, and those governors should be respected by their own people as well as those in other lands.

Second, theonomy should not be interpreted as meaning that we must support America whether it is right or wrong, or that America must be number one in the world. Such positions are abhorrent. We condemn Hitler's Germany for the execution of six million Jews—a terrible atrocity. But our slaughter of the unborn is equally horrible. America is not a Christian nation that has a special place in God's revealed plan. We need to change America and save America for the sake of Christ's kingdom. But we need to do that for Germany, for France, and for every other nation, too.

Q: How Christian was America during its first 150 years?

Bahnsen: Whether or not America ever was a Christian nation is very unclear. To what extent was America living up to the intent of God's law? It probably fell short in many ways. A more objective question would be, To what degree were the actual laws of the founding colonies based on God's law? To the degree that the Founders of the federal government, and of most of the original colonies, believed they could and should use the Old Testament law as a basis for America's law. John Cotton, for example, wrote the Mosaic Judicials verbatim into the Massachusetts law code. We must be more sensitive to contemporary conditions than Cotton was, but his act demonstrates that the actual laws of America were extensively theonomic during the colonial period.

Q: Is Puritan New England in its early stages a proper model for us today?

Bahnsen: Yes and no. I believe in the progress of history. The Puritans are an embarrassment in some ways. Their wage and price controls violated the law of God. But they believed in punishing kidnappers, rapists, and sex offenders, a practice we should revive.

Q: Theonomy stresses the negative role of the state — that government should restrain crime and punish those who hurt others or defraud others. But should the state not also commend the good, as Paul taught in Romans?

Bahnsen: It was a common practice of the Roman Caesars to send out letters of commendations to good citizens in various cities of their empire. It is very likely Paul has this in mind when he talks about commending the good. This suggests that governments should commend the good by recognizing citizens who have not violated the law and by setting them forth as role models for others to follow. Bringing people to the White House and thanking them for their good work among others would be the cultural analogue to which Paul refers.

More importantly, however, the commending of the good takes place when government protects the good. Who are good in the eyes of God? Often, in the Bible, they are the poor and the oppressed. Minorities and the poor are discriminated against terribly in America's courts today. If the courts actually acted to relieve the oppression of the poor instead of catering to high-priced lawyers, then our nation would start commending the good.

We should not, however, commend the good by sending welfare payments to the poor as a way of saying thank you for being good citizens. The positive aspect to the magistrate's job is to protect against foreign aggression and to punish criminal behavior for the sake of the good—whether poor or rich.

Q: How should pastors today apply the Mosaic law to Christians who previously were homosexuals or adulterers?

Bahnsen: God applies His law to the family, to the church, and to the state in different ways. The church should extend forgiveness and reconciliation to a repentant sinner, whether he is a homosexual, adulterer, or murderer. It should take no other action, unless the person's crime has left an outstanding debt. For example, an embezzler must repay what he has stolen, a murderer must turn himself in. The Bible does not, however, teach that those who practice sexual perversion must turn themselves in to public authorities. Paul says in Romans 1 that homosexuals know that what they are doing is worthy of death. He adds in 1 Timothy 1 that the law is lawfully used when homosexuals are punished to restrain their activity. But he tells the Corinthian church not to act like the state and administer punishment, because it is *not* the state. Instead, the church is the arena of redemption where reconciliation is extended to those who are repentant.

Some people object, however, by saying that if you execute a homosexual then you have no chance to evangelize him. The same is true if you execute a murderer. But that is not for us to determine. If a person is going to be converted, he will be converted in God's due time. It is not for us to adjust the requirements of His law because we want to provide occasion for a person to repent. But we must remember that the church is not the state and the family is not the state.

Q: Does not history demonstrate that it is impossible to create a theonomic society? Massachusetts Bay Colony was probably America's most theonomic society, yet as the Puritans lost their power in numbers, their society became much less theonomic.

Bahnsen: It was not power in numbers the Puritans lost but rather their orthodoxy. The development and spread of Unitarianism destroyed the Puritan movement.

Q: Since committed Christians are such a minority in America today, are not all theonomists compelled to believe the postmillennial view that the number of believers will increase tremendously in order to accomplish their goal for society?

Bahnsen: One does not have to be a postmillennialist to be a theonomist. Consider the analogy of a ship. Passengers on a ship may be travelling in a certain direction even when they are looking the other way. It is possible for the ship of God's kingdom to move ahead in a postmillennial direction, even if premillennialists and amillennialists stand at the back and cry, "No, it's that way, it's that way!" It does not require belief in postmillennial eschatology to say that magistrates should obey God. Nevertheless, it is true that people will often not keep working when things are looking bad — unless they have confidence in eventual victory.

Q: The villages and towns of Massachusetts Bay Colony maintained two community chests of food and other necessities. One was for those who fell on hard times but were not church members, and the other was for church members who experienced difficulties. The practice in Massachusetts seems to contradict your argument that civil government should not engage in the business of charity or welfare at all.

Bahnsen: Please remember that I am not here to defend all that the Massachusetts Bay Colony did or what people in Tyler, Texas, maintain. I only wish to defend the practice of going to what the Bible, including the Old Testament, teaches about civil affairs.

Did the state or did the church maintain these community chests in the Massachusetts Bay Colony? Were citizens compelled to contribute to them? I believe that the church, not the civil government, should provide for charity. God will judge the church severely for building great edifices while not ministering to the poor all around us. But when the state undertakes such charitable work, it assumes a messianic complex. A cup of cold water should be given in Jesus' name, not in the name of Caesar.

Q: Granting that the two spheres of church and state exist and that their functions are distinct, are there some penalties and sanctions that are unique to the ecclesiastical sphere?

Bahnsen: Yes.

Q: Would idolatry be one? In *Theonomy in Christian Ethics* you argue that practices such as idolatry, false prophecy, blasphemy, and Sabbath-breaking should be punished by the death penalty. Pluralists contend that church officers, not civil magistrates, have responsibility to enforce God's penalties for these practices, which do not include capital punishment.

Bahnsen: Can you suggest any specific texts that teach that today's civil magistrates cannot punish these acts?

Q: Is there not a contradiction between your argument that the power of the state be limited and your suggestion that, if theonomists take over, the state would be empowered to punish people for publicly worshiping false gods?

Bahnsen: Theonomists do *not need* to "take over." Jesus Christ has already done that. Second, we do not need to *empower* the state to do something. God has already done that. The question separating us is, How do you interpret that fact?

A much better question would be: Is it not very difficult to take these Old Testament laws about idolatry and other matters that are so far from our culture and apply them today? It certainly is.

Q: Should we execute idolaters?

Bahnsen: The *prima facie* understanding of the biblical texts would seem to support the justice of punishing idolatry, even today. But I have not done sufficient homework and reflection on this question. Instead of talking about these theoretical things, we should work to end the slaughter of unborn children, our nation's widespread sexual perversion, and the state's continual intrusion into our lives by, for example, its stealing of our property and intervention in Christian schools. Let us talk to each other about these immediate, real situations first of all. As time goes on, we should together exegete key biblical passages about other important social problems. Killing idolaters is not the agenda.

Q: Do you agree with chapter 19 of the Westminster Confession which states that Christians are obligated to obey only the general equity of the civil legislation of the Old Testament?

Bahnsen: That is precisely my position.

Q: Principled pluralists believe, following the Westminster Standards, that everything — every crossing of the *t* and every dotting of the *i* — is authoritative for us today in terms of its general equity. Why then do you insist that pluralists tend to disregard so much of the Old Testament as not being normative to us today?

Bahnsen: There is very little exegesis of Scripture in pluralist literature. Pluralist objections to theonomic conclusions are primarily based upon generalities and appeals to general revelation. Theonomists are wholly in accord with the Westminster Confession. Pluralists need to consider the Larger Catechism's exposition of the second commandment. It declares that all men, in whatever station, including the magistrate, are to carry out the laws of God against idolatry. The English Puritans who wrote the Confession clearly thought that the magistrate had the right to punish idolatry. I disagree with some of the particular actions of the Westminster divines, but their approach was much closer to the theonomic perspective than to that of the pluralist.

Questions Addressed to Gordon J. Spykman

Q: Would you explain the terms *structural pluralism* and *confessional pluralism*?

Spykman: God created the world as structured and ordered. He created human beings as multifaceted creatures who, under His direction, developed various institutions — such as families, schools, churches, states — to structure and guide life. God did not directly create little red schoolhouses, for example, but He did create people as learning creatures, and eventually schools and universities emerged. The term *structural pluralism* means that various separate institutions are part of God's intended order.

Confessional pluralism, by contrast, is a result of the Fall. It is because of the Fall and redemption — because out of the mass of fallen humankind God calls forth in Jesus Christ a new people — that we have a clash of religious convictions. Thus Christians and non-Christians espouse different confessional traditions. Both of those confessional traditions have been splintered, so that we have many Christian and non-Christian communities. That is why confessional pluralism exists. Religious pluralism is a terrible, anti-normative thing, but we live in that kind of world. You cannot handle this fact by ignoring it.

Q: To what extent, then, would it be possible for the United States to recognize or to tolerate confessional pluralism when our nation includes such diverse ideologies as Marxism, Islam, and various Eastern religions? Does acceptance of confessional pluralism require us to tolerate all religious or political groups and not simply Christian denominations?

Spykman: We faced that problem in America when the Mormons advocated polygamy in the nineteenth century. A moral consensus exists today in America based upon the Judeo-Christian ethos. Every society has a set of mutually agreed upon values that provides social cohesion. When a particular religious community challenges the prevailing ethos of the society, it produces a rock-bottom crisis. If, for example, Islam developed a religious world view that called for the overthrow of our democratic society, a crisis would exist.

As long as non-Western religions, secular ideologies, and Christian sects affirm, or at least do not attack, basic underlying American commitments and values, they must be tolerated. Confessional pluralism is not normative, but it must be accepted as an historical reality, as the tares among the wheat. The tares are not normative, but we should recognize their existence and tolerate them as long as they do not undermine the foundations of the society. A government based upon Reformed Christian principles would be best able to safeguard the religious pluralism of our society.

Q: The Koran teaches that idolaters should be converted at the point of a sword. Do Muslims have the right to propagate or to practice this tenet of their "divinely inspired" book? If they attempt to use force to convert people, should Christian legislators seek to prevent them?

Spykman: Using coercion to convert people is wrong whether practiced in Iran or in this country. If this is done in Iran, the only thing we can do is to try to evangelize that society and help it to accept a new set of values that would change its religious practices. If members of the Islamic community in this country should not only believe in their hearts that people ought to be converted at the edge of a dagger but start carrying it out, then they would violate the laws of this country—insofar as they are still shaped by Judeo-Christian tradition and not by an Islamic tradition. Thus, they must be prevented from doing so. But you cannot make Muslims stop believing this teaching in their hearts, just as a Mormon may still believe in his heart that polygamy is correct. Despite America's secularization, the Judeo-Christian ethos is still strong enough to prevent these practices.

Q: How should American society be structured?

Spykman: We have a strong Protestant, a strong Catholic, and a strong Jewish community in this society. None of these large communities threatens the fabric of our society. The government should treat all of them evenhandedly; it should not favor a Jewish synagogue over a Protestant church, nor a Protestant church over a Catholic one. We have generally treated these groups fairly in this country.

While we have disestablished the church, we have not disestablished the public school system. That is next on the agenda. The government should stand in the same legal relationship to Catholic, Lutheran, and Reformed school systems as it does to a secular and humanist school system. Structurally, the government must relate to all schools alike; confessionally, it must allow various religious communities to carry on programs of education that are consistent with the faith of their members. How to deal with sects and cults such as the Mormons or Satan worshipers is much more problematic.

Q: Is the church one of the mediating structures between the state and the individual?

Spykman: Yes. Peter Berger and Richard Neuhaus—who coined the term *mediating structure*—seem to assume, however, that individualism and collectivism are the normative starting points for defining the issues. I disagree. The biblical account of the creation order reveals instead that marriage, family, work, learning, and worshiping—the original, divinely ordained institutions—are the normative starting point. If there had been no Fall, our society, reflecting the creational order, would have been based upon pluralist structures, rather than upon individualism or collectivism. Church, home, school, and business all mediate between the state and the individual.

Q: Then is it the task of the political sphere actually to define and implement the boundaries between these different groups?

Spykman: No. God established these boundaries at creation. The government is not called upon to define, but rather to honor and safeguard, the lines of demarcation. It is not always easy to mark them out. Sometimes we can. Preaching the gospel is clearly not the task of the state. Some cases clearly violate the separation, or sovereignty, of various spheres. Other cases are problematic.

Q: When you dismiss the Islamic jihad or the Satan worshipers who believe in human sacrifice as peripheral to mainstream American society, you have my emotional support. In California, however, it is not easy to dismiss such groups as simply a lunatic fringe. Is there any other way to determine that a group is part of the lunatic fringe besides simply accepting the opinions of individuals and communities? Is there any objective way for the state to set a limit on what is going to be tolerated?

Spykman: In a religiously diverse society like ours, which is becoming even more pluralist, determining which groups or practices are too extreme to accept will become tougher. Christians themselves cannot agree on abortion or open housing or any crucial public issue. Therefore, it should not surprise us if non-Christians are radically opposed to what we take to be a Christian consensus. This suggests that our society's crisis is becoming deeper and that less and less consensus will exist. The major issues are hermeneutic ones: how do we read, interpret, and understand the Bible together, and how do we develop the Bible's view of society and the role of the state in it?

Q: Have you used the phrase *confessional pluralism* in two different senses? In the one sense *confessional pluralism* describes the sinful world we live in with its many different ideologies and views. This is how the world, because of sin, actually is (*de facto*). In the other sense *confessional pluralism* is a God-ordained way for governments to deal with the multiplicity of religious groups in society (*de jure*). You have clearly stated the first idea. Are you also stating the second?

Spykman: The presence of atheists, secularists, humanists, and various groups of Reformed Christians in our world does not reflect God's intent for His creation. This is an antinormative development, but it is a historical reality.
    The label *principled pluralism* indicates that its advocates believe that pluralism is more than a historical or pragmatic reality; it is a tenet of a Christian view of civil government. This case for pluralism is based on norms rooted in the Scripture.

Q: Do you think that Christians should work to convince our nation to recognize officially the authority of Jesus Christ? Should magistrates confess that their authority comes from God and that He rules in America?

Spykman: If we did include Jesus Christ as Lord of lords and King of kings in the Constitution, what difference would it make? It should not change the Jews' ability to celebrate their Passover on Saturday or the Christians' right to go to church on Sunday. That is to say, Christians in the government should promote the eschatological tolerance that Jesus describes in Matthew 13. Christians should give others who disagree the legal right to be religiously wrong. But where do you draw the lines? That is the ticklish question.

Q: The concepts you have stressed are basically derived from Abraham Kuyper and Herman Dooyeweerd, who attempted to apply them in the Netherlands during the late nineteenth and early twentieth centuries. The Netherlands today, however, is in a horrible mess. Has the practice of principled pluralism produced the Netherlands' problems?

Spykman: It is not because the Dutch followed the principles of Kuyper and Dooyeweerd, but because they violated them, that they are experiencing so much difficulty. Kuyper did not originate principled pluralism. Its roots are found in John Calvin. These three men, however, simply rediscovered and rearticulated biblical teachings, pointers in the Scripture. God gave Adam and Eve a cluster of cultural tasks, cultural mandates, which are the basis for structural pluralism. Eventually, these tasks take on institutional forms.[2]

Q: The term *pluralism* is used in so many different ways in our language today. By *pluralism* do you really mean *principled tolerance*? If so, what prevents a public acknowledgment of Jesus Christ as King of kings and Lord of Lords? On the basis of biblically defined justice, we could protect all other religions — but call it *tolerance* rather than the ambiguous term *pluralism*.

Spykman: Jesus Christ is Lord of all. He admonishes us to provide liberty and justice for all. Acknowledging Christ's lordship does not require us to enforce Christianity upon those who resist it. The only way to bring people to Christian faith and commitment is by the persuasive power of the Word of God and the work of His Spirit, not by legislation.

2. This is evident in the Old Testament with the differentiation of prophetic, priestly, and kingly offices and the respective institutions involved. In the New Testament the single office of apostolic leader is divided into ministers, elders, deacons, and these various tasks are institutionalized.

The rights that I ask for my own Christian community, I must also be willing to advocate for another community.

Q: In their attempts to defend the unborn, Christians are accused of trying to legislate morality. If Christ were explicitly acknowledged in the Constitution, would we not have a stronger foundation for passing legislation that truly insures justice for all?

Spykman: Justice involves more than preserving the life of the unborn. It also involves preventing unwanted pregnancies and helping single mothers. We should stress that abortion is taking life, and taking life is contrary to the will of God. Christians should be in the forefront of preserving the life of all people — old, young, unborn. Given the prevailingly secular mind of American public life, I doubt that an explicit acknowledgment of the lordship of Jesus Christ in our Constitution would do much to stem the tide. Our actions speak louder than the Word.

Q: Historically, America has allowed different denominational practices as long as they were biblically based. This kind of pluralism prevented practices by Mormons, Muslims, and other groups that were contrary to Scripture, yet it did not force people to accept the gospel in their own hearts and minds. Would not your broader conception of pluralism allow and endorse practices and applications that specifically contradict the Word of God?

Spykman: Madalyn Murray O'Hair should have the same right to establish a university dedicated to an atheist world view as Christians do to organize colleges committed to a biblical world view.

Q: Would principled pluralism then allow public blasphemy of God?

Spykman: I would not allow public blasphemy because it offends other people.

Q: On what basis would you disallow public blasphemy?

Spykman: Both Christians and non-Christians should be prevented from doing things that are blatantly offensive to and infringe upon others.

Q: But is your decision about what acts to permit and what acts to disallow based upon any objective criterion?

Spykman: Give me one objective basis that the believer and unbeliever will both accept. Of course, you cannot. The only objective basis, ultimately, would be the Scriptures.

Q: But is the type of pluralism that you are promoting based upon biblical teaching?

Spykman: I am not promoting it. I am only recognizing that it exists in America. Catholics and Jews live in our country. How do we, with the gospel in our hands and hearts, face that?

Q: Should Satan worshipers have the right to establish their own school?

Spykman: Sure, as long as it does not infringe upon the rights of others. The way to stop Satan worshipers is not to restrict their freedom, but to confront them with true freedom in Jesus Christ.

Questions Addressed to Harold O. J. Brown
(and James W. Skillen)

Q: The Christian America position and theonomy seem to agree on many issues. How do you interpret Psalm 2, which calls upon the judges and the rulers of the earth to kiss the Son and to serve Jehovah with fear?

Brown: The Second Psalm seems to be a sort of rhetorical admonition. Kings and rulers are definitely obligated to bow before the Son, but this admonition has not yet been fulfilled on the earth.

Q: Should confessional pluralism be established as a principle?

Brown: Pluralism should not be established as a principle; there should be toleration, however.

Q: Should idolatry be defined in terms of failure to worship the Triune God? Should those who purport to respect the name of Jehovah and honor His Word and law, whether they are Jews, Jehovah's Witnesses, Unitarians, or others, be considered idolaters?

Brown: I think of idolatry in terms of the second commandment. We are prohibited from making and venerating idols. By this definition neither Jews nor Jehovah's Witnesses seem to be practicing idolatry. We should not extend the second commandment into areas that would immediately involve the state in all sorts of unnecessary confrontations. In a Christian America, Jews and Jehovah's Witnesses would continue to be tolerated.

Q: Is it not possible that God the Father and Christ the Son are best revered and obeyed by having our government adopt a principled pluralist approach rather than enshrining Christ in the Constitution or establishing an explicitly Christian nation?

Brown: It is possible, I suppose, to have a legal structure that officially adopts principled pluralism, while the representatives of that government, in their personal commitments and in their deliberations and decisions, honor God the Son, yet without violating the principle of pluralism. Therefore, principled pluralism, as I have heard it expounded, is not per se dishonoring to God; nor does it guarantee that God will be dishonored. But I disagree that the state should be neutral toward all religious commitments and values. All faiths should be tolerated, but the Christian faith should be preferentially treated. I did not advocate my Christian America viewpoint as obedience to the Second Psalm. I advocated it more as a kind of a practical necessity, although all individuals are commanded to honor the Son.

Q: On the one hand, you admit what many people describe as the secularization of America. Yet, at the same time, you believe that Americans still have enough Christian sympathies for a biblical reconstruction of society to occur. Does America not need a fundamental reorientation, not simply a recapturing of residual Christian conviction or sympathy?

Brown: Secularization and residual Christianity are like the wheat and the tares. The public mind is clearly becoming progressively more secular. Nevertheless, Romans 1 to 3 teaches that natural man has the ability to respond to certain principles of divine justice. Consequently, the extensive secularization of our society can be arrested and reversed, and a Christian nation established. My position emphasizes practical political possibilities, while others stress what is commanded in Scripture.

Q: Jerry Falwell, Pat Robertson, and other religious leaders urge people to join their organizations to fight our society's increasing secularization. But they insist that Christians can be successful politically only by devising proposals that appeal to the majority of Americans. Do not these two goals seem to be at war with each other?

Brown: There still may be enough of a Christian consensus in America that some of our current practices could be changed. Some societies that appeared to be going very much in the wrong direction did recover. The Wesleyan revival transformed eighteenth-century England, and the iconoclastic movement brought national renewal to seventh- and early eighth-century Byzantium. So these two things—combating secularization and devising widely accepted political policies—are not necessarily mutually exclusive.

Q: Are you an establishmentarian?

Brown: No. I believe in a certain amount of sympathy and benevolence toward the church, but it is not to be established and state supported.

Q: How would atheist Madalyn Murray O'Hair be treated in your Christian America?

Brown: She would be prevented from public blasphemy and insulting God. It is correct to suppress or punish these actions, whether they be done by O'Hair or anyone else. However, she should have the right to express atheistic opinions, as long as she does not do so in a blasphemous way. Ridiculing God and the faith of Christians should be punished by a fine or in some other way. She should have the right to found an educational institution to propagate her views.

Q: Should government enforce the first commandment in public law?

Brown: In the case of Madalyn Murray O'Hair we are talking about the third commandment—"Thou shalt not take the name of the Lord thy God in vain"—not the first. Government should enforce the third commandment.

Q: You said Christians should have preferential treatment in society. How would this be done in terms of education?

Brown: I envision two school systems. One would be a public school system that rested upon a generally Christian consensus and allowed churches to provide religious instruction during school hours. Islamic, Jehovah's Witnesses, and Hari Krishna views would not be taught in these public schools. Second, independent schools would be established and supported on a voucher basis. The Hindu could take his voucher and use it to support his own school. And so could Christians who want a thoroughly Christian school system.

Q: My question is directed to James Skillen, a proponent of pluralism and one of the respondents to Brown's paper. You made a theological, exegetical argument based on the doctrine of common grace. You used Exodus 23, a command to exterminate the people in the land of Canaan, in conjunction with Matthew 13, the parable of the wheat and tares. You argued that we should not impose these Old Testament sanctions, because doing so violates the common grace order we are now under, which allows the tares to continue to grow instead of eliminating them before their time. The problem I see with your position is this. The common grace order originates in Genesis, in the time of Noah. God says that seed time and harvest, winter and summer, day and night will not cease as long as the earth remains. Because Noah lived before the Mosaic administration, the common grace order was already in place at the time of the Israelite conquest of Canaan. If exterminating the Canaanites did not contradict the common grace order in the Old Testament era, why should placing legal restrictions on unbelievers contradict it in the New Testament era?

Skillen: I argued that what Exodus 23 describes is unique and, therefore, not normative for us. God was bringing His final judgment upon various groups living in Canaan. The Israelites were not supposed to go in and love this enemy, because they were to be destroyed. There is no common grace for them in that sense. We must understand that God had a special purpose in reestablishing His people in the Promised Land and that the common grace order was temporarily set aside. We cannot simply pick out certain laws from the Old Covenant; we must understand it as a whole.

Q: Does the different treatment commanded by the Old and New Testaments involve a common grace/special grace distinction?

Skillen: If you mean by *common grace* that God is protecting even non-Christians and that the same rain and sunshine come to all, I do not object to using that language. But, my point in contrasting the Exodus and Matthew passages was to show that there is an integrality of meaning to the way particular laws are given. I am not now saying that what was love in the Old Testament is not love in the New, or that what was justice here is not justice there. I am not denying the universality of norms. In our attempt to develop case law, however, we cannot ignore the real structural dynamics of history as God unfolded the creation. When Christ came, many things began to change, such as the meaning of who Israel was and of what a civil or political order should be.

Questions Addressed to William Edgar

Q: Does your proposal to have the United States Constitution explicitly recognize the authority of Jesus Christ include the establishment of a state church?

Edgar: No.

Q: You argue that the Constitution is a secular document because it is enacted in the name of no god. Your interpretation drives a wedge between the Constitution and the Declaration of Independence. The Constitution, however, dates the Union from the Declaration of Independence. The Declaration not only mentions God, it declares that we receive all our inalienable rights from our Creator, and it is dated in the year of our Lord. So, the Declaration of Independence cannot be secular. Furthermore, the expression "the law of nature and nature's God" is Calvinistic theology. In terms of legal tradition, the law of nature and nature's God is Christian theology, the separation between Creator and Redeemer. Respond, please.

Edgar: Those who attempt to portray the writers of the Constitution as deliberate secularists are confusing them with the Jacobins (members of a famous group of French revolutionaries organized in 1789). America's Founding Fathers are more like the philosophers of the English Enlightenment who simply ignored, rather than attacked Christianity. The argument that America has been a totally secular country from 1776 onward and that any public expression of religion is contrary to the views of the Founding Fathers is wrong. Nevertheless, a sharp contrast exists between the language of colonial documents, which are unmistakably

Christian, and that of the Declaration of Independence, let alone the Constitution. According to Romans 1, lukewarm public religion, as evident among the Founding Fathers, represents the first half-step in refusing to honor God as God or to give Him thanks. Fail to correct that and things become worse. And this is borne out by the subsequent history of the United States.

Q: We all agree, it seems to me, that the core Christian confession that Jesus is Lord should find expression in statecraft. Given our religiously mixed citizenry, given the largely secular and even anti-Christian prevailing cultural ethos, would not many citizens be violating the ninth commandment if our nation formally recognizes Christ's lordship in its Constitution? How could a Christian amendment ever be the authentic, truthful expression of even a bare majority of the American people?

Edgar: Such a Christian amendment could only be adopted after a tremendous earth-shaking revival in this country. Putting it forward now could be called a propaganda point, challenging Americans to extend their Christian faith even this far. Our final goal is for our whole nation to be Christian. Our aim is this broad because of who Christ is. As Christians, we cannot strive for less. In the next election, Americans will not elect 435 Congressmen pledged to support the Christian amendment. So, in the next election we should also pursue more limited goals, such as an end to the horror of abortions and a voucher system to provide educational justice for Christians.

Q: That Christ is Lord over America should be a plank of a platform of a political party. But that is not quite the same as proposing this as an amendment to the Constitution. There is an essential difference between a party platform, such as those of the socialist parties in Europe, and the Constitution which, in a sense, is a confession of the total citizenry.

Edgar: Socialist aims began as planks of their party. Their final goal, of course, was revolution, the classless society, pure communism. This plank of their party was their goal for the whole society. Political parties in America should adopt this amendment as a plank in their platform, but intend it as a goal for the whole nation.

Q: Does anything in the Constitution prevent the establishment of the theonomic regime for which Bahnsen argued?

Edgar: As originally written, the Constitution is an all-purpose document that might allow a theonomic regime, except for its toleration of the slave trade. But can you imagine a theonomic family or church that remains silent about Christ? At any rate, today's Constitution has been amended a number of times, and the federal government is much more powerful than it was in 1800. Court interpretations, legal opinions, law school teaching, and popular understanding of the Constitution provide an insuperable barrier to instituting a theonomic society based upon our current Constitution. It must be fundamentally changed to make very plain and explicit what was not made plain and explicit two hundred years ago — that there is a definite religious base to our law.

Q: From your perspective, what kind of civil government should we have?

Edgar: The Ten Commandments are the proper foundation for social life. They are special even in the Old Covenant. The rest of the Old Covenant laws apply the Ten Commandments to the situation of ancient Israel.

Calvin applied the Old Testament laws, and the Westminster Larger Catechism obviously made use of them in expounding the meaning of the Ten Commandments. The New England Puritans made a definite effort to develop a Christian law code. They used English common law, some ecclesiastical law, some local village law, and the Bible. All Christian rulers, when they have power and try to exercise it as Christians, use the Old Testament law code. That law code applied the Ten Commandments to an agricultural society with tribal characteristics. What those biblical applications imply for the United States must be considered one by one. The details are crucially important.

Q: Why do you dislike principled pluralism?

Edgar: We live in a pluralistic situation and, therefore, much of the strategy of the pluralist is appropriate. But pluralism should not be the goal. If the church accepts principled pluralism as an ideal for society, certain unfortunate, unintended consequences will result. I warned about some of these in my essay.

Q: Can Christians accept a pluralistic position at the present time?

Edgar: Principled pluralism is a dead end. It unwittingly compromises the lordship of Christ, it leaves the government with no sure guide to justice, and its sociology is incorrect. It cannot be worked out in a society as complex and diverse as America's.

Q: It is quite clear that questions about how to exegete and interpret the Scripture are going to be fundamental, and Reformed Christians must keep working to unfold what the Bible teaches about law and politics.

One of the dilemmas of the Christian amendment approach is that we must consider the nature of the state, not just our confession about it. This brings us back once again to the question, What does God expect the state to be and to do? Our laws are reflections of the purposes and goals of our nation. The Association for Public Justice encourages Christian citizens to work to change public laws. That is a different kind of act than trying to draw platforms, write constitutions, or exegete the Scriptures — things that politicians or biblical scholars might do. Do we have to settle all exegetical questions and all the details of case law and frame platforms before we can challenge apathetic fellow citizens to become active politically?

We are paralyzed because theologians exegete Scripture without taking political action, while others engage in political activity without scriptural guidance. How do we combine scriptural interpretation with political participation? How can we inspire Christians to fulfill their civic responsibilities?

Edgar: Many Christian groups are working on one issue or another of great moral and political importance for our country. Most of them are single-issue groups, like the Christian Action Council's opposition to abortion or the various anti-pornography groups. The APJ and the NRA are unusual in trying to address a number of issues. All these groups need to expand their work, but they should do so within the larger context of national submission to Christ and obedience to the Bible. In that way, Christians will see more clearly that all these issues have to do with our relationship to Christ the King and His law.

Theologians and political activists should pay greater attention to one another's contributions. The theologians of the Reformation such as Calvin and Knox were much more involved with immediate social and political application of the truth than today's theologians are. On the other hand, such Christian leaders as Governor John Winthrop of Massachusetts Bay Colony really knew their Bibles. We need men who understand the larger picture and have big goals, not just narrow specialists.

Q: Does America's current crisis mean that God is giving up on our nation, or does it instead indicate that He is seeking to redirect our country? How do we sort out what is a sign of blessing and what is a sign of judgment?

Edgar: It is never possible to sort out fully God's blessings and curses in history. For one thing, the same occurrence may be a blessing to a believer and a curse to an unbeliever. All things, even calamities, work for the good of God's children. They are blessings in that they strengthen our faith and character. On the other hand, even blessings such as the sun shining and crops growing may become curses to unbelievers as they imagine that they do not need God. So, maybe we should look at the responses of people to Christ's providential acts. Were people brought to repentance? If so, then a disaster was God's blessing.

According to Romans 1 the main curse of God on thankless people who will not honor Him is a religious and moral one. He gives them over to worshiping idols and gives them up to evil and destructive lives. If we see a society growing in wickedness, we know it is receiving God's curse, even if it is prospering and at peace for the moment.

Has God given up on our nation? Not at all. But the axe is laid to the root, and our nation must change its ways.

Q: You and others have persistently and unfairly misrepresented the purpose of principled pluralism. This position has been criticized for advocating alternative kings (Jesus versus a nation's leader), promoting political polytheism, and undercutting evangelism. The early church was born in a pluralistic climate, but Christians during the first three centuries did not depreciate the uniqueness of Christ. And significant pluralism characterized both Europe and America in the nineteenth century, but this period was the great age of evangelism and mission.

There is a simple reason why the notion of pluralism has been misunderstood. Principled pluralism demands and guarantees for everyone the right to follow the dictates of his conscience and belief. Moreover, it allows people to advocate public policy positions shaped and influenced by those beliefs. That is the heart of pluralism. But the right to propagate one's view is held in tension with the equal right to consider those views as being philosophically nonsense, ethically monstrous, theologically blasphemous, or just plain dumb. Thus principled pluralism is not intellectual pacifism, wishy-washy ecumenism, or political polytheism. Instead, it is a way of taking on the powers and the idolatries of our age through the Word and Spirit alone. Principled pluralism has repeatedly been seriously mischaracterized.

Since the resurgence of Christian influence in the public arena in the 1970s, our greatest weakness has been the lack of an articulated public philosophy, particularly about religion and public life. Would you not agree?

Edgar: Today's pluralists seem to be trying to persuade people to accept certain values; being a pluralist, apparently, does not keep one from going into the public arena and trying to argue for biblically based positions. This is what theonomists have been saying, too. They do not advocate taking the sword and beating the nation into submission. They urge Christians to go out into the public arena and argue for the goodness of God's law and show people that biblical norms are far better than our current practices. Apparently, both theonomists and pluralists believe in using persuasion to try to show people the importance of Christian values. Now, if that is true, why do pluralists continue to reject the theonomic approach?

Q: Your proposed preamble to the Constitution states that God's "revealed will" would be the supreme authority." Unless the Supreme Court justices become biblical scribes and understand what God's revealed will is for government, or the masses become theonomists, how will this preamble work?

Edgar: This proposed preamble could only be adopted if the spiritual climate of our country changed dramatically. These words cannot be put into the Constitution in the present environment. Amending the Constitution in this way would change the terms of debate as Congressmen make laws. Instead of considering only the latest opinion polls or sociological research, lawmakers would also consider biblical teachings. They will not all suddenly agree. But the basis for debate will shift, at least in part, to a proper basis. Yes, this would require lawmakers to know their Bibles. Adopting this amendment would set the boundaries of what is acceptable discourse and pressure the people to conform. If this amendment were adopted and Christianity became much more influential in our country, the pressure would be on the unbeliever to support his positions from the Bible. The issues would be framed differently and argued differently.

Appendix B

A Summary of Agreements and Disagreements

The following summary of areas of agreement and disagreement among the four positions was drafted at the conclusion of the consultation.

Areas of Agreement

1. The Word of God is authoritative.
2. Scripture of the Old Testament and New Testament speaks to all of life, including politics.
3. There are continuities and discontinuities between the Old Testament and the New Testament.
4. The ascended Christ is King over all creation.
5. God has ordained various institutions, at least family, church, and state.
6. God is sovereign governor and judge over the universe and over all nations.
7. God requires civil officials to conduct their offices as His servants, ruling justly and recognizing the dignity of all persons as created in His image.
8. Christians should resolutely resist the secularizing of society, as we presently see it, for example, in humanistic state education and disrespect for unborn life.
9. Christians should obey and promote biblical precepts in political life, including its institutions and policies.
10. To promote the goals in 8 and 9, Christians should develop strong families, churches, and organizations.
11. Persuasion, not violence, is the only legitimate means to form and correct the civic mind in favor of a biblical position on issues or to obtain religious conversions.
12. The United States is *de facto* a religiously pluralistic society.

Areas of Disagreement

1. What is the meaning of "peoples" and "nations in the Bible?

2. What is the nature of the continuity and discontinuity between the Old Testament and the New Testament, especially regarding the Mosaic law?

3. How does Christ exercise His kingship over the nations? How should nations respond to His kingship?

4. How may the creedal distinction between the moral, ceremonial, and civil laws of Old Testament Israel be applied to contemporary political life? In what sense?

5. What is the biblical view of civil justice and of the legitimate task and power of the state?

6. What is confessional pluralism? Is the concept of confessional pluralism biblical? To what extent should the state tolerate the practice and promulgation of non-Christian world views and religious confessions?

7. Should the Constitution formally recognize Christ as supreme authority over the nation?

8. What was the original nature of the U.S. Constitution—to what degree is it Christian or secular?

Index of Scripture

Index of Topics and Proper Names

discontinuities between the Old and
New Testaments, 31-36, 57-59,
62-63, 242-43, 285-86
idea of office, 92, 95, 104
infallibility of, 23, 31, 39, 47, 51-52, 64
relationship between the Old and New
Testaments, 24, 33-41, 49-51, 155
Secularism, 21, 30, 66, 69, 81, 115-16, 134,
174, 183-84, 186, 188, 205, 208, 218,
220, 245, 259-61, 270, 279
Secularization
American, 5, 135, 150, 173-74, 182, 187,
197, 213, 219, 248-49, 259-61, 270,
274, 275-77, 285
European, 129, 182, 248
Seward, William, 218
Sider, Ronald, 36, 43, 45, 50, 65
Simon, Paul, 7
Sin, 1-3, 25-27, 39, 49, 58, 64-65, 69, 75,
82-83, 89, 104, 112, 160-61, 163, 166,
168-69, 180, 183-84, 190, 193-96, 199,
215, 219, 229, 238, 248-49, 261, 266,
272
and crime, 42-43
Slavery, 5, 179, 184, 262, 281
Smith, Al, 6
Smith, Gerald, L. K., 6
Snow, C. P., 254
Social contract, 90, 93, 181
Social gospel, 5
Social sciences, 108, 118, 188, 261
Sojourners, 7
Sphere sovereignty, 54, 75, 79, 95-96,
102-3, 117, 235
Sphere universality, 75, 80, 96, 117
State, 1-14
biblical basis for, 4-5, 22, 44, 46-47,
85-86, 95, 100, 106, 112, 123, 139,
142, 144, 148, 152, 159, 162, 168, 174,
182, 193-95, 213-15, 218, 222, 227-29,
245-46, 258, 272, 281
Canadian Constitution, 185
Christian aspects of American
government, 123, 134, 147, 202
civil disobedience, 85
colonial charters, 174, 184-85, 205, 226,
258-59
and education, 98-99

limited, 5, 13, 18, 42-44, 63, 66, 72,
95, 97, 101, 103, 123, 139, 146, 151,
159-60
magistrates as God's servants, 24,
41-42, 48-50, 60, 77, 133, 139, 267,
285
nature of, 97, 108, 136
origin and basis of, 89-91
political activism, 6, 8, 12-13, 53,
194-95, 210, 250, 282, 285
political reform, 52-53
role of, 2
administer justice, 13, 18, 76-78,
86-89, 91, 97, 105, 114, 138-39,
213-16, 251
balance rights and responsibilities of
other societal spheres, 97, 111, 215,
271
coin money, 193
commend the good, 265-66
dispense capital punishment, 42-43,
102, 139, 141, 143, 268
insure equal rights, 76-77, 86-89,
105-6, 213, 215, 251, 264
insure peace, 2, 44, 114, 194
help the poor, 86-89, 105, 110, 214
not to control the marketplace, 245
not to encourage interpersonal
virtues, 42, 263
not to enforce the gospel, 45
not to police the world, 45
not to preach the gospel, 271
not to promote charity toward
neighbors, 18, 45, 47-48, 64, 263,
267
not to provide education, 45, 64
not to redistribute wealth, 245
preserve order, 2, 18, 44, 89, 214-15
promote a moral climate conducive
to furthering God's kingdom, 114
promote education, 60, 147-48, 151,
154, 244
promote good health, 147
promote goodness, 2, 139, 149, 167,
193
promote human dignity, 114
promote morality, 2
promote reconciliation, 250